HEREWARD

VICTOR HEAD

ALAN SUTTON PUBLISHING LIMITED

To Peggy

First published in the United Kingdom in 1995 by
Alan Sutton Publishing Ltd · Phoenix Mill · Far Thrupp · Stroud · Gloucestershire

Reprinted 1995

British Library Cataloguing in Publication Data

Head, Victor
Hereward
I. Title
942.021092

ISBN 0-7509-0807-6

Library of Congress Cataloging in Publication Data applied for

Typeset in 11/13pt Garamond.
Typesetting and origination by
Alan Sutton Publishing Limited.
Printed in Great Britain by
Hartnolls, Bodmin, Cornwall.

Contents

List of Illustrations   v

Preface   vii

Acknowledgements   ix

CHAPTER ONE
1066 and All That   1

CHAPTER TWO
Sources   16

CHAPTER THREE
The Outlaw   37

CHAPTER FOUR
'Valiant Hereward'   51

CHAPTER FIVE
The Avenger   69

CHAPTER SIX
The Guerrilla Leader   90

CHAPTER SEVEN
Betrayal   107

CHAPTER EIGHT
The Legend   123

CHAPTER NINE
A Forgotten Hero?   141

APPENDIX A
Late Saxon Weapons from the Ely Area   153

APPENDIX B
Family Matters: The Genealogical Argument   156

Notes   170

Bibliography   177

Index   178

List of Illustrations

Page

1   Saxon axemen in the Bayeux Tapestry (Bayeux Tapestry).

7   Brixworth Church, Northamptonshire (Author).

8   Late Saxon Thetford (Alan Sorrell drawing, reproduced by courtesy of the *Illustrated London News*).

9   Edward Augustus Freeman, the eminent Victorian historian (By courtesy of the National Portrait Gallery, London).

16 The Scribe Eadwine from Canterbury copy of the Utrecht Psalter made in 1147 (Courtesy of the Master and Fellows of Trinity College, Cambridge).

17 Illustrated page from the Utrecht Psalter (Courtesy of the Master and Fellows of Trinity College, Cambridge).

20 Opening page of the *De Gestis Herwardi* (Courtesy of Peterborough Cathedral authorities).

23 Orford Castle, Suffolk (Courtesy of The Conway Library, Courtauld Institute, London).

24 York Minster (Courtesy of The Conway Library, Courtauld Institute, London).

26 The Domesday volumes and the chest in which they are stored (Crown Copyright photograph, reproduced by permission of the Controller of Her Majesty's Stationery Office).

28 A page from Domesday Book showing one of the Hereward entries (Alecto Historical Editions).

32 Bishop Odo's prominence in the Bayeux Tapestry suggests that he commissioned the work (Bayeux Tapestry).

32 Bayeux Tapestry's decorated borders (Bayeux Tapestry).

44 Edward the Confessor depicted on a silver penny (British Museum).

46 Eustace, Count of Boulogne (Bayeux Tapestry).

61 Abbey at Bury St Edmunds (Courtesy of St Edmundsbury Borough Council, Manor House Museum, Bury St Edmunds. Photograph copyright Graham Portlock).

65 William the Conqueror as depicted in the Bayeux Tapestry (Bayeux Tapestry).

65 Head of William I on a silver penny (British Museum).

70 The old church at Bourne (Author).

72 Hereward's vengeance at Bourne (Cambridgeshire Collection).

74 The girding of a knight with a sword – medieval drawing (British Library).

75 Castle at Conisbrough, Yorkshire (Courtesy of The Conway Library, Courtauld Institute, London).

76 Seal of a Warrenne, Earl of Surrey (Crown Copyright photograph, reproduced by permission of the Controller of Her Majesty's Stationery Office).

79 Peterborough Cathedral (Courtesy of The Conway Library, Courtauld Institute, London).

83 Late Saxon Palace at Cheddar (Alan Sorrell drawing, reproduced by courtesy of the *Illustrated London News* Picture Library).

84 Earls Barton Church, Northamptonshire (Author).

93 February at Queens Holme (Cambridgeshire Collection).

94 The Lode, near Reach (Cambridgeshire Collection).

97 Late Saxon sword (Norwich Castle Museum, Norfolk Museums Service).

98 The Temple Pyx (Courtesy of Glasgow Museums, The Burrell Collection).

99 Viking battleaxe (Norwich Castle Museum, Norfolk Museums Service).

103 Aerial view of the causeway to Aldreth (Cambridge University Collection of Air Photographs: copyright reserved).

113 Ely Cathedral (Courtesy of The Conway Library, Courtauld Institute, London).

114 The heart of the Bruneswald today (Author).

116 Leighton Bromswold, Cambridgeshire (Author).

117 Newton Bromswold, Northamptonshire (Author).

121 Bedford Castle in the eleventh century (Artist's impression, courtesy of Bedfordshire Archaeological Trust).

124 Victorian view of Hereward (Cambridgeshire Collection).

129 Hereward wooing Torfrida (Cambridgeshire Collection).

130 Charles Kingsley (By courtesy of the National Portrait Gallery, London).

133 Great Ouse, Offord Cluny (Cambridgeshire Collection).

134 Reflections at Morley's Holt (Cambridgeshire Collection).

135 Reminder of the medieval Fen (Cambridgeshire Collection).

139 Crowland Abbey (Courtesy of The Conway Library, Courtauld Institute, London).

143 Wicken Fen sketch (Cambridgeshire Collection).

144 Aerial view of Belsar's Hill (Crown Copyright – courtesy of Ministry of Defence).

146 Sketch map of the Fens around Ely (Author).

147 Map showing probable route into Ely taken by Norman attackers (Author).

148 The Holmes Fen Post (Author).

150 Trevor Bevis, the Fenland historian.

168 The John Harvard commemoration window, Emmanuel College Chapel (Courtesy of the Master and Fellows of Emmanuel College, Cambridge).

Preface

The name of Hereward 'the Wake' is one that strikes a chord in most people's memories, as does the year AD 1066. They may recall from school history lessons that he was the patriot who resisted the Norman invaders after the battle of Hastings and, thereby, salved some Saxon pride in a chapter of otherwise unmitigated gloom and disaster. From this episode, it has been argued, stems the outlaw myth that spawned Robin Hood and other guerrilla fighters resisting oppressive overlords. Beyond that, they will probably recall little and this is unsurprising since apart from a name there is nothing tangible upon which to reconstruct a biography.

Attempting to tell the story of Hereward is, necessarily, largely an exercise in deduction, surmise and speculation, as professional historians will acknowledge. The historic footprints are barely discernible, amounting to a few perfunctory references to 'Hereweard', a landholder in Domesday Book, and to his reputation for valour in some of the monastic chronicles. No castle remains to command awe, no tomb suitably engraved, no depiction in stone or coin – Hereward has vanished completely from this earth like the smoke from a woodland fire. Yet somehow the essence of his life has remained to infiltrate folklore, legend and literature.

This book is, therefore, an academic exercise only in the theoretical sense. The accepted facts relating to 1066 and the Norman Conquest form a background to the story and the question we investigate is why this obscure figure came to symbolize resistance in an hour of greatest peril and how in subsequent centuries he still had the power to inspire minstrels and writers like Charles Kingsley, and cause the Victorians to rediscover him as an icon of national heroism. The efforts of a family with an impeccable Norman pedigree, such as the Wakes of Courteenhall, to associate themselves with this Saxon hero and the strenuous attempts by General Harward to refute all claims to such kinship may not customarily be the stuff of historical research but they tell us something about Hereward's enduring legacy and how it links us, even today, with those distant antecedents who lived in this island a millennium ago.

Acknowledgements

During the research for and writing of this book the writer has received much help from many individuals and institutions, and particular thanks are due to the following:

Bedford Central Library, Trevor Bevis, The British Library, The British Museum, British Tourist Authority, Cambridge Antiquarian Society, Cambridge University Library, Cambridgeshire Collection (Cambridge Central Library), J. Carman (Hon. Curator, Ely Museum), The Conway Library (Courtauld Institute), Emmanuel College Library, Professor Christine E. Fell, Fenland District Council, Professor Peter Gordon, James B. Graham (Cecil Higgins Art Gallery, Bedford), Harvard University Archives, Dr Mary Hesse (Cambridge Antiquarian Society), Canon J. Higham, Professor Sir James Holt, Ann Inscker (Bedford Museum), The London Library, Sue M. Margeson (Keeper of Archaeology, Norfolk Museums Service), Richard Muir, National Portrait Gallery, Dr Dorothy Owen (Ely Cathedral Archivist), Peterborough Museum Society, Public Record Office, C. Rowsell (Ministry of Defence), Shakespeare Centre (Stratford upon Avon), Dr F.H. Stubbings, Alison Taylor (Cambridgeshire County Archaeologist), Trinity College Library (Cambridge), Sir Hereward Wake, Bt., Miss R. Watson (Northamptonshire County Archivist).

CHAPTER ONE

1066 and All That

In the year AD 1070 Saxon England lay prostrate under the heel of the Norman invader. Four years after King Harold's defeat by William the Conqueror at the battle of Hastings all opposition had seemingly withered away, crushed with a ruthless cruelty that eclipsed even that of Caesar's campaigns in Gaul a thousand years earlier. Only one last centre of resistance remained – the Isle of Ely in the Fens of East Anglia to which refuge stout hearted men of all kinds and from various parts made their way. Once there, they assembled under the banner, not of Edgar the Ætheling, the last Saxon claimant to the throne of England, nor under that of any of the remaining Saxon nobility such as Earl Morcar or his brother Earl Edwin; inexplicably, their chosen leader was, as the eminent scholar of the Middle Ages, Sir Frank Stenton, records, 'a Lincolnshire thegn of moderate estate, named Hereward, who in history as well as tradition represents the spirit of the native resistance to the Conqueror'.

'The redoubtable housecarls, the same axemen of the Bayeux Tapestry slaughtered by the dozen beneath Harold's dragon banner at the battle of Hastings.'

Hereward of Bourne in Lincolnshire, popularly known as Hereward the Wake, is an historical footnote, a man almost overlooked against the complex background of national upheaval surrounding the pivotal date of 1066. Yet a simple recital of his deeds casts him firmly in the heroic mould and arouses a keen curiosity about this shadowy figure whose struggle against enormous odds wins our admiration and flickers like candlelight in the enveloping gloom of Norman oppression.

Much of Hereward's life is closer to legend than reality and partly for that reason it has not concerned the professional historian too deeply. This is a pity because the few facts of which we are certain hint tantalizingly at a personality who, for a brief moment, became the incarnation of Anglo-Saxon defiance and therefore part of the matrix that creates folk heroes and helps to define a national identity.

For the rest of that fateful year of 1070 and well into the next – some versions of the story suggest a much longer siege but these are generally discounted – Hereward's small army, which was scarcely more than a guerrilla group, held out against repeated Norman attacks. An alliance of sorts was formed with the fleet of King Swein of Denmark and this may well have been seen to pose a potential threat to the lasting success of the whole Norman Conquest. Swein, as the nephew of King Cnut, ruler of England for twenty years until 1035, doubtless felt he had something more than a token claim to the English throne.[1]

The gravity of the situation, from a military and political standpoint, is underlined by William's decision to take personal command of the fenland operations. Some see it as the first assembly of an 'English' national *fyrd* (army) following the Norman invasion, although any native Anglo-Dane or Saxon assisting the invaders must surely have been regarded as a quisling. Eventually the Conqueror's superior forces, aided by treachery among the defenders, breached the defences and killed or captured most of the partisans. Hereward and some of his followers managed to cut their way to freedom and for some time continued to fight a bushwhacking campaign from the depths of the Bruneswald, the ancient forest that approached his home at Bourne and extended for perhaps 50 miles south-west across Northamptonshire and Buckinghamshire.

So, at a crucial watershed in British history and out of apparent obscurity steps this larger-than-life successor to King Arthur. He makes his sudden impact on a violent time and then exits, just as abruptly, leaving behind few clues to his existence yet an image powerful enough to become a model for Robin Hood and all England's popular champions thereafter.

The inclination of historians is to dismiss Hereward as merely another folk figure, born of the despair and barren hopes of a downtrodden people. Otherwise his career begs awkward questions. Why did the Saxons pin their faith on someone of such apparent unimportance, ignoring those of higher rank and greater authority? Or did Hereward have more powerful connections than we suppose?

Who was he really and how did he achieve the kind of renown that first made men of power, such as Earl Morcar, flock to his side and then enabled him to withstand the full impact of the Norman fighting machine?

Legend he may have become but even the more sceptical writers admit that someone called Hereward undoubtedly lived. The Domesday Book records that he held land near Bourne, his ancestral Lincolnshire home, and also in Warwickshire, and contemporary chroniclers, both Norman and Saxon, agree on some of the main elements of his story. While long after his death he was remembered best in the verses and tales of the common people, such traditions are often rooted in the memory of actual events. It is surely remarkable that a figure of potentially epic stature should not have been even more celebrated by writers of history and fiction.

Putting Hereward into perspective requires first a look at the two societies, Saxon and Norman, that collided at the battle of Hastings and then some explanation for the Conqueror's campaign of terror that followed, a veritable 'ethnic cleansing', involving the wholesale massacre of the vanquished and the removal and destruction of their means of livelihood. The degree of barbarity prompted even Norman scribes to recoil in horror and brand William for 'an act which levelled both the bad and the good in one common ruin'.

Some measure of Hereward's – albeit temporary – defiance is possible by comparing it with other doomed attempts at rebellion that sparked and spluttered in the post-Hastings period. It contrasts starkly with the general subjugation that saw the Old English society in all its forms buried by an alien one.

The Normans may have begun their rule as an occupying garrison living for the most part behind hastily thrown-up defensive ramparts, but within twenty years they were to permeate and dominate the fabric of England's society, replacing the Saxon aristocracy that had enjoyed similar powers and privileges. Pockets of that old governing class probably lingered here and there, each thane making what compromises his conscience could stomach in order to protect his kinsfolk in a changed and hostile world. But the majority were either slain in battle, exiled, or usurped and uprooted. This must have provided a ready recruiting ground of dissidents, such as those who flocked to Hereward's banner, and prompts us to wonder how R.J. Adam[2] can so readily assert that their Norman successors could disperse over the face of England 'without fear of racial war' to insert themselves into the old framework of English government. 'They were warriors of a new type, but lords of a familiar pattern,' he claims, 'and for the great majority of Englishmen they can have appeared little different from the men they displaced. More even than the king who led them, these men were the real makers of the Norman Conquest, and the real gainers from it.' The reality must have been a great deal more complicated than this even if it is all too easy, in the light of subsequent events, to be persuaded by the resonance of G.M. Trevelyan's summation that

England 'still needed to be hammered into a nation, and she had now found masters who would do it' (*A Shortened History of England*, Pelican, 1943, p. 109).

Historians, working with the advantage of hindsight, have a perspective denied to those who make history or live through it. Their horizons are not foreshortened and we should remember this in order to have any conception of what it must have felt like to be a Saxon or a Norman during those turbulent times. Hereward must be seen against the familiar background of invasion and the different reactions of a populace to losing their freedom and coming to terms with an occupation that was to prove permanent. To our eyes it was, of course, a very different and unfamiliar society whose conception of loyalties was still evolving from the old ties of kinship and tribe to the considerably more complex idea of one nation under one king. The land was divided internally by rival factions and threatened externally, not merely by a Norman invasion, but by Denmark, the Scottish king and still, in theory, by the warlike Welsh, inflamed by the recent exploits of their hero Gruffydd ap Llywelyn who had been defeated only four years before Hastings.

Hereward's motivations – he was a landholder deprived of his family estates by the Normans – are understandable but less significant, perhaps, than his apparent ability to attract substantial support where luminaries of the Saxon nobility had failed. His capacity to organize a long rearguard campaign and inflict minor yet embarrassing defeats on a hitherto invincible invader may suggest unusual military cunning. Even if only some of his reported exploits were factual he seems to have utilized the fenland's natural advantages for guerrilla warfare in a manner seldom equalled before or since. The tradition of Ely as a place of refuge was to continue for centuries.

Hereward's attempted alliance with the Danish King Swein indicates a wider vision than might have been expected from a minor thane, and his eventual defeat – due in part to Swein's defection but ultimately, according to popular tradition, to betrayal by monks who led the Normans to his fenland stronghold along secret pathways – is a romantic tale that has been embellished by legend. Even so, Hereward's escape and subsequent career as an outlaw is recorded in some versions of his life. These also report his earlier exploits on the Continent as a hired mercenary and his eventual reconciliation with William who restored his lands and titles – one of the occasions when the Conqueror's cruelty was allegedly tempered by chivalry towards a doughty opponent.

Borrowing descriptions such as 'cruel' and 'ruthless' to describe historical characters such as William requires caution. By any standards such terms are doubtless true, but it is unlikely that the Conqueror was markedly different from his contemporaries and the trail of rapine and devastation that he left behind, particularly in his campaigns in the north of England, occurred at a time when such atrocities were not unknown. If he were a monster, he lived in monstrous times.

Rediscovering Hereward's story and trying to disentangle it from myth is an exercise in which we have to balance the sometimes contradictory views of historians who, down the ages, may have been swayed by political or other influences. In the end our assumptions must recognize that even primary sources of intelligence, such as the medieval chronicles, are full of quicksand. Those original scribes may themselves have been misled or mischievous in their handling of facts and subsequent translations from Old English or Latin agree to differ often enough to make this kind of detective work far from an exact science.

However, awareness of such difficulties should not deflect our aim which is in some small way to acknowledge the life and achievement of this forgotten hero and perhaps even to help elevate him from a footnote to a place in the pages of history. We shall look at the attempts made to trace Hereward's origins and descendants and identify those places in East Anglia and elsewhere that figured significantly in his life. Above all we shall try to put ourselves in the shoes of Hereward and his kinsmen at the time of the Norman assault on England. Invasion is more than a violation of sovereignty; it leaves scars on the psyche of individuals and nations that can be indelible. Occupation by an invading army with its inevitable loss of freedom, its impact on home, family and friends, deepens such wounds and it is arguable that the passage of years may not completely erase them from what might be called the collective folk-memory.

Even in Britain where such memories, if they indeed survive, are nearly a thousand years old, the fear of invasion still exercises a powerful hold. In recent times its phantoms have become all too real for Channel Islanders and the British inhabitants of the Falkland Islands. A decade after Argentine armoured vehicles rattled past her window a housewife in Port Stanley admitted that the sound of Spanish being spoken was enough to revive her worst memories of 1983. To the writer, an English schoolboy in the 1940s, the notion of invasion carried images of jack-booted German storm troopers marching up the village High Street, ordering the postmistress to hand over her takings, plundering the vicar's apple orchard and commandeering both Farmer Tongue's shire horses and his Fordson tractor.

During the darkest hours of the Second World War such pictures engaged the imagination rather more sombrely than did Jules Verne, the *Wizard* comic or even the sepulchral radio tones of Valentine Dyall and, although we never truly believed that the Germans would descend from the skies, the possibility was strong enough to worry even the unworldly. This was especially true at bedtime when lamps were switched off and we prepared for sleep. Then the prospect of invasion became more real and we tried to imagine what it would be like to have foreigners trampling on our everyday lives.

At the county library we would consult the history section devoutly, hoping to discover a comparable national disaster that might put the current threat into comforting perspective. No such comparisons could be found until the search went back almost a millennium to 1066 and the battle of Hastings. That event exerted a special fascination missing from other pages of history. The Spanish Armada, for example, had a fancy-dress quality and in any case represented the threat rather than the reality of invasion. Hastings was different. It evoked – albeit illogically – almost a sense of shame. National pride was bruised at the notion that this island of a million people could be subdued apparently so quickly and so completely by a Norman expeditionary force of fewer than ten thousand men.[3] After all, we lived in that selfsame island, itself besieged and threatened with invasion, and patriotism was an unspoken but potent undercurrent to our lives. Jingoistic contemporary cinema newsreels reflected the attitude of ordinary people in 1940 no more accurately than do the headlines in today's tabloid newspapers. But we had inherited assumptions of an invincibility that was implicit in the Empire's benevolent pink dominance of the classroom globe. A generation later things had changed and more sophisticated children of the 1960s onwards may not have identified so readily with either Saxon or Norman.

A naïve schoolboy of the 1940s was a not altogether unreliable barometer of popular emotions, being much influenced by them. To him the broadcasted taunts of a Herr Goebbels had much less impact than the condescension of the Norman chronicler William of Poitiers, whose boast it was that by this battle at Hastings Duke William conquered all England in a single day 'between the third hour and the evening'.

If it were not such a familiar fact we would, like R.H.C. Davis,[4] have thought it incredible that England, or any other State, could have been completely overwhelmed after a single battle. 'But this', writes Davis, 'was what happened after the Battle of Hastings. Apparently as the result of one day's fighting (on October 14, 1066), England received a new royal dynasty, a new aristocracy, a virtually new Church, a new art, a new architecture and a new language.' By 1086, when Domesday Book was made, less than half a dozen of the 180 greater landlords or tenants-in-chief were English. By 1090 only one of the sixteen English bishoprics was held by an Englishman, and six of the sees had been moved from their historic centres to large towns. By the end of the twelfth century almost every Anglo-Saxon cathedral and abbey had been pulled down and rebuilt in the Norman style (many Saxon village churches escaped and can be seen today).

Nothing was allowed to stand which might remind the English of the glories of their past. The Normans put it out that the Anglo-Saxons had been used to wooden palaces and wooden churches, that they had lived by a 'natural' economy, and that since they had no money they had been forced to pay their taxes in kind. They claimed that their military prowess had been ineffectual

Anglo-Saxon parish churches, unlike the more prestigious cathedral and abbey, survived Norman destruction. Brixworth Church, Northamptonshire, in the heart of Mercia, dates from around AD 675 and is regarded as one of the most impressive seventh-century buildings that survives north of the Alps.

and their culture non-existent, and they relegated the English language to the underworld of the lower classes. For almost two centuries the language of polite society – the aristocracy and the court – was French, and the reality of the English past was smothered with romantic stories about King Arthur and the ancient Britons

Davis wrote these words many years after we were obtaining a roughly similar impression from earlier historians. Further reading was to reveal a somewhat different story, but that initial reaction was intuitive and, being ignorant of, was therefore uninfluenced by the centuries of historical debate. This experience may, perhaps, sustain the assertion of R. Allen Brown[5] that the historians' interpretation of events filters through into public consciousness to establish, as it were, a common knowledge. Depending upon which historians one reads – and fashions of opinion change over the years as we shall see – this would explain our unwitting adoption of the Whig view of the past in which 'the Anglo-Saxons tend to become "us", the Normans "them", with William the Conqueror cast as a foreign tyrant winning a regrettable victory over clean-limbed Englishmen with marked liberal and Protestant leanings.'

Edward Augustus Freeman, the eminent Victorian whose five-volume tome *The*

Late Saxon Thetford: part of the ironworkers' district, as it might have appeared in the tenth century.

Norman Conquest was published between 1867 and 1879, stands indicted for so interpreting the past through the distorting mirror of his own contemporary political sentiments as, indeed, his seventeenth-century predecessors had done. Freeman, as R. Allen Brown points out, saw the struggle in terms of a 'national party' versus the Normans, and presented as the 'patriotic leaders' and champions of that party the unlikely figures of Godwin, Earl of Wessex, and Harold his son 'with the result that to this day Harold is popularly regarded as a national hero rather than as an over mighty subject usurping the English throne. For Freeman the Norman Conquest was "only a temporary overthrow . . ." and "in a few generations we led captive our conquerors; England was England once again, and

Edward Augustus Freeman, the eminent
Victorian historian.

the descendants of the Norman invaders were found to be among the truest of
Englishmen".' As G.K. Chesterton remarked, a man 'may end by maintaining that
the Norman Conquest was a Saxon Conquest'.

Perhaps Freeman did see English society as a flowing stream to which the
Conquest was merely a temporary obstruction, a tree falling into the water causing
a splash but ultimately not diverting the direction of the current. His view can
also, if you are so inclined, be identified as antidote to the venom of Thomas
Carlyle, his famous contemporary. Carlyle observed that 'England itself . . . still
howls and execrates lamentably over its William Conqueror, and rigorous line of
Norman and Plantagenets; but without them . . . what had it ever been? A
gluttonous race of Jutes and Angles, capable of no great combinations; lumbering
about in pot-bellied equanimity; not dreaming of heroic toil and endurance, such
as leads to the high places of the Universe and the golden mountain-tops where
dwell the Spirits of the Dawn.'

That lofty view could readily be adopted by a Calvinist Scot, and perhaps it was
no great hardship for Carlyle, the Lord Rector of Edinburgh University, to tweak
the nose of Oxford's Regius Professor of Modern History as Freeman then was.
Indeed, the belligerence of historians seems to borrow some of its vigour from the
long-dead combatants of whom they write. Thus a modern historian such as

R. Allen Brown can declare, tongue in cheek, that if it were necessary to take sides he should be with Duke William at Hastings, 'thus to find myself locked in mortal combat with E.A. Freeman, who declared he would gladly have fought upon the other side'.

Of course no such conceits entered those faraway schoolboy considerations. Ours was a cowboys-and-Indians view of history and we readily identified with whomever were the 'home' side at the time. Thus we shouldered arms with the Britons against the Romans and later the Angles and Saxons, then cut our elderberry spears with the Saxons against the Vikings and naturally with the Saxons against the Normans. It was therefore easy for us to sympathize with that deeply sinister schemer Godwin, Earl of Wessex, and share the view that his son Harold was cast in the identical mould from which Drake, Nelson, Wellington and other heroes were later to emerge.

Recent Anglo-Norman scholarship has tended towards the view that the Norman Conquest was not simply a Norman–Saxon struggle since an English nation as we know it did not exist in the mid-eleventh century; rather, seen through Hereward's eyes, it may have appeared to be at first a private war between Wessex and Normandy. Later scholars, notably W.H. Stevenson, have acknowledged the importance of the Norwegian and Danish impact on the battle for the English kingdom, and R. Allen Brown identifies a swing from Freeman's preoccupation with political events and constitutional implications to the effects of the Norman Conquest upon a wider range of matters, including social and economic factors, Church, government and State and the very nature of society itself.

At the same time the past few decades have seen a striking increase in the awareness and appreciation of the Saxon pre-Conquest achievement in almost every sphere, a change reflected in Stenton's own writings. When his *William the Conqueror* was published in 1908 little could be said in favour of England before William's armada set sail. J.H. Round[6] had declared that the Normans were essentially superior and that in a sense English political history only commences with them. By 1943, however, Stenton[7] was stigmatizing the harsh and violent Normans as 'closest of all the western peoples to the barbarian strain in the continental order. They had produced little in art or learning, and nothing in literature, that could be set beside the work of Englishmen. But politically, they were the masters of their world.' Twenty years later, as Trevor Rowley[8] remarks, the pendulum swung even further against the Normans and H.G. Richardson and G.O. Sayles[9] could affirm: 'For half a century or so, from 1066 the English way of life was not sensibly altered, the Normans had very little to teach even in the art of war, and they had very much to learn. They were Barbarians who were becoming conscious of their insufficiency.'

Norman propaganda's efficiency in portraying the Conquest as the restoration of civilized Christianity to a rude Saxon backwater of Europe is unmasked as cynical mendacity. The tragedy of Saxon England was, paradoxically, that it was too well organized and possessed an administrative machine unsurpassed in the whole of western Europe. Trained officials ran both central and local administration; a royal Exchequer received taxes, and a Chancery (or writing office) produced standardized writs conveying instructions around the provinces where local officials had been trained to obey them. Shire reeves or sheriffs controlled the shires which, in contrast to other parts of Europe, covered the whole kingdom and had precisely defined boundaries. 'There was no vagueness about what belonged to where, and as a result it was difficult, if not impossible, for any person or place to evade the control of the sheriff,' observes R.H.C. Davis. Every shire was divided into hundreds composed of neighbouring villages and the hundred court met every four weeks. In turn each hundred belonged to a shire with its twice-yearly court which all the principal men were compelled to attend. At such gatherings judgements in lawsuits were given and the king's orders received.

These institutions provided the monarch with the means to exercise enormous power best exemplified by taxation and coinage. The administrative divisions enabled him regularly to levy a land tax or geld on the whole kingdom which was divided into hides or carucates – taxable units of a notional value usually some 120 acres in size. Central government knew how many hides were in every shire and its tax demands sent to the shire court were there divided among the component hundreds. The hundred courts next subdivided the tax among the component tithings; and within each tithing each landholder knew what proportion he had to pay. 'When, in the tenth century,' says R.H.C. Davis, 'Anglo-Saxon kings had declared that every man had to be in a hundred and tithing, they were ensuring not only that all men could be brought to justice but also that they could be taxed. As a system it was unique in Western Europe.' The Conqueror must have been elated to discover that all he needed to do to replenish his Treasury was to proclaim a geld year and then sit back and await the harvest of money that followed.

For the coinage in which taxes were collected all moneyers were appointed by the Crown and obtained their dies from a strictly controlled die-cutting agency. Coin types were apparently changed at six-yearly intervals, and to facilitate re-minting there were perhaps as many as seventy minting places scattered throughout England. Few places would have been more than a day's ride away from one or other. 'Such elaborate control of the coinage was almost unprecedented in a medieval state.'[10] This flatly contradicts the impression given by Norman scribes of a rudimentary system in which the Anglo-Saxons sometimes had to pay their taxes in kind.

William soon realized the potential of the governmental machine that had fallen into his hands. Devised to provide England with an army for its defence, it could now be employed to speed the transfer of the lands of the English to Norman ownership. Comments Davis: 'Countries which are well governed should be able to resist invading armies more easily than countries which are not, but if by any chance they fail they are easier for a conqueror to control. They do not lend themselves to guerrilla resistance, because efficient governments remove the opportunities for such activities. . . .'

The historians' verdict is that the logical explanation for the success of the Norman settlement lay in the legitimacy of William's claim to the English Crown. After Harold's death, the only possible alternative was the Ætheling Edgar, and, says Davis, 'since he was too young and too much of a simpleton to inspire confidence, the English had no option but to accept William as their king. But his accession would have had little practical effect if it had not been for the fact that the English kingdom had an efficient system of government.'

The layman can be excused his confusion at the contradictions that abound in the historians' interpretations of what happened and why. He may well conclude that perhaps one of the reasons for the lack of agreement over the Norman impact on England is due to the difficulty of answering the question, Who were the Normans? The enigma of this powerful yet curiously impermanent race is that their capacity to subdue others and appropriate both property and institutions was matched by the ease with which they were themselves eventually absorbed into the supposedly conquered society.

It has been asserted that the Norman monarchy had ceased to rule in England within a century of the battle of Hastings and its empire, which once touched lands as far apart as Wales and Syria, had all but evaporated by 1200. In fact Normandy as an independent State ceased to exist when it was wrested from King John by France in 1204 and F.W. Maitland has even suggested that for at least fifty years before Hastings the Normans were more French than Norman in their language, law and customs. Coinage of the period discovered in Normandy also indicates an increasing detachment from Scandinavia and a strengthening of ties with the Romance world. We should therefore perhaps begin this quest by looking at the origins of the Normans, why they were so effective and what made others fear them.

Normandy sits astride the lower Seine river, whose natural access to the very heart of France had been exploited in turn by Celt, Roman, Visigoth, Vandal, Hun and eventually the Norse pirates. When in 911 the king of the Franks ceded territory on the lower Seine to a Norseman called Rollo, Normandy effectively came into being with all its momentous consequences for European history.

It was, writes Trevor Rowley, a State with well-defined borders and internal administrative divisions and this secular and ecclesiastical administrative heritage considerably aided the dukes in their creation of the Norman Empire. Normandy was the cooking pot in which Roman, Carolingian, Frankish and Scandinavian elements were combined in a brew that under forceful and single-minded rulers was to prove too powerful for the stomachs of its neighbours.

This may explain to some extent the riddle of how so few overcame so many both in France and England in the tenth and eleventh centuries. Although we have only a dim picture of the nature of Scandinavian settlement, Rowley's interesting question is how much was the creation of Normandy accompanied by significant incursions of people from the north? Or was it, as in England after 1066, largely a matter of an alien aristocracy imposing itself on the indigenous people, in this case the Franks, who had held the land for the previous four centuries? The fact that French seems to have remained the dominant language suggests only a limited immigration. Early eleventh-century writers record 'Roman' rather than Danish as the language of Rouen, although reputedly Scandinavian was being spoken in Bayeux.[11]

Norsemen intermarried freely with non-Scandinavians, indeed none of the wives of Normandy's dukes came from Scandinavia, and it has been observed that it was only in the eleventh century, when the Normans were no longer Scandinavian, that they began to acquire some of their most 'Norman' characteristics. As the great families emerged, so did the great abbeys, with their distinctive style of art and architecture. The plunder of England financed a huge building programme and most of the Romanesque churches of Normandy were built after the Conquest.[12] By the time of the Conquest the Normans, who had become Christian with typical vigour, appear to have distanced themselves from their wild Nordic origins.

Rowley's analysis of place-name evidence shows that names once regarded as purely Scandinavian have been found to have parallels in non-Scandinavian parts of France. While most Scandinavian place-names in Normandy are hybrids, in England, especially in the north, is to be found a distinctively Scandinavian pattern that has no counterpart in France. The picture that emerges is interpreted as being one of Scandinavian overlords governing a population who spoke neither Frankish nor Scandinavian, but French.

The situation in England was to prove not dissimilar for ultimately the native tongue was equally resilient despite being ousted by Latin (used in lawmaking since the seventh century) and French at the law courts, the first universities and in early parliamentary procedures. This, after all, was the language of the Anglo-Saxon Chronicle, described by the American critic F.P. Magoun, Jun., as 'the most important work written in English before the Norman Conquest'. G.N. Garmonsway's introduction to his translation of the Chronicle,[13] describes it as 'the first national continuous history of a western nation in its own language' and 'the first great book in English prose'. R.W. Chambers remarks, 'The historians insist that English literature was dead at the time of the Conquest, yet, so long as there is any Chronicle at all, they cannot get on without its telling phrases.'[14] The restoration of English was signalled by a trilingual proclamation issued by Henry III in 1258, and at the opening of Parliament in 1362 the Chancellor was to read his speech in English for the first time.

'Old English' is a preferable term to 'Anglo-Saxon' for the language spoken in England before the Conquest because it reinforces the fact that it is an older form of our present tongue and not a different language. Most words and expressions commonly used today existed in Old English although pronounced and spelt differently as part of an altered vocabulary and grammar. Old English rather than adopting foreign words as Modern English does (e.g. *royal* from France, *piano* from Italy) preferred to translate the idea a foreign word might convey. Thus instead of adopting 'trinity' the Anglo-Saxon translated it as 'three-ness'. This language with its runic past and its heroic links with Norse saga and Saxon story-telling was the tool with which the English, long before the Norman Conquest, fashioned a literature which survives in the poetry of Caedmon from before AD 700 and in the epic *Beowulf*.

It is from such literature that we begin to obtain a picture of the England that existed before the coming of William, and of the men who lived there, especially the thanes, the class of Saxon lords and landholders to whom Hereward belonged. 'The Battle of Maldon', a poem lamenting the death in battle of the ealdorman Brihtnoth in 991, offers a window at which we can listen to and perhaps even see Hereward and his peers. Its words may well have been known to them and the lives and values it describes mirrored their own:

> Brihtwold spoke . . . (he was an old companion): 'Thoughts must be the braver, hearts more valiant, courage the greater as strength grows less. Here lies our lord, all cut down, the hero in the dust. Long may he mourn who thinks now to turn from the battle-play. I am old in years; I will not leave the field, but think to lie by my lord's side, by the man I held so dear.'[15]

Loyalty to their king earned such men honour, fame and estates as recorded by book or charter, and with it society journeyed towards feudalism. Below them toiled the peasants, and foremost among these was the *geneat* who may have originally been attached to a royal entourage, and carried out such official duties as shepherding his lord's visitors. The only free man below aristocratic rank was the *ceorl* a property-owning peasant whose economic status varied widely. He, and those above him, owned slaves who may have been debtors or prisoners taken in battle, for slavery was an essential part of that society.

Britons, descendants of an earlier conquered race, still survived in parts of

Wessex, some as slaves (*Welsh* became synonymous with *slave*), some free. Danish society was not dissimilar although the Danelaw in eastern England appears to have had a higher proportion of free men, which could explain the sokeman of the Domesday Book. He was more free though not necessarily richer than his English neighbour.

The bonds linking lord and man, leader and follower, held this society together and near its apex were the king's most trusted followers who would include the redoubtable housecarls, the same axemen of the Bayeux Tapestry slaughtered by the dozen beneath Harold's dragon banner at the battle of Hastings. The king and his Court were supported, in part at least, by food rents due from villages and it seems that since the days of Alfred peasants laboured on their lord's land after the fashion that became the norm in medieval records. Kinship was the cornerstone of everyday life, hence the pragmatic method of dealing with murder: the *wergild* payable in cases of homicide by the guilty person to the kin of the deceased.

This may or may not have been the wisest way of avoiding a prolonged vendetta but in any event it offered some compensation for the loss of a breadwinner. Vendettas were far from unknown, however, and retribution for wrongs could be carried on into succeeding generations and conducted by such eminent and posthumously saintly men as Waltheof, Earl of Northumbria, whose execution by William was to cast him in the role of Saxon martyr.

While such an overview gives an impression of rigidity, it appears that in reality Saxon society was fluid and that climbing the social ladder was not impossible. For instance, a trader showing enterprise and crossing the open sea three times at his own expense prospered accordingly and afterwards might claim the rights of a thane. Similarly, a ruined harvest or bad investments could lead to just as sudden a fall to serfdom or even into slavery. But the slaves themselves had a possible alternative: some ran away and joined the free enterprise brotherhood of Vikings.

Living in eleventh-century England was thus very much a snakes-and-ladders affair and no better illustration of this can be found than the life of Hereward.

CHAPTER TWO

Sources

The task of rediscovering Hereward must begin with the primary sources of our knowledge of medieval history, the monastic chroniclers, who, as recorders of their age, in a sense combined the functions of today's newspaper, radio and television reporters, political commentators and, indeed, gossip columnists. Like modern journalists they must at times have allowed their personal bias or prejudices to lure them into fiction, if only by adding imaginative touches to brighten otherwise prosaic records. We should not be too hard on them, however, remembering the difficulties under which they worked. And they are the closest we can get to those distant events since they lived through them or in the years immediately following, or spoke to people who may have fought with Harold at Hastings or Stamford Bridge, and survived the evil days that followed William's conquest.

Monastic chroniclers were the recorders of their age. The Scribe Eadwine from the Canterbury copy of the Utrecht Psalter made in 1147.

Few would doubt the sincerity and probity in this voice that addresses us across the millennium through the early twelfth-century Peterborough Chronicle of Hugh Candidus:

For I call truth herself which cannot lie, to witness that I write nothing and I speak nothing, save that which I found recorded in the writings of old time, or heard from the lips of ancient and faithful witnesses. Whoso desires to study these matters with care, he will still be able to find the record, and to relate the story or to test its truth.

It is easy to empathize with the views of the fenland historian Trevor Bevis when he says 'I put more value on the words of those old chroniclers than I do on those of later historians. They were men of God who valued the truth and were enthusiastic searchers after it.' In 1981 Bevis published his own revision of a nineteenth-century translation of the *De Gestis Herwardi* [1], which he described as undoubtedly the oldest existing manuscript touching upon the exploits of Hereward and

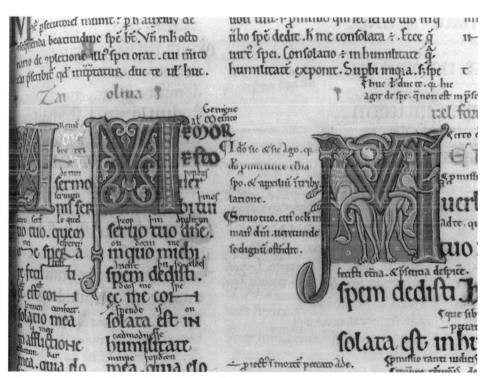

The monastic scribe often embellished his work with handsome decoration as in this page of the Utrecht Psalter.

preserved for centuries in Peterborough Cathedral library (it is now at Cambridge University Library).

H.W.C. Davis in commenting on the Hereward legend[2] included 'the Latin romance' *De Gestis Herwardi* printed in the Rolls edition of Gaimar among the principal sources of information. The others were the 'False Ingulph' (1300–70); 'John of Peterborough', a fourteenth-century compilation; the *Historia Eliensis*, a local Ely chronicle written between 1174 and 1189; the *Liber de Hyda*, written at Lewes before 1136; and Gaimar's own *L'estoire des Engles*.

To Davis's selection we must add, for a wider view, the writings of such men as Orderic Vitalis (1075–1143), the Anglo-Norman historian; Florence of Worcester (??–1118), an English monk of Worcester, who wrote a chronicon which comes down to 1116; and William of Malmesbury (*c.* 1090– *c.* 1143), another English monk-chronicler, born probably near Malmesbury, Wiltshire, whose *Gesta Regum Anglorum* provides a lively history of the kings of England from the Saxon invasion to 1126. Hugh Candidus, or Hugh White, the author or compiler of the first local chronicle of Peterborough, lived during the reigns of Henry I (1100–35), Stephen (1135–54) and Henry II (1154–89). What little knowledge we have of Hugh lies in a paragraph in the text of Hugh's chronicle inserted by the unknown scribe, who copied it into the Peterborough Cartulary, destroyed during the burning of part of the Cottonian library at Ashburnham House, Westminster, on 23 October 1731. This unknown scribe referred to Hugh as a 'man who has just died, who also gathered the materials for this book, and when they were gathered wrote it'. After describing at some length Hugh's miraculous recovery in youth from a serious haemorrhage, the scribe concluded:

> When he had thus recovered from his illness, he was well and truly instructed by good counsellors, to wit:—Abbot Ernulph [1107–15] brother Reinald, and the rest of the elders, and he was called Hugh White, because he was white and of a fair countenance. . . . In boyhood and in youth he was the son of the elder monks, and the brother of them of his own age, but now he is the oldest of them all, and father to them all, loving his people as his friends, and being loved by them . . . he held and maintained through the changes of the times for as long as he could, offices, obediences and possessions of the church within and without, that were entrusted to his hands. At last he reached the office of sub-prior, at first, under abbot Martin, and later under abbot William de Waterville . . . he departed this life in happiness enriched with all those virtues in the times of William the abbot.[3]

Davis preferred Gaimar as the most trustworthy of these authorities. The latter wrote between 1135 and 1147 and shows a special familiarity with the events of north and eastern England during the Conqueror's reign, and his account of Hereward 'cannot be traced to any extant source'. The implication of some exclusive line of information is intriguing.

Doubts about the veracity of the *De Gestis Herwardi Saxonis* arise because it professes to be based in part upon an Old English poem about Hereward; but the author says that of this he had only been able to discover a few leaves, which were mildewed and otherwise defaced. Davis says,

> The poem was written, according to its title, by Leofric the chaplain of Hereward. But since the author of the *Gesta* tells us that the fragments at his disposal related to the early adventures of Hereward, and these as reported in the *Gesta* are purely fabulous, it is probable that the poem, whether contemporary with Hereward or not, was a mere romance. Leofric the Deacon is in fact described in the *Gesta* as a romancer who wrote for edification. But the author of the *Gesta* also mentions information derived from two of Hereward's followers, Siward and Leofric the Black, and from monks who had seen and conversed with Hereward.

We can come to our own conclusions only by reading the words of the deacon Leofric ourselves, even if we have to rely on the versions offered by translators. If nothing else, the preface to the *De Gestis Herwardi Saxonis* as presented by Bevis offers an intriguing picture of the difficulties faced by the monkish scribes even a generation or so after the events they describe and the zeal with which they pursued their task:

(Addressed to the Abbot)

> Here begins the preface of a certain work concerning the exploits of Hereward the renowned Knight. Some of us desiring to learn of the deeds of the noble Hereward, an Englishman, and his renowned men, and to hear of his generous actions and doings, the brethren of your house have helped us by enquiring if any man had left anything in writing about so great a man in the place where he once lived. For when we declared that we had heard in a certain place that a short account had been written about him in English, straight-away you sought the whereabouts of that writing and before long translated into Latin, adding also the things which we had heard from our own people with whom he [Hereward] was well known, living nobly as a soldier.

The search for documentary evidence was only partly successful:

> We enquired in many places, and yet found nothing except a few scattered leaves, partly rotten by damp, and decayed and partly damaged by tearing.

'*Incipit præfatio cujusdam opusculi de gestis Herwardi incliti militis . . .* Here begins the preface of a certain work concerning the exploits of Hereward the renowned knight.' The original source – a page from the story of Hereward related in *De Gestis Herwardi*, now contained in the Peterborough Manuscript (the Book of Robert of Swaffham), kept at Cambridge University Library.

When the pen had been put to its task we have with difficulty extracted from it his descent from his parents and his character among other things; that is to say the early achievements of the very famous outlaw Hereward, edited in English by Leofric the Deacon, his priest at Bourne. For the intention of this well known priest was to collect all the acts of the famous warriors from stories, or from trustworthy narration, for the edification of his hearers, and for their remembrance to commit them to the English language.

And although insufficiently skilled in this, or rather incompetent to decipher what is obliterated of the unfamiliar language, we have gathered concerning Hereward on his return to that place and to his ancestral home where he had found his brother murdered. We leave this material, written in rude style, to your care and to the zeal of some man's trained ability to be interpreted in simpler and plainer language. We have been able to decipher nothing further than this, ever hoping for greater results but as yet finding nothing thoroughly.

It is a daunting thought that within a generation or so of Hereward's death would-be biographers encountered such obstacles. Leofric the Deacon, as a Bourne man, would have been proud of his local hero, but his efforts were intended for a wider audience and the scribes now hint at the existence of some undiscovered work that seems to have been an early biography of Hereward:

For they, deluded for a long time, derived hope from others who said that in a place there is a great book of his [Hereward's] exploits from the beginning, found nothing of what they had been led to expect, although they sent to the place. We eventually abandoned the search completely and put away the work we had begun. But some of our men did not want us to do this, and unexpectedly you kindly directed that at least the commencement should not be denied you.

Thank heavens for the abbot's encouragement for the next passage brings us as near to Hereward and his men as we are likely to get:

It was then an object of care to us, for want of great ability that you might see our incomplete work, and take up the pen once more and again to present to you a little book in the manner of a history, concerning these things which we have heard from our own men and from some of his [Hereward's] with whom they had associated from the beginning of his career and were in many ways his comrades. We have seen some of these men, tall in stature and huge and of exceeding courage, and you yourselves have seen also two men conspicuous for their form as you yourself told us, namely Siwate, Bother of St. Edmunds, and Leofric Niger, his Knights, although injured by enemies, being bereft of some members by trickery, through envy. Indeed of these and others, proved and seen, it is given to you to understand of what valour their lord was, and how much greater were the things that he did what they reported of him [*sic*]. We think it will encourage noble deeds and induce liberality to know Hereward, who he was, and to hear of his achievements and deeds, and especially to those who are desirous of living the life of a soldier. Wherefore we advise you, give attention and you who the more diligently strive to hear the deeds of brave men, apply your minds to hear diligently the account of so great a man: for he trusting neither in fortification, nor in garrison, but in himself, alone with his men waged war against Kingdoms and Kings, and fought against princes and tyrants, some of whom he conquered.

The allusion to fortification is perhaps a scornful reminder of the Norman practice of consolidating gains by quickly throwing up a motte-and-bailey castle, first of timber and later of stone, to defend themselves against reprisals. These were important instruments of subjugation and Orderic Vitalis even suggested that the English would never have been conquered if they had possessed castles of their own. Such dominating features had been almost unknown in England before the Conquest, being quite different from the fortified towns or boroughs favoured by the Anglo-Saxons.

The boroughs were large because they had been designed to accommodate people from a wider area seeking refuge from invaders. The smaller castle, on the other hand, was intended as a strategic position from which the few could dominate the many. In its simplest form it became merely a wooden tower erected on a mound of earth (or motte). From there defenders could fire down on to their attackers who were denied the impetus of a cavalry assault by the steepness of the mound.

Despite its relatively modest scale, such a motte must have required a major building operation, involving the forced labour of local people, working with spades, baskets and wheelbarrows. That at Oxford measured 64 feet in height with a diameter of 81 feet at the top and 250 feet at the base. An upturned cooking bowl conveys a mind's-eye picture since the proportions are roughly similar. Typically, the site of Oxford's motte was on the perimeter of the old borough, so offering its Norman occupants a link with possible outside assistance in the event of revolt by the town's citizens.

At York a vivid impression can be obtained of just such a menacing sentinel from Clifford's Tower whose heights still offer the finest view of the ancient walled city with its Minster floating like a grey battleship above the orange-brick sea of

The Norman castle was a strategic position from which the few could dominate the many. Orford Castle, Suffolk, dates from a century after Hastings and its polygonal keep was an experimental design (square keeps were vulnerable to collapse when besiegers burrowed beneath their corners).

modern sloping rooftops. Today's surviving tower was built by Henry III in the thirteenth century on the site of the keep which in its turn had replaced the Conqueror's wooden tower, burned down by the mob attacking the besieged Jews in the pogrom of 1190. It had been designed as an instrument of oppression, a gaoler posted on the city's doorstep, and it ably fulfilled its grim purpose.

It is ironic that Leofric the Deacon, the scribe nearest in time to Hereward and the one most personally and emotionally committed to perpetuating the memory of his deeds, should in fact be the cause of much of the scepticism which the Hereward story evokes. For it contains two elements – material that could be fact and episodes that can only be fiction. The latter are the fabulous early adventures of Hereward as a wandering exile and they are found only in the *Gesta* and, therefore, must derive from Leofric alone. Some may dismiss Leofric as an over-enthusiastic and misguided admirer but another interpretation is possible. Perhaps this obscure cleric had the vision to foresee that presenting the Hereward story as a popular legend would give it enough buoyancy to float on the stream of time until some future inquirer might separate truth from myth and so give Hereward his due.

It is indeed unsurprising that much of the more believable material is found in that other local history, the *Historia Eliensis*, which contains many details about the

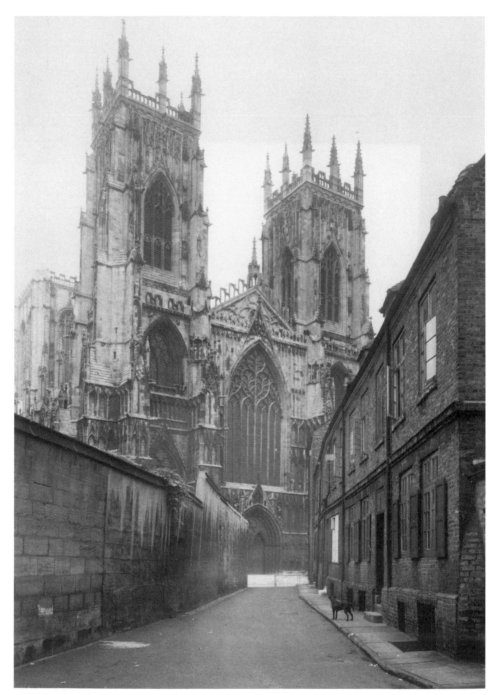

York Minster 'floating like a grey battleship above the orange-brick sea of modern sloping rooftops'.

siege of Ely not found in the other sources. It would, in fact, be surprising if this were not so since we would expect an Ely writer to be especially well informed about this incident. The great mistake of the *Historia Eliensis* is in describing two sieges of Ely. It was evidently composed long after the event, and used the *Gesta* among its sources. Nevertheless H.W.C. Davis feels that 'some of the stories for which the *Historia* is alone responsible have all the marks of verisimilitude'.

Most authorities seem to agree broadly over Hereward's subsequent career in the Bruneswald, the main problem arising from the contradictory account of his end given by Gaimar which is at variance with that in the *Gesta*. According to the latter Hereward died in peace while Gaimar gives the heroic version with which the novelist Charles Kingsley[4] has made us familiar. 'The natural course would be to prefer the story of Gaimar,' says Davis, 'but it is hard to suppose that a Croyland writer was mistaken about the death of a man who was buried in the church at Croyland.'

Historians may lay stress upon the inconsistencies and demonstrable errors of the traditional account but Davis recognizes that we are dealing with a genuinely popular tradition in which there is much truth intermixed with fable; that the siege of Ely did occur around 1070–1, and Hereward, its hero, may have survived (dying sometime before 1109); and that the historical Hereward must have possessed great qualities to become the popular champion of the English.

We are left wondering whether the *Gesta*'s Siward (Siwate) and Leofric the Black were, indeed, the men who fought alongside Hereward at Ely and escaped the final carnage. The chronicler's words have conviction, conjuring up as they do a compelling picture of grizzled veterans, scarred by battle, whose innate strength and bearing impressed all who saw them. It is only a glimpse, for at once they slip into history, unsung and unrecorded even in the Domesday Book which was compiled some twenty years after Hastings.

It is to the Domesday survey that we turn for more factual evidence. The Anglo-Saxon Chronicle records that in 1085 'at Gloucester at midwinter   the King had deep speech with his counsellors and sent men all over England to each shire . . . to find out . . . what or how much each landholder held . . . in land and livestock, and what it was worth. . . . The returns were brought to him [before he left England for the last time, late in 1086].'

William showed meticulous attention to detail in his search to discover what he now possessed in his conquered land and who held it. He dispatched a second set of commissioners 'to shires they did not know, where they were themselves unknown, to check their predecessors' survey, and report culprits to the King'. The information was collected at Winchester, corrected, abridged and fair-copied by one writer into a single volume, but William died before the task of abridgement and codification was completed and work stopped.

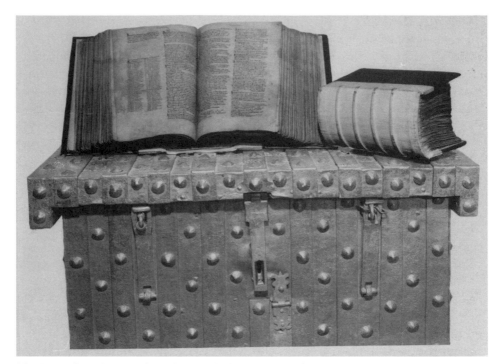

The Domesday volumes and the chest in which they are stored.

The remaining material, left unabridged, was copied in a second volume, smaller than the first, usually now referred to as 'Little Domesday Book'. This massive audit was completed with remarkable speed (in less than twelve months), though the fair-copying of the main volume may have taken longer. Both volumes are now preserved at the Public Record Office. Some versions of regional returns also survive.

Commissioners inquired into all the possessions of the king, the churches, plough-land, wood, meadow, sokemen, villeins, serfs and cattle, and estimated the value of each estate at three different dates – when King Edward was alive (1065), when its present holder first took possession, and as it actually was in 1086.[5] William used the basic machinery of the Anglo-Saxon government to discover precisely what he had given his followers and who had seized more than their rightful share. Undoubtedly there was a real need for such a survey since in the confusion and terror of the Conquest and its aftermath the plundering of Saxon-held lands was compounded by opportunist Normans taking possession of manors that should have gone to others. 'In some cases', writes R.H.C. Davis, 'this seems to have been done with no attempt to conceal the use of naked force in a cloak of legality, but in others the Normans concerned attempted to secure their position by forcing the shire court to give false evidence with threats and intimidation.' An account preserved at Rochester Cathedral tells how a Norman sheriff, Picot, attempted to rob the cathedral of its manor at Freckenham, in Suffolk, by claiming it as royal demesne and keeping the profits himself. He was able to get away with this fraud until the overawed Anglo-Saxon bishop was succeeded in 1076 by a bolder Norman who immediately complained to the king.

An inquiry was held and amid an atmosphere of legal chicanery the witnesses summoned to give evidence, terrified by threats from the sheriff, perjured themselves in the assembled court. There things might have rested had not the resourceful Norman bishop of Rochester discovered the Saxon monk who had previously managed the estate for the cathedral. His evidence persuaded one of the jurors to confess his lie and Rochester recovered its land. The twelve jurors were fined £300 – an enormous sum for a time when £20 a year was considered a suitable income for a Norman knight.

Fortunately it is possible to study a modern translation of the Domesday Book from which can be pieced together a reasonably persuasive impression of what life could have been like in eleventh-century England. It provides a detailed picture of the old Anglo-Saxon society under new management, in minute statistical detail. Although the manorial dwelling might house a foreign lord, not much else had altered. The principal landholders and their tenants are named and a head count taken of those lower in the social scale. Most people lived in villages, their cottages huddled close together; as we have seen, villages were grouped in administrative districts called hundreds, forming regions within shires, or counties, that survive today, their outlines barely changed. Thus men had a local voice that could be amplified up through the administrative hierarchy and was certainly listened to by the commissioners. The survey was the fruit of a proficient English administration and for centuries it was unmatched elsewhere in Europe.

The Domesday survey examined the details of the rape of Saxon England and gave its approval to that which had been done by authority, hence its name – 'The Book of Judgement Day'. Every Norman had to explain how he had acquired his English lands in order to get approval and have his claim upheld for ever by the hundred, the shire, the king's justices and the king.

A commonplace of history, as R.H.C. Davis reminds us, is that starting a revolution is not nearly as difficult as getting it to stop. The instigators are swiftly overtaken by those who follow, and the rapidity of change increases as the revolution gathers momentum. Davis identifies signs of this phenomenon happening almost immediately after the Norman Conquest, in the evidence that some lands had changed hands two or three times between 1066 and 1086. Chaos of another dimension may well have occurred if William the Conqueror had lost control of the situation. That he did not, says Davis, was due to the fact that he recognized the potentiality of the Anglo-Saxon machinery of government and exploited it to the full. It became his tool in the expropriation of the English, the framework for the Domesday survey, and it enabled him to start his revolution and to bring it to a conclusion. 'In so doing', says Davis with a touch of irony, 'he demonstrated to the English what a formidable weapon their kings had devised for their undoing.'

Many Siwards and Leofrics appear in the Lincolnshire survey but linking them with the men described by the *De Gestis* manuscript has to be conjectural. Bother, if incorrectly recorded, could be that Bothildr who held land at Thurlby barely 3 miles south of Bourne itself. We can all make suppositions but at least Domesday offers the following solid evidence about our chief character:

In WITHAM (on the Hill), MANTHORPE, and TOFT and LOUND Hereweard had 12 bovates[6] of land taxable. Land for 1½ ploughs. Asfrothr, Abbot Thoraldr's man has 6 villagers, 4 smallholders and 2 Freemen with 2 ploughs; and meadow, 20 acres; woodland, 40 acres. Value before 1066, 40s; now the same.

In LAUGHTON Toli and Hereweard had 4 bovates of land taxable. Land

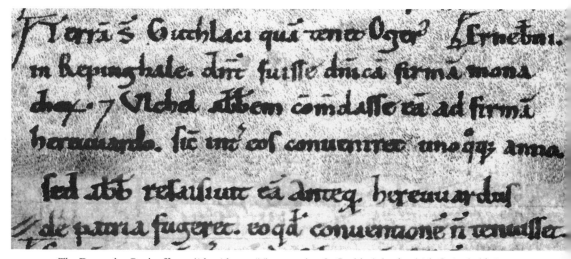

The Domesday Book offers solid evidence: 'They say that St Guthlac's land, which Ogier holds in Rippingale, was granted to Hereweard at farm. . . . But the Abbot took possession of it again before Hereweard fled the country. . . .'

for ¹/₂ plough Odger has 2 ploughs in lordship; 4 villagers who have ¹/₂ plough and the fourth part of 2 churches; meadow, 10 acres; underwood, 6 acres. Value before 1066 and now, 40s.

The Wapentake states that Hereweard did not have Asfrothr's land in BARHOLM hundred on the day he fled. The Wapentake states that Halfdan's land in DUNSBY, which Bishop Remigius holds and the Abbot of Peterborough claims was not St. Peter's before 1066. They state that St. Guthlac's land which Odger holds in RIPPINGALE was lordship revenue of the monks, and that Abbot Ulfketill assigned it to Hereweard at a revenue as might be agreed between them each year, but the Abbot repossessed it before Hereweard fled from the country because he had not held to the agreement.

('Wapentake' appears to have been an alternative term to hundred found in the heart of the Old Norse areas that lay between the Rivers Welland and Tees. It derived from the Old Norse *vápnatak*[7]: the flourish of arms at an assembly, a gesture made by free men. In the mid-tenth century occurs the Old English form *waepentac*, which denoted an administrative unit with its own court.)

Of the places mentioned in this passage, Witham, Manthorpe, Toft and Lound are found today as adjacent villages just outside Bourne, and Barholm is a few miles beyond. Laughton is in the north of the county near Gainsborough. All this seems to reinforce part of the legend, the traditional Hereward link with Bourne. Perhaps it should persuade us to look at the rest with less scepticism. Certainly, the historian J.H. Round accepts that the 'Hereweard' mentioned in Domesday and Hereward the Wake are one and the same person. (The appellation 'Wake' is not contemporary, as we shall discuss in Appendix B.)

Asfrothr, who appears to have benefited from Hereward's absences, is portrayed by Hugh Candidus as a 'man of the monks' and Domesday describes him as Abbot Thoraldr's man. The abbot's apparent acquisition of land once held by Hereward is understandable if one accepts part of the legend that Hereward had once captured Abbot Turold (Thorald) of Peterborough and held him to ransom. The connection is underlined by the phrase 'the day he fled' which has to refer to Hereward's flight after the fenland rebellion of 1070/1. 'who with a few men escaped through the marshes' as Florence of Worcester records.

When a monastery decided to make its own record of significant happenings — what Orderic Vitalis called 'the exacting task of investigating past events' — the abbot would no doubt appoint one monk to be responsible for the composition of such a chronicle. We can only speculate on how much this appointment depended upon worldly experience, or knowledge of ecclesiastical and state affairs. The man selected faced a demanding routine, sitting in the cloister or scriptorium, painstakingly working away by hand to produce his manuscript. Perhaps he provided rough drafts that more skilled penmen finished off or perhaps he himself was chosen because he possessed this special talent.

Such a monk seems to have been largely free to select his subject and lend it whatever emphasis or bias he wished or he may have reflected the views of his superiors. But in an age when communication was sparse his chief problem would have been finding sources of information. This would not have been too difficult when describing events in the monastery or its neighbourhood. Details of flood, famine, or fire, visits by important people, domestic mishaps and ailments and problems with livestock around the monastery and its local community would have been straightforward enough to collect. However, when it came to writing about the larger world outside, he would have depended for his material on word-of-mouth accounts, sometimes from eye witnesses but probably more often on second- or third-hand reports or even hearsay. Thus Orderic, referring to the progeny of William the Conqueror and his wife Matilda, daughter of Baldwin, Count of Flanders, writes self-deprecatingly: 'Skilful historians could write a memorable history of these great men and women if they applied themselves with energy to the task of handing on their exploits to future generations. We, however, who have no experience of the courts of the world, but spend our lives in the daily round of the cloisters where we live, will briefly note what is relevant to our purpose, and return to our chosen topic.'

Monastic scribes had to rely for information on passing travellers, perhaps refugees fleeing from pestilence or Viking raids, foot soldiers returning from faraway wars, or a lord's retainer riding along the highway and requesting a night's accommodation. The arrival unannounced of such a stranger would have been an exciting highlight in the chronicler's secluded life and doubtless he would bustle down to obtain whatever news and gossip he could. It would be surprising if such visitors did not feel obliged to embellish their tales to repay the monks' hospitality.

One can imagine how eager for news those chroniclers were around the time of the battle of Hastings and we have accounts of William and his activities after the Conquest from both the Norman and Saxon perspectives. Normans writing about this period can be excused a certain tribal exultation because the mid-eleventh century saw the high point of Norman power not only in the art of warfare. Church and ruler had been able to combine their interests in achieving political and economic advances. Such unity gave strength and enabled Normandy to gain acceptance as a European State that could embark on its English adventure with the blessing of the Pope and the support of neighbouring nations (much as a modern crusade, such as that of 1991 to liberate Kuwait, would require the United Nations' stamp of approval).

The Anglo-Saxon Chronicle was written by English monks and so tells what Englishmen thought about William, while monks in Normandy also wrote about the Norman Conquest and provide us with their viewpoint. They wrote in Latin or medieval French or Old English which means that for the layman their stories have been passed through the sieve of various translations. Bruce Dickins[8] is particularly scathing about some eminent historians who have 'followed grotesquely antiquated translations and given a fresh lease of life to extraordinary misrenderings'. He cites as examples the rendering of *Then they committed every atrocity* as *Then did they all wonder* and the transformation of *coats of mail* into *burning things*. Admittedly, both put a different slant on what is being described although to what extent they distort our perception of the past is debatable, especially as the veracity of the documents they were quoting is not beyond dispute.

Fortuitously, the unfolding drama of the Conquest and Hastings has come down to us in the more accessible form of that needlework mural, the Bayeux Tapestry, which takes us outside the area of vernacular argument. Before the advent of the printing press and photography only the artist could offer a pictorial representation of his times and the women who spent years at the tapestry with needle and thread did a similar job, making pictures of the great stories that society's leaders wished future generations to remember. It was made to be displayed when some of the dramatis personae were still living, a fact which some historians, including Stenton, regard as an indication that it was unlikely to stray too far from the truth. On the other hand cynics might argue that it provided an opportunity to massage the egos of those in positions of authority.

Who these painstaking workers were is not known although the tapestry is thought to have been commissioned around 1080 by William's half-brother, Bishop Odo of Bayeux, who had been made Earl of Wessex. Odo's prominence in the tapestry might be a clue and while the story related is distinctly pro-Norman – it gives the Norman version of Harold's ill-fated visit to the Continent in 1064 in which he allegedly swore his oath of allegiance to William, and promised to help him gain the throne of England – the quality of its work suggests the skilled fingers of Saxon needlewomen, famous for their embroidery. Indeed, some letters in the embroidered words have a distinct English character.

The embroidery was on coarse linen in pieces about $19^{1}/_{2}$ inches (about half a metre) wide, sewn together in one long strip, a fact which conjures up an appealing (if, perhaps, mistaken) picture of a row of needlewomen with the tapestry spread across their knees, gossiping and perhaps arguing over details of dress and events that had occurred fifteen years earlier. They produced a piece of embroidery that is now about 231 feet (70 metres) long; it was longer when completed, but some of the later pictures have been lost.

These seamstresses used wool in eight colours (three shades of blue, two greens, red, yellow and grey), partly in outline or stem stitch and partly filled in with a method not unlike a modern satin stitch. An elegant favour to later generations

Bishop Odo's (third from left) prominence in the Bayeux tapestry suggests that he commissioned the work.

The seamstresses of the Bayeux Tapestry performed an elegant favour to later generations by decorating its borders with vignettes of contemporary life.

was to fill the borders with vignettes of contemporary life, pictures of birds and animals, ploughmen, huntsmen and so on, quite apart from the momentous happenings they had been commissioned to depict. People figure prominently in the tapestry and the chief scenes show some 623 human figures, 202 horses and mules, 55 dogs, 505 other animals, 37 buildings, 41 ships and 49 trees.

The tapestry is a unique memorial that has apparently survived from this period and could well be the same work as that described in a poem, addressed by Baudri, Abbot of Bourgueil, to Adela, King William's daughter, a possibility to which Stenton gives some weight:

> Baudri's verses do not seem to have been intended, and should not be taken, for a precise description of a real piece of stitchwork, but they show that such representations of history were possible at the date when he was writing – that is, between 1099 and 1102.

There is no reason to think that Baudri had seen the Bayeux Tapestry itself. His account of the battle of Hastings reflects the language of William of

Poitiers, but he was not exclusively dependent on William's narrative. The early date of the poem gives importance to a definite statement that Harold was killed by an arrow. But, on the whole, Baudri adds remarkably little to the information supplied by contemporary writers.

We must turn to these contemporary writers for our information and, of the Anglo-Norman scribes writing in the twelfth century, Stenton and Freeman agree that one of the most important is Orderic Vitalis (1075–1143). He was born near Shrewsbury, the son of a French priest and an Englishwoman, and sent as a child oblate to the Norman abbey of St Evroul, where he spent most of his life. He visited England to collect material for his *Ecclesiastical History* (1123–41), an account of monastic life in his day and of the Anglo-Norman feudal world. It has been called the greatest social history of the Middle Ages and is an invaluable source for a narrative of the Conquest and the settlement of England up to 1075.

Stenton regrets that William of Malmesbury, 'the finest scholar of the group', contributes so modestly to the history of periods earlier than his own. William (c. 1090– c. 1143) was probably born near Malmesbury, Wiltshire, becoming a monk in the monastery, and in due time librarian and precentor. He took part in the council at Winchester against King Stephen in 1141. His *Gesta Regum Anglorum* tells of the kings of England from the Saxon invasion to 1126; the *Historia Novella* brings the narrative up to 1142. The *Gesta Pontificum* is an ecclesiastical history of the bishops and chief monasteries of England to 1123.

Chronicles written from a local standpoint can sometimes be more valuable sources of fact. History and tradition were preserved in written form in most religious houses, some being written down within a century of the Conquest. This would give the manuscripts at Peterborough and Ely extra weight and, indeed, perhaps we should not dismiss out of hand the so-called 'False Ingulph', Abbot Ingulph who became abbot of Crowland in 1086. Long regarded as the author of *Historia Monasterii Croylandensis*, printed between 1596 and 1684 and translated in 1854, he acquired the 'False' sobriquet when scholars cast doubt on its reliability and proved that the surviving manuscript had been written in the thirteenth or fourteenth century. Some idea of the difficulty of piecing together the events even of the recent past which these scribes must have encountered is illustrated by the experience of modern writers.

Almost fifty years after the Second World War Alderney historian Colin Partridge was trying to research evidence of Nazi atrocities on the island from July 1940 at a place called Sylt Camp, the only German concentration camp built on British soil. Most of the inhabitants of Alderney had departed before the Germans arrived and the camp was built for foreign (mostly Russian) slave labourers. Some three hundred and fifty inmates are said to have died there 'in obscene conditions'. Some were allegedly shot as sport by the guards, others thrown into setting concrete. Imagine the problems of tracing any surviving eye-witnesses and although the Czechs issued a wanted for murder order on the camp commandant Kurt Klebeck, he was said to be still living in Hamburg in 1992. Colin Partridge would have some sympathy for the chroniclers of around 1116 trying, with far scantier records, to assemble a factual account of the Norman atrocities after 1066.

However, it must not be forgotten that Ingulph was in a uniquely privileged position from which to record the events of his day. He had been a secretary to no less a person than King William himself [9] and it was the Conqueror who made him abbot of Crowland, doubtless for services rendered. Ingulph's chronicle gives us this fascinating piece of information: 'Hereward . . . ended his days in peace and was very recently, by his especial choice, buried in our monastery [at Crowland] by the side of his wife.' This at least suggests that Hereward survived the Ely campaign and puts his death (aged anything from forty-five to seventy) at somewhere before 1109, the date of Ingulph's own death.

Ingulph's chronicle gives us other insights that have the weight of local tradition as when he tells of the pre-1066 ravaging of the villages along the Fen border by the Danish marauders, and of the defence of the fenmen upon the island refuges, protected by reeds and rushes, and aided by unusual floods. For anyone trying to understand what conditions must have been like for Hereward and his men defending the Isle of Ely against the Conqueror, Ingulph's account of the earlier defence of Crowland is illuminating:

> It happened, fortunately, that this year the inundations had increased to an unusual degree in consequence of the frequent showers, and consequently rendered the neighbouring fens, as also the marsh-lands adjoining thereto, impassable. Accordingly, all the population repaired thither, and infinite multitudes flocked to the spot; the choir and the cloisters were filled with monks, the rest of the church with priests and clerks, and the whole abbey with laymen; while the cemetery was filled night and day with women and children under tents. The stoutest among them, as well as the young men, kept watch among the sedge and alder-beds upon the mouths of the rivers; and every day, not to speak of other expenses, one hundred monks sat down to table.

Ely's reputation as a place of sanctuary was already established and later, in the reign of Edward the Confessor (1042–66), the abbot of St Albans, as Matthew Paris relates, on hearing rumours of another Danish incursion sent relics of his monastery to Ely because of its safety.

Among the other contemporary writers whose material sheds light on Hereward is the English chronicler Florence of Worcester. While the *Gesta Herewardi* gives us much more detail it is interesting to compare the way Florence of Worcester and Orderic Vitalis deal with the momentous events of 1071. Thus Florence (*see page 101*) has Earls Edwin and Morcar fleeing from court 'because king William sought to put them in confinement', and for some time continuing in rebellion against him. Edwin dies in an ambush laid by his own people but Morcar takes ship, and goes to the Isle of Ely to join 'the valiant Hereward'.[10] Orderic's account, less succinct and objective, is nonetheless fascinating:

But in truth, since the enemy of mankind walketh about the earth as a roaring lion seeking whom he may devour with his cruel teeth, another great and lasting disturbance arose among the English and Normans, and the false Furies stormed over the land, destroying thousands. For King William, ill-advisedly relying on evil counsellors, brought great harm to his reputation by treacherously surrounding the noble Earl Morcar in the Isle of Ely, and besieging a man who had made peace with him and was neither doing nor expecting any harm. Crafty messengers went to and fro between them, and infamously proposed treacherous terms: namely, that the earl should surrender to the king, and the king should receive him in peace as a loyal friend. For the besieged could have held out almost indefinitely thanks to the inaccessibility of the place; or if the attacking forces seemed too great might have slipped away by boat along the surrounding rivers to the sea. But he in his simple honesty believed these false stories, and peacefully led his men out of the island to seek the king. The king, however, fearing that Morcar might wish to avenge all the wrongs that he and his fellow countrymen had endured, and might foment further hostile risings in the realm of Albion, flung him into fetters without any open charge, and kept him in prison to the end of his days under the charge of Roger castellan of Beaumont.

When the fair youth Earl Edwin learned of this he determined to prefer death to life unless he could free his brother Morcar from unjust captivity, or avenge him fully in Norman blood. So for six months he sought support amongst the Scots, Welsh, and English. But during this period three brothers who were his most intimate servants betrayed him to the Normans; and they slew him with twenty knights, all fighting desperately to the last. The Normans owed their success in part to a high tide, which penned up Edwin beside a tidal stream and prevented his escape. When the news of Edwin's death spread through England, Normans and French alike joined the English in mourning and lamenting him as though he had been a close friend or kinsman. For he, as I have already told, came of pious parents, and had devoted himself to all the good works that were possible for one caught up in so many worldly duties. He was so handsome that few could compare with him: and was a generous friend to clergy and monks and to the poor. King William, when he heard of the treachery that had brought this Mercian earl to his death, was moved to righteous tears, and when the traitors brought the head of their master to him, hoping for a reward, he angrily commanded them to leave the country.[11]

Orderic took many of his basic facts from the William of Poitiers who served King William as chaplain and subsequently as eulogistic biographer. Orderic clearly admired him:

William of Poitiers has brought his history up to this point, eloquently describing the deeds of King William in a clever imitation of the style of Sallust. He was a Norman by birth, a native of Preaux, and had a sister there who became abbess of the nunnery of St Leger. We call him 'of Poitiers' because he drank deeply of the fountain of learning there.

When he returned home he was conspicuous for his learning in his native parts, and as archdeacon helped the bishops of Lisieux, Hugh and Gilbert, in the administration of their diocese. He had been a brave soldier before entering the church, and had fought with warlike weapons for his earthly prince, so that he was all the better able to describe the battles he had seen through having himself some experience of the dire perils of war. In his old age he gave himself up to silence and prayer, and spent more time in composing narratives and verse than in discourse. He published many subtly linked verses.

These, then, are among the chief primary sources on which our Hereward quest must be based, but the trail leads into unexpected by-ways.

CHAPTER THREE

The Outlaw

For someone who in so many respects is such a blurred figure we have a remarkably precise if somewhat ambivalent picture of Hereward painted by the writer of *De Gestis*:

> He was as a boy remarkable for his figure and comely in aspect, very beautiful from his yellow hair, and with large grey eyes, the right eye slightly different in colour to the left; but he was stern of feature and somewhat stout, from the great sturdiness of his limbs, but very active for his moderate stature, and in all his limbs was found a complete vigour. There was in him also from his youth much grace and strength of body – and from practice of this when a young man the character of his valour showed him a perfect man, and he was excellently endowed in all things with the grace of courage and valour of mind. As regards liberality he was from his father's possessions and his own, bountiful and most liberal, giving relief to all in need. Although cruel in act, and severe in play, readily stirring up quarrels among those of his own age, and often exciting contests among his elders in cities and villages; leaving none equal to himself in deeds of daring and pursuit of brave actions, not even among his elders.

The image conjured up is of a fair-haired, healthy, extrovert teenager, somewhat stocky in build but athletic, excellent at outdoor sports, a bit of a show-off and perhaps more than a shade delinquent. This differs only slightly from that of his first appearance in Charles Kingsley's novel, *Hereward the Wake*:

> The next moment the door of the bower was thrown violently open, and in swaggered a noble lad eighteen years old. His face was of extraordinary beauty, save that the lower jaw was too long and heavy, and that his eyes wore a strange and almost sinister expression, from the fact that the one of them was grey, and the other blue. He was short, but of immense breadth of chest and strength of limb; while his delicate hands and feet and long locks of golden hair marked him of most noble, and even, as he really was, of ancient royal race.

Kingsley dresses Hereward as a kind of Highland chieftain, his wrists and throat tattooed in blue patterns and carrying sword and dagger, a gold ring round his neck, and gold rings on his wrists. Support for the tattooing comes from William of Malmesbury (who stated that the English 'adorned their skins with punctured designs'), and Kingsley concludes that the secret marks by which Harold's mistress, Edith the Swan-neck, is said to have recognized his bloody corpse on the field of Hastings were tattoos, although modern writers have naturally jumped to other, racier, conclusions.

De Gestis goes on to describe how the young Hereward progressed in courage from day to day and, excelling in manly deeds, at times spared no one whom he knew to be at all a rival in courage or in fighting. 'For these reasons he very often stirred up sedition among the populace and tumult among the ordinary people.' We can interpret this either as an excess of high spirits or as evidence that Hereward was, in truth, somewhat truculent and fractious; and the fact remains that he apparently alienated his parents to such an extent that they could not abide having him in the house:

> By this [sedition] he made his father opposed to him and his parents very
> ungracious. Because of his deeds of courage and boldness they were daily
> contending with their friends and neighbours and amongst the country folk
> who behaved like enemies and tyrants because of him, almost always
> protecting their son when returning from sport or fighting with drawn
> swords and arms. At length, his father, unable to endure this, drove him from
> his presence. Nor then, indeed did he keep quiet, but taking with him those
> of his own age when his father was away on his estates, he sometimes
> preceded him and distributed his goods amongst his own friends and
> supporters, even appointing in some of his father's possessions stewards and
> servants of his own, to supply corn to his men.

Matters must have become intolerable because eventually

> His father begged King Edward that he might be banished, making known
> all the harm he had committed against his parents, and against the country
> and people. This was done. From then on he was known as the Outlaw, being
> driven from his father and country in the 18th year of his age.

This story of banishment and exile begs a few questions. If Hereward had, indeed, been simply an obscure thane's son, would his banishment have involved a petition to the king? Surely not. Such exiling was not uncommon for prominent figures, often being the result of political manoeuvring by rivals for royal favour, and Hereward's subsequent appearance in Flanders had many precedents. A long list of disaffected noblemen – including Godwin's sons Sweyn and Tostig, and Godwin himself – had sought temporary respite on the Continent before bouncing back to try to reclaim land and status redistributed in their absence.

The case of Sweyn was particularly notorious. In 1046 this disreputable young man was returning from an expedition against the south Welsh and while passing through Leominster was taken by the beauty of the abbess of the local convent, one Edgiva (or Eadgifu). As the chronicler Florence of Worcester reports, 'he ordered the abbess of Leominster to be brought to him; and he had her as long as he listed; and after that he let her go home.'

Such an act was considered monstrous even in those barbarous times and although Sweyn apparently insisted he wished to marry the lady such a belated attempt to mitigate what was in essence kidnap and rape would not have carried any weight since the abbess was a dedicated member of her order and not a novitiate nun. Cloistered women had never been entirely safe from predatory knights but King Cnut's decree of 1020 declared that 'no man be so presumptuous as to take to wife a professed nun or a woman who had taken religious vows' and Saxon noblewomen were to seek refuge in nunneries after the coming of the Normans. In fairness to William we must remember that an Englishman writing in the Anglo-Saxon Chronicle was to praise William's kingship for bringing peace and security: 'Any honest man could travel over his kingdom without injury with his bosom full of gold, and no one dared strike another, however much wrong he had done him. And if any man had intercourse with a woman against her will, he was forthwith castrated.'

Sweyn escaped comparatively lightly, spending the next three years in exile but his character, never noticeably elevated, went downhill from then on. Life's unruffled tenure could not be resumed at the convent, it was felt. Somewhat unfairly, it would seem, the scandal led to the religious house at Leominster being dissolved and becoming a royal property. Forty years later at the time of Domesday the unfortunate Edgiva was still living there in a tiny holding tended for her by four villeins.

The key to the enigma of the Hereward story is surely hidden in this early banishment. Assuming that the repeated accounts of his exile are founded in fact and that his departure from his native shores was indeed speeded by royal authority, we are left with intriguing questions. What, for example, was the true nature of his offence and his punishment? The answer could tell us a great deal about Hereward, his place in Saxon society and politics, and go a long way towards explaining his later actions. General Thomas Harward, who sought among other things to establish his descent from Hereward in his work of 1896 entitled *Hereward; The Saxon Patriot* (see Appendix B), explores the matter in detail. He finds it necessary to return to Hereward's early training and surmises, reasonably enough, that he received the instruction necessary for a youth intended to bear arms and that he became highly accomplished in these exercises:

> His physique was well developed, and he showed great strength of body and mind. His feelings against the Norman usurpers were aggravated by his early quarrels, and subsequent Norman insults offered to his mother at Bourne. That his character was impetuous and daring beyond measure we have ample proof, but there is no indication of weakness of character, malice, recklessness, or folly in any of his hair-breadth risks and schemes.

He denies that there is any evidence that Hereward ever robbed a servant of the Church as stated by Kingsley with an 'utter disregard of facts'. We must assume that this tale of Hereward accosting the Steward of Peterborough and divesting him of his purse and palfrey was part of Kingsley's poetic licence which helped to explain Hereward's ambivalence towards the clergy, hence his well attested part in the attack on Peterborough and its abbey.

The General's own military experience might well have warned him against making extravagant claims on his ancestor's behalf although the following accolade borders on the fulsome: 'He understood the art of soldiering better than the flower of the Norman army, and his character stands out in high contrast from the Normans, who were rapacious, prodigal, debauched, and cruel, without any redeeming feature.'

We can perhaps agree more readily with the argument that Hereward's high spirits and English breeding would have made it impossible for him to have found favour at the Court of King Edward the Confessor, who is described as being 'of a cold and unsympathetic nature, with the habits of devotion and the observances of the cloister'. Suggesting that Hereward spent some time at Court is, of course, supposition, but would not be unreasonable if he was the son of Leofric, Earl of Mercia, who apparently shared the king's taste for austerity and discipline. A nobleman's son would not be a rare sight at Court, and indeed he might even have been brought up in Edward's household. Sending an unruly youngster to experience such authority would be logical, although the Hereward we are beginning to know would no doubt 'have rebelled against restraint and priestly counsel, preferring exercises of arms, and the sports of the field, to the discipline of a monastic life'.

Whether at Court or at home, Hereward would presumably have progressed as a matter of custom through the stages of page and esquire in his training for the profession of arms. Kingsley himself might have sympathized with the General's explanation of what probably transpired at Court to put Hereward out of favour:

'The King was surrounded by effeminate youths who had accompanied him from France, and there could have been little friendship between these fops and the sturdy young Saxon. They probably excelled in dancing, playing on the harp, and in the meaner offices of the household, while Hereward was distinguished in field sports, and the pastimes of wrestling, tilting with spears, etc.'

Among other manly exercises an esquire was taught to vault on a horse in complete armour,[1] to scale walls, and spring over ditches, similarly encumbered. Hereward appears also to have favoured throwing French pages on to the low roof of a Saxon house, and then admiring the way they rolled off. Rough horseplay, suggests the General, would not have been appreciated by the effeminate youths at Court, who had probably been brought up with the king in France, and complained to him of the prowess of young Hereward in cowardly and un-English style. 'Such a poor creature as King Edward the Confessor could find little sympathy for a youth who openly showed a distaste for religious austerities, and seldom observed the fasts and festivals of the Church. The hostility of the sons of Godwin, his father's rival, was also in his disfavour at Court.'

Boyish pranks do not seem any more plausible than boorish behaviour around the local neighbourhood at Bourne as a very likely reason for such a peremptory dismissal from his native land and there is no suggestion of more heinous crimes such as those committed by Godwin's son, Sweyn. One suspects however, a whisper of truth in the notion that the Godwins were somehow implicated.

General Harward makes a connection with the previous expatriation of Earl Ælfgar, the eldest son of the Earl of Mercia, which was brought about by the intrigues of Godwin and his sons. If Harward's contention that there was an undoubted relationship between Edward and Leofric is correct it would have been perfectly logical for Harold and his brothers to attempt to have both of Leofric's sons dismissed from Court in order to prevent any favour being shown to them over possible succession to the Crown. This would explain why so severe a punishment was inflicted for a venial offence. Comments General Harward:

He was certainly expatriated, but without any sentence of outlawry, which would have entailed the forfeiture of his estates. Moreover, so far as we know, Hereward's case was dealt with solely by the King, at the instance of Leofric. A more normal procedure would have been for it to be brought before the Witan. This could be taken as further corroboration of the belief that Hereward's father was the Earl of Mercia. If he had been an ordinary thane the King would not have interfered with the ordinary course of law.

The word outlaw has now slipped from our legal vocabulary and the form of law which embodied the process of outlawry was abolished in the 1880s. Outlawry meant literally being put outside the law's protection by a legal decision of the king or his courts. The outlaw was denied his ancient inherited privileges at law, which, as Maurice Keen[2] points out, were part of every man's birthright.

Being thus an outcast from society the outlaw became as vulnerable as any hunted beast. Indeed, as Keen shows, the price upon his head was originally as that upon a wolf; whence it was said commonly that an outlaw 'had a wolf's head': 'and so in the *Tale of Gamelyn* we hear that Gamelyn's wolf's head was cried about the county. Another favourite phrase to describe the outlaw was that he was civilly dead (*civiliter mortuus*); hence he could be killed with impunity. . . .' An outlaw's only hope of survival was his ability to evade capture for long enough to buy time. By negotiation he might, with luck, sue for pardon from his judges. Until then he must rely on his own skill and wit, for anyone who offered him help put themselves in peril from the law.

While outlawry was therefore a fearful sentence, its imposition was an admission of weakness. Keen argues that by disowning the outlaw the governing power confessed its failure to bring him to book, an inability of medieval society to curb its own unruly elements. A powerful and determined man could defy the law by retreating to a safe hideaway and if it appeared to be in his interest to do so he would. 'The sentence of outlawry for this reason passed into desuetude after the end of the middle ages, because the law and the government became strong enough to enforce their own decisions. It belonged to the old, disordered age of society, when a strong castle or a forest retreat could put a man outside the reach of authority.'

Sentence of outlawry was a banishment from society but Hereward's banishment could not have been in the same category. *De Gestis* in its perfunctory manner says of his expulsion that 'from then on he was known as the Outlaw', not that he was declared an outlaw, and there is no mention of 'wolf's head'. These are inventions by Kingsley who also, in explanation of his hero's delinquency, hints that he was starved of maternal affection. The punishment imposed on Hereward was somewhat less than full outlawry, which would necessarily have involved forfeiture of estates, and the proceedings would have been conducted before the Witan which had the power to inflict it. The sentence was somewhere between being blackballed from club and being rusticated from university. It gave the victim an opportunity to stretch his wings and seek his fortune in fresh surroundings without severing all ties with hearth and home.

Harward finds an earlier precedent for the king's unusual action when the Witan of Kent, having found that it was powerless to deal with offenders of the highest rank, sent the following appeal to King Æthelstan (who reigned AD 925–39): 'If any man be so rich or of so great kin that he cannot be punished, or will not cease from his wrong doing, you may settle how he may be carried away into some other part of your kingdom, be the case whom he may, villein or thane.'[3] Such a solution would largely explain the Hereward example, and being sent to travel in foreign countries for an indefinite period, whether or not the result of a Court intrigue, matches the nature of his offences while at the same time supporting the view that he was indeed attached to one of the country's powerful families. Indeed, Kingsley offers the fact of Hereward's high birth as an explanation of William's strong desire to spare his life and receive his homage in the years ahead – 'as an atonement for his conduct to Edwin and Morcar and a last effort to attach himself to the English nobility'.

Assuming that King Edward the Confessor's authority had indeed been invoked to get rid of Hereward it is tempting to agree with General Harward and see in this evidence of the political intrigues that marked the years leading up to the Norman Conquest and to a large extent contributed to its success. Perhaps Leofric, a more understanding father than history has painted, was trying to get his younger son out of harm's way? Certainly his heir, Ælfgar, had endured temporary exile as a result, it would seem, of the machinations of the Godwin family.

The version which has the young Hereward incurring royal disapproval for his rough handling of effete young Frenchmen may be fanciful yet it reminds us that the seeds of the tragedy of 1066 were, indeed, sown as early as the year 1004 when King Æthelred was presented with a son, Edward, who was to become 'the Confessor'. His birth 'was in the fullness of time to prove the year's greatest disaster'.[4]

Following the argument that Hereward must have had lofty connections to explain this regal intervention we need to look at some of the other personalities involved in the politics of the day, central among whom was, of course, King Edward himself. Half Norman by blood – his father was Æthelred II the 'Unready' and his mother the remarkable Emma of Normandy – Edward became probably wholly Norman in outlook and spirit since circumstances conspired to have him spend his formative years across the Channel. If this training had been accompanied by a stronger personality history might well have been different.

Had the Confessor unequivocally recommended Duke William to the Witan as his preferred successor it is not impossible to envisage a more or less peaceful accession and the unifying of English and Norman under a King William who might then have claimed the allegiance if not the undiluted affection of all his subjects. This would have been preferable to what happened when a Norse scribe could write memorably, 'Cold heart and bloody hand now rule the English land.'

It is one of history's misfortunes that Edward was not able to provide such leadership when he came to the throne in 1042. To what extent he alienated his subjects by favouring Norman above English candidates for positions of importance at Court, in State and Church, is debatable. More critically,

The head of King Edward the Confessor wearing a pointed helmet on a silver penny minted at Hereford (moneyer: Wulfwine).

religious fervour occupied his attention at the expense of State affairs in which arena he appears to have been outflanked and even outfaced by the influential nobles whose ambitions divided the country at a time when unity was most needed.

Foremost among these men were the powerful earls, Godwin of Wessex, Leofric of Mercia and Siward of Northumberland. Siward, the doughty old Danish warrior, was probably least involved in national politics, possibly a reflection of the swing away from Danish back to English ascendancy with a return to the English line of kings following Cnut (1016–35) and the brief reigns of Harold 'Harefoot' (1035–40) and Harthacnut (1040–2). In any case, Siward was too preoccupied keeping order in his turbulent northern domain which was ever under threat from the Scots and Vikings. Both Godwin and Leofric were veterans whose eminence in national affairs went back to the time of King Cnut.

Godwin, whose origins are obscure, may have been driven by the doubts about his background as William was sensitive about his own bastardy. Godwin's elevation was due to the patronage of Cnut who also made Leofric earl of Mercia. With the exception of Siward, no new Danish earls appear at Court in Cnut's last years, and at the end of his reign the upstart Godwin and the establishment figure of Leofric were apparently his chief advisers. They were still entrenched when Edward was crowned and the scene was set, not only for a power struggle between their houses, but also for a more complicated game of political chess between them and their monarch. Stenton writes:

> Through its ultimate consequences the promotion of Godwin and Leofric was of momentous significance for English history. The rivalry of the families which they brought to eminence fatally weakened the possibility of a united

English resistance to the Norman invasion of 1066. Leofric himself was regarded by contemporaries as an upright man; he was the son of an ealdorman, and he seems to have maintained himself in power for more than twenty years without violence or aggression. Godwin had no ancestral claim to political influence; he could be unscrupulous in action, and the career of aggrandisement which he opened to his family accounts in great part for the sense of strain and unrest which colours the reign of Edward the Confessor.

The contrast between Godwin and Leofric was dramatic, with the latter cast as loyal patriot and Godwin depicted as the self-seeking, unscrupulous villain of the piece. Doubtless this is an oversimplification but Godwin's recorded actions are those of someone with a keen appetite for power and a shrewd awareness of how to acquire it.

Soon after Godwin attained his earldom, around 1018, he married Gytha, the sister of Cnut's brother-in-law, a marriage which linked him to the centre of influence. Two years after Edward's coronation Godwin was equally swift to establish a firm power base with the new monarchy: the country was probably startled to learn of the king's marriage to Godwin's daughter, Ealdgyth. At Cnut's death Godwin had supported the cause of his widow Queen Emma's son Harthacnut[5] while Leofric led the magnates of Mercia and the north in declaring for Harold 'Harefoot', Cnut's son by his English mistress Ælfgifu. Neither appear to have given much encouragement to Edward who made a lame bid for the Crown, crossing the Channel with a squadron of forty ships. 'Perhaps fortunately for the peace of England he received no encouragement' is the withering comment of Harold R. Smith, who dismisses Edward, perhaps too readily, as a timid, indecisive man sailing back to Normandy with his tail firmly tucked between his legs. Nevertheless, six years later he ascended the throne of England and became known to posterity as Edward the Confessor, a man who in Smith's judgement has possibly received more undeserved praise than any other king in history.

Edward's first action, which some historians see as a contradiction of his supposed saintly nature, was to visit his mother's residence at Winchester and take possession of her considerable treasure, apparently in retribution for her previous indifference to him. The forceful Queen Mother, then almost sixty, lived on at Winchester for another nine years but never again was she to cut much of a political figure. On this somewhat shabby mission the king was accompanied by Siward, Leofric and Godwin whose former loyalty to the queen was thus easily forgotten.

Godwin did not have things all his own way. Such a godly man as the king could not overlook the scandalous behaviour of Sweyn, the eldest of the earl's sons. Sweyn, expelled in 1046 for his abduction of the abbess of Leominster, was apparently unrepentant since he committed further crimes such as raiding the shores of his homeland and murdering his cousin Beorn, one of the beneficiaries of the re-allocation of Sweyn's properties. Yet inexplicably – or perhaps the insidious hand of Godwin can again be detected – the king reinstated Sweyn in 1050. 'Only a feeble brain such as the Confessor's could have been capable of so grave an error of judgement' is the comment of Harold R. Smith.

But the signs were that even this weak monarch was growing impatient with the Godwins. His insistence that Robert of Jumièges be elected Archbishop of Canterbury over Godwin's choice, Ælfric, was significant although he may have exchanged one baneful influence for another. A crisis came in 1051 after a curious incident involving the Confessor's brother-in-law Eustace, Count of Boulogne, that same dark figure alleged to have been among the Norman knights who were to hack down King Harold at Hastings fifteen years later.

Eustace, Count of Boulogne, points excitedly to indicate to the wavering troops that Duke William is alive and still in the saddle.

Eustace complained to the king of insult and injury received at the hands of the townsfolk of Dover, part of Godwin's domains. The Confessor's reaction would appear strangely immoderate, unless he was advised that this was a heaven-sent opportunity to test Godwin and perhaps curb his power. Without waiting to hear both sides of the story he commanded Godwin to punish the citizens of Dover and raze the town. Unreasonable or Machiavellian? The king could not have contrived to put Godwin in a more awkward position.

Even if the townsfolk had been at fault the sentence was absurdly harsh and Godwin's refusal to comply was inevitable. A showdown seemed unavoidable and Godwin, aided by his sons Sweyn and Harold, quickly summoned his levies to confront the king's forces which included the *fyrds* of Siward and Leofric, who were doubtless not unhappy to see the likely downfall of the Godwins. Civil strife was averted by a compromise truce but the Godwins, seeing their forces gradually diminish, thought it prudent to seek refuge overseas, Sweyn and Tostig in Bruges with their father and Harold in Ireland. The king's momentary triumph was celebrated vindictively. His Queen, Godwin's daughter Ealdgyth, was dismissed to religious confinement in the convent of Wherwell in Hampshire, and perhaps to emphasize his new-found independence the king invited his cousin Duke William of Normandy to England for a visit whose purpose and content remain open to speculation.

Stenton was not alone in finding it difficult to form a clear picture of English internal politics during this period. He describes the king's personality as an enigma that has led different historians to reach very diverse opinions about his character and ability. In contrast to Harold R. Smith, for instance, Stenton concedes that the Confessor may have been generally underestimated, and that reserves of latent energy were cloaked by the benign manner which attracted so many and the asceticism which earned him sainthood: '. . . there fell upon him the responsibility of governing an unfamiliar country through a group of men firmly established in their respective spheres of influence, and experienced in the elementary statesmanship of their time. Throughout his reign Edward was required to deal with men who at first or second hand represented the traditions of the Anglo-Danish monarchy.'

Duke William's visit was brief as was the king's temporary elation. By the following summer Godwin and Harold had combined forces to sail up the Thames where they were welcomed by the Londoners and once again a confrontation developed with Edward on the north bank of the river facing his rebellious earl. Popular opinion was apparently against the king whose eventual climb-down involved the reinstatement of the Godwins and Queen Ealdgyth, and the departure of many foreign favourites including Robert of Jumièges.

The next few years were to see changes in the cast but the underlying drama continued. Earl Godwin enjoyed his return to Wessex only briefly and died in 1053, being succeeded by Harold. Siward, having led a famous victory over the Scots at Dunsinane, died in 1055 calling for his armour and weapons as he sensed death approach, so that he could meet it like a warrior. His heir Osbeorn had fallen at Dunsinane 'with all his wounds in front' as Siward had observed with pride, and his younger son Waltheof was still a child.

The power vacuum thus created in Northumbria was filled, unwisely it seems, when the king bestowed that earldom on Earl Godwin's third son, Tostig, a character who shared the wilder blood of Sweyn. This move was not welcomed by the Northumbrians and must have irritated Leofric of Mercia who no doubt perceived himself as outmanoeuvred in the political gambits of those later years.

Leofric may well have been in decline physically. He died in 1057 doubtless saddened by the exile of Hereward (if, indeed, the two were father and son) and certainly by the chequered career of his elder son, Ælfgar, who had been outlawed for treason by the Witan 'well-nigh without guilt' according to one account. There is some suggestion that Ælfgar resented Tostig's appointment having coveted the vacant Northumberland earldom himself. He would no doubt have seen Tostig's elevation as part of a re-grouping of Wessex influence that threatened to encircle Mercia. The family feud between the Godwins and Leofric thus had much to fuel it and further trouble was not long in coming. Ælfgar, who seems to have been in the same mould as the fiery Sweyn and Tostig, engaged in a little profitable piracy before linking forces with King Gruffydd and the Welsh. Together they crossed the border and defeated the shire levy near Hereford which they then put to the sword. Ælfgar, with his traditional allies the Northumbrians under new and hostile management, needed to seek fresh partnerships and the Welsh were always willing to pepper the stew of English politics.

The operation backfired somewhat since it presented Harold Godwinson with the chance to demonstrate his abilities and leadership and strengthen his relationship with the monarch whose strong right arm he soon became. Harold was dispatched with a large force to put a stop to this Welsh nonsense and the sides met at council and agreed terms, part of which was to grant Ælfgar a general pardon and return to him his lost earldom. However, he had other reasons for disquiet. Much of the land in East Anglia, the Midlands and elsewhere, formerly under his control, had been chipped away and parcelled off to make new earldoms for Gyrth and Leofwine, Harold's younger brothers. Thus the Godwin quest for power survived the old earl and Ælfgar was encouraged to seek other alliances.

He strengthened his friendship with the Welsh by marrying his daughter, the beautiful Ealdgyth, to Gruffydd, probably around 1058 and his final years according to Stenton were obscure: 'Although it seems certain that he died in 1062 no chronicler noted the date of his death. Nevertheless it is one of the determining events of eleventh-century history. If Ælfgar had survived King Edward, it is on every ground unlikely that he would have acquiesced in the choice of Harold as king . . . his interests had always clashed with those of Harold.'

This is very probable, for apart from the long-standing rivalry of these two mighty families, Ælfgar had twice been banished by the Godwin-dominated Court. One can speculate that he would certainly have prevented Harold from obtaining the immediate recognition which gave him the chance to reign. Stenton does not believe that Ælfgar would have put himself forward as a rival claimant for the throne but the fact that such a notion is even considered puts a new light on the events at Ely if Hereward had, indeed, been Ælfgar's kin.

Ælfgar's eldest son Edwin – Hereward's 'nephew' – succeeded him as Earl of Mercia but his youth and inexperience gave Harold the chance, with some help from Tostig, to deal permanently with Gruffydd, who was killed during the campaign, and at least for a time with the Welsh menace without Mercian interference. He showed something of his father's careful planning by taking as wife Gruffydd's widow. He thus reduced the possible menace of Edwin and Morcar by marrying their sister and, incidentally, thereby became himself a nephew by marriage of Hereward according to the Harward pedigree.

Harold's stature in the country was thus substantially enhanced to ensure that when the moment came his claim to the throne would at least challenge those of William of Normandy and the King of Norway. It was around this time that occurred the strange episode of Harold's mission to Normandy and his alleged oath of allegiance to William. The circumstances are so clouded and contradictory that even Stenton falls back on the Bayeux Tapestry as the most probable evidence that Harold took a solemn oath to observe the duke's interests.

The tapestry does not explain why Harold took this journey and what his mission was, nor what duress if any may have been imposed upon him to exact such a promise. Says Stenton: 'It is possible that even in 1064 – the probable date of the oath – he may have doubted whether his following in England was strong enough to carry his election as king. In a Norman environment he may have felt that, in view of the danger from the king of Norway, his wisest course was to ally himself with the duke and work for his succession.' A cynical view might be that Harold simply took the soft option to escape from an awkward corner, leaving future events to decide whether an oath made under duress was binding or not.

Events were to take a sudden swing in the following year, 1065, when Harold's strong position was threatened by a rebellion in Northumbria against the unpopular Tostig. The rebels hunted down his retainers, seized his treasury and then invited Morcar, brother of Edwin of Mercia, to become Earl of Northumberland, a revival of the old Siward–Leofric alliance against Godwin.

The fate of this rebellion may have been decided by the fact that Edwin himself, with an army of Mercians, including the men of Lincolnshire (a fact which must have interested the exiled Hereward), joined them as they marched southwards to confront the king. Negotiations in which Harold played an important role resulted in Morcar's appointment being confirmed and the angry Tostig left England for Flanders, there to brood on his usurpation and plot his revenge.

Thus the portentous year of 1066 dawned with England ruled by an ailing king, his attention dominated by his plans for the new cathedral at Westminster, and the country once again riven by the conflicting interests of Wessex and Mercia, which now had the Northumbrians firmly on its side. The prospects were such as to make any would-be invader lick his lips in anticipation. Across the Channel and over the North Sea were hawks waiting to swoop.

CHAPTER FOUR

'Valiant Hereward'

While Anglo-Saxon England was suffering the political tug of war that inexorably weakened her capacity for self-defence, if not tearing her apart completely, we must suppose that Hereward was condemned to wander abroad as an exile, cut off from the events at home. This was not an unusual experience for well-born younger sons whose thwarted hopes found buoyancy in foreign lands, and certainly in the post-1066 period such an exodus could have increased significantly, as Charles Kingsley graphically speculates: 'Hot young Englishmen began to emigrate. Some went to the court of Constantinople, to join the Varanger guard . . . some went to Scotland to Malcolm Canmore, and brooded over return and revenge. But Harold's sons went to their father's cousin, Ulfsson of Denmark, and called on him to come and reconquer England in the name of his uncle Canute the Great; and many an Englishmen went with them.'

Kingsley's account, if credible, is conjectural and we have no firm knowledge of Hereward's movements during the eventful year of 1066. However, if we assume that he was living near the Court of Bruges, it is safe to suppose that he kept himself well briefed on what was happening in England. The news of the death of Edward the Confessor on 5 January in his riverside palace outside London was the signal that set in motion the tidal wave of change. Because he was childless and his kinsman, Edgar the Ætheling, deemed too young and inexperienced to succeed him, the throne was open to the claims of four powerful men. Two of them, Harold and Tostig, were brothers of the queen and another was Harold Hardrada, King of Norway. The fourth was Edward's cousin, William, Duke of Normandy. King Edward, however, nominated his brother-in-law, Harold, and this choice was accepted by the Witan. With a haste that reflects the urgency of the time Harold was consecrated at Westminster on the day following Edward's death and the king was buried the same day. Volumes have been written about the momentous months that followed but we cannot do better than return to Florence of Worcester,[1] one of the chroniclers who wrote about events that were still in living memory:

AD 1066. On Thursday, the vigil of our Lord's Epiphany [5 Jan.], in the fourth indiction, the pride of the English, the pacific king Eadward, son of king Æthelred, died at London, having reigned over the Anglo-Saxons twenty-three years, six months, and twenty-seven days: the next day he was buried in kingly style, amid the bitter lamentations of all present. After his interment, the subregulus Harold, son of earl Godwin, whom the king had nominated as his successor, was elected king by the chief nobles of all England; and on the same day was crowned with great ceremony, by Aldred, archbishop of York.

On taking the helm of the kingdom he immediately began to abolish unjust laws and make good ones; to patronise churches and monasteries; to pay particular attention and yield reverence to bishops, abbots, monks, clerics; to show himself pious, humble, and affable to all good men; but he treated malefactors with the utmost severity, and gave general orders to his earls, ealdormen, sheriffs, and thanes to imprison all thieves, robbers, and disturbers of the kingdom; and he himself laboured by sea and by land for the protection of his country.

On the 8th of the kalends of May [24 April] in this year, a comet was seen not only in England, but, it is said, all over the world, and shone for seven days with exceeding brightness. Shortly afterwards earl Tosti [Tostig] returned from Flanders and landed at the Isle of Wight. After making the islanders pay tribute and stipend, he departed and went pillaging along the sea-coast until he arrived at the port of Sandwich. As soon as king Harold, who was then at London, heard this, he assembled a large fleet and an army of cavalry, and he prepared to go in person to the port of Sandwich. When Tosti was informed of this he took some of the shipmen of the place, willing and unwilling, and bent his course towards Lindesey, where he burned many vills and put many men to death. Thereupon Eadwin, earl of the Mercians, and Morcar, earl of the Northumbrians, hastened up with an army and expelled him from that part of the country.

Departing thence he went to Malcolm, king of the Scots, and remained with him during the whole of the summer. Meanwhile king Harold arrived at the port of Sandwich, and waited there for his fleet. When it was assembled, he crossed over with it to the Isle of Wight, and inasmuch as king Eadward's cousin William, earl of the Normans was preparing to invade England with an army, he watched all the summer and autumn for his coming; and in addition distributed a land force at suitable points along the sea-coast. But about the feast-day of the Nativity of St. Mary [8 Sept.] provisions fell short, so the naval and land forces returned home.

After this Harold Harvagra,[2] king of the Norwegians and brother of St. Olaf the king, arrived on a sudden at the mouth of the river Tyne, with a powerful fleet, consisting of more than five hundred large ships. Earl Tosti, according to previous arrangement, joined him with his fleet. They hastened their course and entered the river Humber, and then sailing up the river Ouse against the stream, landed at a place called Richale. King Harold, on hearing this, marched in haste towards Northumbria; but before his arrival the two brothers, earls Eadwin and Morcar, at the head of a large army, fought a battle with the Norwegians on the northern bank of the river Ouse near York [at Fulford], on Wednesday, being the vigil of the feast-day of St. Matthew the apostle [20 Sept.], and they fought so bravely at the onset that many of the enemy were overthrown. But after a long contest the English were unable to withstand the attacks of the Norwegians; and fled with great loss; and more were drowned in the river than slain in the field. The Norwegians remained masters of the field of carnage, and having taken one hundred and fifty hostages from York, and leaving there one hundred and fifty of their own men as hostages, they went to their ships.

Five days afterwards, that is, on Monday, the 7th of the kalends of October [25 Sept.], as Harold, king of the English, was coming to York with many thousand well-armed fighting men, he fell in with the Norwegians at a place called Stamford-bridge, slew king Harold and earl Tosti, with the greater part of their army, and gained a complete victory; nevertheless, the battle was stoutly contested. He, however, permitted Olaf, the son of the Norwegian king, and Paul, earl of Orkney, who had been sent off with a portion of the army to guard the fleet, to return home without molestation, with twenty ships and the remains of the army; first, however, taking hostages and oaths [of submission] from them.

In the midst of these things, and when the king might have considered that all his enemies were subdued, it was told to him that William, earl of the Normans, had arrived with a countless host of horsemen, slingers, archers, and foot-soldiers, having brought with him powerful auxiliaries from all parts of Gaul, and that he had landed at a place called Pefnesea [Pevensey]. Thereat, the king at once, and in great haste, marched his army towards London; and though he well knew that some of the bravest Englishmen had fallen in his two [former] battles, and that one half of his army had not yet arrived, he did not hesitate to advance with all speed into South Saxony against his enemies; and on Saturday the 11th of the kalends of September [22 Oct.], before a third of his army was in order for fighting, he joined battle with them nine miles from Hastings, where they had fortified a castle. But inasmuch as the English were drawn up in a narrow place, many retired from the ranks, and very few remained true to him; nevertheless from the third hour of the day until dusk he bravely withstood the enemy, and fought so valiantly and stubbornly in his own defence, that the enemy's forces could hardly make any impression. At last, after great slaughter on both sides, about twilight the king, alas! fell. There were slain also earl Girth, and his brother earl Leofwin, and nearly all the nobility of England. Then earl William returned with his men to Hastings.

Harold reigned nine months and as many days. On hearing of his death, the earls Eadwin and Morcar, who had withdrawn themselves and their men from the conflict, went to London and sent their sister queen Algitha to Chester; but Aldred, archbishop of York, and the said earls, with the citizens of London and the shipmen, were desirous of elevating to the throne Eadgar the etheling, nephew of king Eadmund Ironside, and promised that they would renew the contest under his command. But while numbers were preparing to go out to fight, the earls withdrew their assistance and returned home with their army.

Meanwhile earl William was laying waste South Saxony, Kent, South Hamptonshire, Surrey, Middle Saxony, and Hertfordshire, and kept on burning the vills and slaying the natives until he came to a vill called Beorcham. There archbishop Aldred, Wulstan, bishop of Worcester, Walter, bishop of Hereford, Eadgar the etheling, earls Eadwin and Morcar, the chief men of London, and many more came to him, and, giving hostages, surrendered and swore fealty to him. So he entered into a treaty with them; yet, nevertheless, he permitted his army to burn the vills and keep on pillaging. But when the feast of our Lord's Nativity [25 Dec.] drew nigh, he went to London with his whole army in order that he might be made king. And because Stigand, the primate of all England, was accused by the pope of having obtained the pall in an uncanonical manner, he was anointed king at Westminster with great ceremony on Christmas day (which in that year fell on a Monday) by Aldred, archbishop of York, having previously (for the archbishop had made it a condition) sworn at the altar of St. Peter the apostle, in the presence of the clergy and people, that he would defend the holy churches of God and their ministers, and would also rule justly and with royal care the people who were placed under him, and would ordain and maintain right law, and utterly prohibit all spoliation and unrighteous judgements.

From this detailed and graphic account the inescapable conclusion is that deep-rooted mistrust between the houses of Mercia and Wessex was the chief cause of the defeat of Anglo-Saxon England. If not, why did the army of Edwin and Morcar operate separately from that of Harold? Having dealt with Tostig's initial spring raid, Edwin and Morcar could well have delayed their showdown at York and waited a further five days for Harold's arrival before taking on the might of the Scandinavian invaders. The precise numbers of men and ships is a subject of much debate among historians but the figure of 500 Norwegian ships suggests an armada rivalling that of the Conqueror, whose fleet can only be guessed at. Robert Wace (*c*. 1115–*c*. 1183) offers a figure of 696 (learned from his father) while admitting that nobody, not even at the time of the invasion, knew the exact number.

Harold caught up with the Norwegian force less than a week after Edwin and Morcar had been so savaged at Fulford and those few days spelt the doom of the nation. Although his victory was overwhelming – a mere twenty vessels were sufficient to take home the surviving invaders – the price in fighting men killed and wounded was a heavy one. The Norwegians would have been less able (or willing) to take on a combined army of Mercians, Northumbrians and men of Wessex and consequently the Saxon army at Hastings would have been much larger and fresher.

Harold's haste in dashing southwards after Stamford Bridge to confront the Normans at Hastings has been criticized as imprudent, rash and militarily inexcusable. It was also out of character for such a seasoned and experienced warrior. The truth may well be that he had little cause to believe that Edwin and Morcar were prepared to commit themselves, despite the family ties forged by his marriage to their sister. William of Malmesbury gives a possible clue to the uncharacteristically haphazard preparation when he writes: 'Harold, elated by his successful enterprise, allowed no part of the spoil to his soldiers. So many of them, as the chance came, stole off and deserted the king as he was proceeding to the battle of Hastings.'

Again we are faced with questions to which there are as yet no answers. Is this an indictment of Harold's meanness, denying his soldiers their just rewards? Surely not, since the 'spoils' taken from a defeated invader would have been chiefly weapons and armour. Any other more marketable booty would have been plundered from fellow-Saxons, clergy and laity and, arguably, Harold was displaying kingly virtue in attempting to restore such property to its rightful owners. We shall never know.

We must, however, assume that throughout that summer and autumn Hereward remained overseas and this invites another obvious question: why in the nation's hour of need was the greatest of all Anglo-Saxon heroes not by his king's side defending the realm at Stamford Bridge and Hastings? It may seem even stranger that he was not helping his nephews in their struggle at Fulford.

His absence and apparent disinterest prompt us to re-examine the accepted interpretation of the events surrounding 1066. Seen through contemporary eyes these become much more complicated. Hereward's loyalty to Edward, the king who banished him, may have been tenuous but he, like Edwin and Morcar, would have found it even more difficult to identify with a land ruled by a son of the hated House of Godwin.

To rush home sword in hand to support Harold's personal ambitions would have been a grotesque *volte-face* and he probably found little to choose between Harold and Duke William. Possibly he deluded himself, as it seems others may have done in Mercia and Northumbria, that William had conquered not England, but Wessex, and that the future could offer a mutually beneficial compromise between Norman and Saxon. The confusion about the immediate aftermath of Hastings is increased by William of Malmesbury's allegation that when Edwin and Morcar went to London, upon learning of Harold's death, their intention was to get one or other of themselves made king. Having failed, they retreated to Northumbria believing that they would be out of harm's way.

Later historians have discounted these charges pointing out that the brothers had suffered heavy losses at Fulford in their attempts to hold off the Norwegian invaders, who also were badly mauled, but in so doing had made Harold's task at Stamford Bridge correspondingly easier. They would have needed time to reorganize, lick their wounds and recruit fresh troops and this was a respite that Harold, for whatever reasons, failed to give them.

Hopes that far-off places such as Northumbria would be beyond the reach of William's sword were of course to prove groundless, although some historians believe that the Conqueror's original intentions could have embraced a more peaceable solution; his early attempts to accommodate some Saxon interests and enlist co-operation tend to support this view. However, he relaxed his vigilance at a crucial time six months after his landing at Pevensey when, says Stenton, he was so far the master of England that he felt able to pay a visit to Normandy, although matters there could not have been pressing.

His error was to leave the newly won land in the hands of subordinates whose personal ambitions made their reliability and judgement suspect and whose harsh methods alienated even those who might have been prepared to come to terms with a new regime. And in the time-honoured manner of thieves falling out, the plunderers themselves were to squabble over the loot and this ensured that the troubled times would continue indefinitely.

King William divided the responsibility for governing England between his seneschal, William fitzOsbern, whom he made Earl of Hereford, and whose especial duty it was to defend eastern England against invasion from Denmark, and his half-brother Odo, Bishop of Bayeux, whom he made Earl of Kent, and who was ensconced in Dover Castle in order to guard the Kentish ports. He took with him to Normandy those Saxons of any rank who might have become a focus for revolt including Archbishop Stigand, the boy Edgar the Ætheling, Edwin, Morcar, and Waltheof, Earl Siward's son.

But, says Stenton, 'the whole country was in a state of suppressed rebellion, and . . . a serious uprising broke out in Kent. Count Eustace of Boulogne, who had been prominent in the Battle of Hastings, had quarrelled with King William. Convinced that the native dynasty could never be restored and that the devil they had known for many years was preferable to those they had recently encountered, a number of Kentishmen decided that the count would be the most tolerable of foreign rulers, and persuaded him that with their help he could seize and hold the port of Dover.'

This flourish ended in fiasco when Eustace refused to wait for promised reinforcements and was defeated by the garrison. But when King William hurried back across the Channel there was 'a new determination to check his progress by local resistance'. Exeter openly defied him and held out for eighteen days before being granted reasonable terms of surrender. The highest ground in the city was taken for a castle, which was strongly garrisoned but the army was denied its plunder and customary payments to the Crown were not increased.[3]

One of the more gripping descriptions of the state of affairs in England comes from Orderic Vitalis whose account differs from that of William of Poitiers which praises the administration of fitzOsbern and Odo. In contrast, Orderic described how the people were flinching under the Norman lash, and suffering oppressions at the hands of the disdainful and petty lords who were so swollen with pride that they ignored the king's injunctions and would not listen to the appeals of the English for impartial judgement.

> And so the English groaned aloud for their lost liberty and plotted ceaselessly to find some way of shaking off a yoke that was so intolerable and unaccustomed. Some sent to Swein, king of Denmark, and urged him to lay claim to the kingdom of England which his ancestors Swein and Cnut had won by the sword. Others fled into voluntary exile so that they might either find in banishment freedom from the power of the Normans or secure foreign help and come back and fight a war of vengeance. Some of them who were still in the flower of youth travelled into remote lands and bravely offered their arms to Alexius, emperor of Constantinople, a man of great wisdom and nobility. . . .[4]

The English exiles were warmly welcomed by the Greeks and were sent into battle against their old enemy, the Normans, who, under Robert Guiscard, Duke of Apulia, were fighting for the deposed emperor, Michael VII. Some conflict of views exists over the precise details of this struggle but various sources confirm that the exiled Saxons earned a high reputation for valour and formed an important element in the Varangian guard of the Byzantine emperors.

Hereward's mercenary career in Europe reflects the experiences of such men and his eventual return and entry into recorded history were spurred by tales of

Norman persecution and injustice especially in his Lincolnshire homeland. This saga of a returning hero is an aspect of the movement of withdrawal and return that fascinated Professor Arnold J. Toynbee,[5] who drew a parallel between Giuseppe Garibaldi, the mid-nineteenth-century Italian patriot, and Hereward: 'Garibaldi stepped straight into that place in the hearts of his countrymen and in the history of his age which he was to occupy from that time onwards. . . . [C]ompare the life history of Hereward the Wake, who left England before the Norman Conquest as a young sprig seeking his fortune on the Continent, and returned to England after the Norman Conquest to step at once into the position of being the one Englishman who knew how to defy the Conqueror.'

If, indeed, Hereward was the only patriot with the will and the military experience to defy William, he must have acquired a formidable reputation before setting foot once more in Lincolnshire. It is unfortunate that most of the chronicles are silent about those years in which he seems to have established his name. We can deduce that his exile started some time before 1057, the year of Leofric's death at the great age of eighty or thereabouts, and we are told that he was still young, under twenty. General Harward suggests a date some years after Ælfgar's banishment in 1052, but the *De Gestis* is unhelpful and merely records that Hereward was exiled in his eighteenth year. Yet it is to the *De Gestis* that we must turn for any information on those fateful fifteen or so years in Hereward's life from perhaps 1055 to 1070 when he enters the centre stage of history.

The *De Gestis* obliges with a lively, confusing and sometimes contradictory account, a confection of events in which it is impossible to separate fact from fable. The marvellous adventures recounted are part of the process by which later writers transformed historical characters into figures of legend. It appears that, accompanied by his faithful servant Lightfoot, Hereward began his exile by riding north apparently with some notion of seeking fame and fortune across the Border where Malcolm and Macbeth were struggling for the Scottish crown. General Harward suggests that he may also have intended to involve himself in the power struggle in Northumbria where Harold's brother, the unpopular Tostig, had been made earl. This would put the date of exile after Siward's death in 1055, and, if Hereward was in fact eighteen, his birth might be fixed at around 1037.

Attributing such political motivation to a feckless youth seems questionable and in any case wiser counsel prevailed for Hereward was invited to the home – in York according to General Harward – of his godfather, Gilbert of Ghent, who was related to Baldwin V, Count of Flanders. This fact is significant since Gilbert's Flemish base was close to the Baldwin headquarters in Bruges, at that time perhaps one of the best-informed centres of international intelligence. The Flanders connection with Anglo-Norman politics was a long and involved one, King Alfred's third daughter having married into that family. During the eleventh century the Court at Bruges became a haven for English exiles – Queen Emma in 1039, the dastardly Sweyn ten years later, the Godwin family during their brief decline in 1051, and Tostig and his wife, herself a sister of Baldwin, in 1065.

By giving Tostig sanctuary Baldwin earned a small stake in the Scandinavian bid for the English throne, although his major investment was almost certainly in a Norman victory. While he had a sister in the Scandinavian camp, his own offspring was in that of the Normans. Baldwin V's daughter Matilda had married William around 1053 and was thus to become Queen of England and mother of William Rufus and Henry I. Such links indicate the power and influence of the counts of Flanders. Baldwin, who was then Regent of France, was in a position to give his son-in-law critical aid at the time of the 1066 invasion, not least by guaranteeing that his rear was not threatened by attack from a France under hostile leadership. Intriguing light is thrown on this part of the Hereward legend by a recent booklet written by L.R. Cryer[6] in which he quotes the following extract from Domesday:

> The land of Gilbert de Gand, a manor in Folchingeham where Ulf has 12 caracutes of land to be taxed and as many ploughs. Gilbert has there in demesne 5 ploughs and 14 villeins and 5 sokemen and 9 bordars with 7 ploughs.

Cryer makes the following claim:

> Gilbert de Gand (or Ghent or Gaunt) was the son of Baldwin, the Earl of Flanders and nephew of the Conqueror's wife, Matilda. He came to England with William in 1066 and was certainly well rewarded. Rawnsley[7] said that only Bishop Odo of Bayeux had more favour shown. At the time of the Survey his possessions included a lordship in Berkshire, 2 in Oxfordshire, 3 in Yorkshire, 6 in Cambridgeshire, 2 in Buckinghamshire, 1 in Huntingdon, Rutland, Leicester and Warwickshire, 18 in Nottinghamshire.

In Lincolnshire de Gand held some 120 places, including Folkingham[8] which became his seat and was later strengthened, for once the Normans had subdued an area they made sure of holding it by the building of fortified places. In this part of Lincolnshire alone there were castles at Spalding, Bolingbroke and Tattershall as well as those at Lincoln, Sleaford, Bourne and Castle Bytham. Gilbert not only played his part in the Conquest but continued to serve the king and was present at the siege of York which surviving Danes eventually destroyed in 1069. He was one of the few Normans to escape from the city, but soon died in the reign of King Rufus to be buried at Bardney Abbey which had been restored by him after pagan

Danes, led by Inguar and Hubba, had demolished it in 1087.

Identifying this Gilbert as the godfather of Hereward and making him a son of no less a person than the Count of Flanders would create a fascinating scenario completed by the geographical coincidence that Folkingham is barely 8 miles from Hereward's home at Bourne. However, enthusiasm must be restrained since the identity of this Gilbert de Gand is debatable. He could not, as Cryer claims, have been both the son of Baldwin V *and* the nephew of Baldwin's daughter Matilda. He could, however, have been Matilda's brother. Stenton agrees that a Gilbert de Gand was one of the barons who came over at the Conquest and 'obtained a great fief in the northern Danelaw and many possessions elsewhere', but says he was 'the son of Ralf, count of Alost'. Gand (or Ghent) lies roughly mid-way between Bruges and Alost and perhaps there is scope for confusion here.

The name Ralf invites further speculation since a dominant landowner at the time was Ralf de Gael, created Earl of East Anglia soon after Hastings but who later fled to Brittany after participating in the abortive rebellion of 1075. Ralf's father was Earl Ralf the Staller, a powerful minister and magnate in Edward the Confessor's day. And it will be recalled that *De Gestis* described Hereward's father as 'Leofric of Bourne, grandson of Earl Radulf surnamed Scalre', which Freeman translates as Ralph the *Staller*.

Freeman confirms that Gilbert of Ghent was established at York in King Edward's reign and was indeed Hereward's godfather. Freeman, however, can only swallow parts of the tale and puts Hereward's exile at a later date: 'Hereward held lands in Lincolnshire; part of them was held of the Abbey of Crowland, of which Abbot Ulfcytel resumed possession because Hereward did not keep his agreement. At some time later, therefore after 1062, the year of the appointment of Ulfcytel, Hereward fled from the country, but for what cause we are not told.' This would absolve Leofric, already five years in his grave, from any involvement in his son's banishment, but this in any case becomes irrelevant to Freeman who does not accept that Leofric of Mercia was Hereward's father.

Whatever the exact date of his departure it is certain that the following years were important in establishing Hereward's reputation among his peers as a warrior; and also, if incidentally, they were necessary as the fertile seedbed in which his legend took root and grew. According to the *De Gestis* account, Hereward spent this period in performing numberless deeds of derring-do against formidable foes in Cornwall and Ireland, including a legendary encounter with a monstrous bear, possessed of human intelligence, which Freeman sees as a cipher for Earl Siward of Northumbria and his son Waltheof. However, such episodes are perhaps more appropriately studied through the lenses of literature and mythology (see Chapter 8).

Hereward's role as a model hero is unusual in that it combines both the elements of saga and medieval outlaw, the saga element inevitably being concerned with his early adventures in which damsels in various degrees of distress are rescued, warriors are felled and his courage and prowess earn universal acclaim. While at the home of the King of Ireland's son he learns of his father's death, but his wish to return home is deferred by a war against the Duke of Munster in which he again distinguishes himself so that the *De Gestis* reports, 'The valour of his ancestors could not approach that of Hereward.'

Other adventures follow but, despite the offer of marriage to the king's granddaughter, Hereward, now equipped with two ships and a company of men, makes his farewells and sails for England. The *De Gestis*, having previously noted the death of Leofric, curiously gives the reason for this departure as 'a great desire to visit his dependants and parents'. Ironically, the narrative begins to falter now that some evidently factual strands are woven into it.

The mention of *parents* can only mean his widowed mother and the reference to *dependants* is interesting since Ælfgar, Hereward's elder brother, succeeded Leofric

The Abbey of St Edmund at Bury as it would have appeared in the thirteenth century. Watercolour by Arthur Lankester, 1895.

and was, with some interruption when he fell from royal favour, Earl of Mercia until his death in 1062. Hereward's post-Conquest claims to any of the estates in Lincolnshire would not have been prejudiced by any participation in the battle of Hastings. The lands of the Englishmen who had fallen at Hastings were by royal command subject to confiscation, and among the feudal documents of the Abbey of Bury St Edmunds survives a grimly worded writ in which William orders the abbot to surrender the holdings of all those under his jurisdiction 'who stood against me in battle and were slain there'.

This was part of William's cynical efforts to legitimize his claim to the throne while depicting Harold as an illegal usurper. The staff work fell down occasionally for, as David Bates[9] points out, one writ issued in William's name makes the mistake – from a Norman standpoint – of calling Harold 'king', a slip repeated in that otherwise expert piece of propaganda, the Bayeux Tapestry. Bates comments:

> The consigning of Harold's reign to legal oblivion had the sinister implication, which is set out clearly by William of Poitiers, that anyone who had fought against William at Hastings was a rebel. The fact that this theory can be shown to have evolved suggests that, although rooted in William's claim to succeed Edward, it was in reality an expedient device developed to justify the transfer of lands from Normans to English. In this context, it is obvious that once William was securely installed as king, and his followers' appetite for English wealth grew, few English landholders can have felt secure when the Normans' definition of treachery was set so widely as to include defending one's kingdom against an invader.

Any land claimed by Hereward would presumably have involved a responsibility for the welfare of those living on it, a responsibility possibly shared with Ælfgar's son, Edwin, who had succeeded his father as Earl of Mercia. In the events of 1070 it would, therefore, be logical for Edwin and his brother, Morcar, to become identified with Hereward's struggle in the Fens, which is indeed what happened. Edwin, however, is said to have met his fate elsewhere and could not have taken part in the fenland resistance as *De Gestis* suggests.

Edwin's death in ambush, probably at the hands of some of his own followers somewhere in the north of England, is generally accepted although some support for the view that he was indeed among the defenders in the Fens came from the discovery of what appeared to be the boss of a shield dug up on the Isle of Ely in 1694. It carried an Old English inscription and was thought to be a love-token given to Edwin by William's daughter who had supposedly been promised to him in marriage. But Duke William failed to honour the pledge which caused Edwin's not unnatural disaffection; as to the feelings that existed between him and the maiden we can only guess. The supposed love-token of a shield boss throws a strange light on Norman romance and makes an enticing tale that, alas, does not withstand Professor Freeman's scrutiny. He dismisses the discovery as having nothing to do with Edwin: 'the name of the owner is not Eadwin or its Mercian form Ædwine, but Æduwen, and Æduwen or Ædwen is a woman's name.'

Hereward's return home was again postponed when savage storms drove his ships first to the Orkneys, no doubt by way of Cape Wrath, and then southwards to be shipwrecked on the coast of Flanders. Here this band of warlike strangers was viewed at first with understandable suspicion, soon to be dispelled by Hereward's magnetic personality and even more persuasive military prowess. *De Gestis* again contributes a lyrical account of Hereward's knightly deeds in war and single combat which earn honour from the Count of Flanders. Mercenaries often lead charmed lives but the description of Hereward's career on the Continent is particularly glittering and General Harward points to the earlier interview with Gilbert of Ghent, his godfather, as having a very important bearing on Hereward's future.

The journey to Flanders, would have been a logical step, with or without the aid of a tempest. Gilbert's position in England was that of a nobleman of great wealth and influence, and he was, says the General – echoing Cryer – related to Baldwin, Count of Flanders. He describes Baldwin as

probably the lord and chief man in Ghent. Not far from Ghent was Bruges, the principal residence of the Counts of Flanders, the fortress or castle of Lille being their chief stronghold of defence, while they had a country residence at Marle, two miles from Bruges.

Gilbert must have been an intimate friend of Hereward's family, as his son afterwards married the grand-daughter and sole heiress of Lucia, sister[10] of Hereward, and thereby he succeeded by right of his wife to the Earldom of Lincoln. We may therefore rest assured that Hereward had the full benefit of this friendship, and that Gilbert's kinsmen and connections in Bruges and Ghent received Hereward most cordially. He was probably lodged in one of Gilbert's houses, and became acquainted with the Flemish nobles and leading burgesses, and about this period of his history he came under the notice of the fair lady Torfrida, who subsequently became his wife.

At this time, also, his love of arms and the sports of chivalry met with encouragement from the martial spirit of the Flemish people. The Flemings were hard men, and whether as artisans, traders, or men-at-arms, they held their own with credit amongst the nations of that day. They also maintained a character for bravery and independence conspicuous amongst all the tribes of Germany, and in such a school Hereward's military training must have been completed under the most favourable conditions, and his martial ardour and lofty spirit stimulated by surrounding influences.

Although the chronicles, *De Gestis* apart, throw scant light upon Hereward's life in Flanders, partial investigators such as General Harward are able to infer a surprising amount from the few facts that survive. Whether Hereward's exploits were as a mercenary attached to Count Baldwin, or to his son Robert, or to the Count of Guisnes, becomes of subordinate importance to be clarified at some future time 'when Flemish records hitherto unknown may enlighten us'.

The 'valiant Hereward' of the Florence of Worcester account inspires General Harward to construct a fine plinth on which to put his heroic figure and from Florence's *vir strenuissimus* he extracts strength and vigour, energy of body and mind, patience, perseverance and endurance, as well as unflinching resolution, indomitable courage, capability of resource in conception, and tenacity of purpose in execution:

> In tournaments and knightly exercises, who more skilful than Hereward? In feats of strength, who bore off the palm? If hard blows were exchanged, who more ready than Hereward to receive and pay back with interest? . . . If the adjective *strenuissimus* is allowed to bear most or all of the meanings here assigned to it, it is by no means impossible to form a fair ideal presentment of the Saxon hero as he stood in his lifetime, with actively working mind, his eyes bright with intelligence and resource for every emergency. No thought for danger troubled his smooth brow.
>
> His features must have indicated the character of the man, and if there is any truth in physiognomy he must have borne a well-formed mouth of decided character, a straight or Saxon nose, and a full chin somewhat projecting, while the jaw, square and massive, gave determination to the lower part of the face, and the well developed head and moderately high forehead indicated his mental capacity and ready wit, not only in deeds of arms and in overcoming difficulties, but in the subtle military arts of stratagem and surprise, of personal self-control, and complete self-sacrifice on emergency, as over and over again he risked himself in the power of his enemies, when reconnoitring their camp or testing their resources.

While it is easy to smile at the writer's self-indulgence we should remember that even sober historians such as Freeman allow themselves some licence in this area. Medieval artists were evidently less concerned with physical likenesses than the symbolism of authority and majesty as represented on manuscripts, seals and coins, yet despite the absence of any contemporary portrait, here is Freeman providing his sketch of Hereward's great foe, Duke William:

Of the man himself our one personal portrait clearly belongs to his later years.[11] William's height was tall, but not excessive; he was neither a giant like Harold Hardrada nor a small man like Eadgar and Cnut. His countenance was stern; the fore part of his head was bald; whether standing or sitting his look was worshipful and kingly.

Such he appears in the Tapestry; such he is described by one who may have looked on the great King with childish wonder. But in his latter days his majestic figure was disfigured by excessive corpulence. Still, unwieldy as he became, he never lost the power of motion like Henry the Eighth; he was able

William the Conqueror as depicted in the Bayeux Tapestry.

William I depicted in profile on a silver penny minted at Hastings (moneyer: Dunnine)

65

to mount a horse to the end of his days. At the times of the three great yearly Assemblies William appeared in all his glory. All the great men of his realm were gathered together, not only for counsel on the affairs of the Kingdom, but to join in their sovereign's royal feasts, when the ambassadors of foreign lands came to see his magnificence, and when William showed himself affable and courteous and bountiful to all. Yet perhaps it is not without significance that the historian who gives us this splendid picture goes on immediately to speak of his avarice and extortions in words hardly differing from those of the native Chronicler.

Modern scientific evidence can fill in the gaps a little. William's tomb was first opened in 1522 and revealed the skeleton of a large man with exceptionally long arms and legs. Later in the sixteenth century the tomb was despoiled by Calvinists and only a single thigh bone survives. David Bates[12] describes how recent examination of this remnant produced the conjecture that William was around 1.75 metres (5 ft 10 in) tall, a remarkable height for a medieval man. 'Meagre as it is, this information does at least confirm the literary sources' statements that William was a man of exceptional appearance and strength. William of Poitiers, for example, related that Count Geoffrey Martel of Anjou believed William to be the greatest warrior on earth and that after an arduous foraging expedition during the Hastings campaign, William was still strong enough to carry back the hauberk (coat of chain mail) of an exceptional warrior such as William fitzOsbern, who was presumably exhausted by his exertions!'

Another chronicler, William of Malmesbury, offers a supporting testimony that William possessed such powerful arms and shoulders that he could draw a bow which defied other men's efforts while riding a horse. This manoeuvre would have required William to control his mount with legs and thighs, leaving both hands free to draw the bow – an exercise demanding great strength and superb horsemanship. Since William became corpulent towards the end of his life such feats must have belonged to his youth and prime when he fought at Hastings and around Ely.

There is no evidence that William and Hereward ever came face to face, although during the siege of Ely they may well have been within bowshot of each other. If a reconciliation did eventually take place and Hereward joined in the Conqueror's military campaigns in Maine we can assume a meeting between them was more than likely. Given that they both had connections with Baldwin it is tempting to conjecture that they may well have met some time before Hastings during Hereward's Continental exile. Such secrets will remain hidden but it was in Flanders that Hereward met the person who did come to exert the greatest influence on his life.

This was the noble and beautiful Torfrida, who was to be his wife and chief adviser before darker days came between them. Torfrida appears to have been an exceptional woman 'much devoted to liberal knowledge and skilled in mechanical arts' says the *De Gestis*. It would seem that she was better educated than most, more so indeed than Hereward, which would help to explain to modern minds any subsequent marital problems. 'Mechanical arts' were in those days linked with astrology and magic, a black art forbidden by the Church.

'Those whose consciences were tough and their faith weak' writes Charles Kingsley, 'had little scruple in applying to a witch, and asking help from the powers below, when the saints above were slack to hear them. Churchmen, even, were bold enough to learn the mysteries of nature, Algebra, Judicial Astrology, and the occult powers of herbs, stones and animals, from the Musselman doctors of Cordova and Seville; and, like Pope Gerbert, mingle science and magic. . . .' Here, perhaps, are echoes of that racial and religious prejudice noted by Kingsley's biographer Brenda Colloms, but, interestingly, the old chroniclers largely resisted the temptation to cast Torfrida as an enchantress. *De Gestis* simply says 'She fell in love with Hereward, having heard of his achievements, and she displayed many of her accomplishments, as they say, for love of him, and by so doing secured his affection for herself.'

It is not too difficult to imagine how a sophisticate of Flanders might dazzle a young Saxon but *De Gestis* does not overlook a pragmatic aspect to the affair: '. . . she (Torfrida) led him away to the inside of the house and showed him all her father's riches in gold and silver, or of other material, belonging to her mother, and also a corselet of excessive lightness and very fine work, and much brighter and purer than any steel or iron, and a helmet of similar beauty and strength.' While this part of the chronicle appears to be dealing largely with invention and fiction it does give us an untypically realistic account of a Flemish campaign in Scaldemariland (Zeeland). In another context it could be taken as an authentic description of a military operation of the period

It describes the outrage of the Scaldemariland islanders at the threat of foreign invasion – 'like the English people to the French' – and refers to a scorched-earth policy of ravaging and laying waste their borders to deny the enemy sustenance. Having achieved a tactical advantage, the islanders offered amnesty if the men of Flanders handed over their leaders, including Hereward, for execution plus their possessions and arms. At Hereward's suggestion the wagons and chariots brought for conveying away this booty were burned and the negotiators detained by some pretext to gain time to prepare for battle.

Peace talks having broken down, battle commenced with the Scaldemariland spearmen advancing in pairs wearing coats of felt dipped in pitch and resin, or leather tunics, their spears studded with nails and twisted for thrusting and striking. They also carried three or four squared javelins for throwing. Between each couple so armed, and protecting them with his shield, was another soldier swinging a sword or axe. But their strategy was inferior and they allowed Hereward's forces to gain the high ground.

Hereward's stratagem of a fake retreat and sudden counter-attack is reminiscent of the celebrated Norman ploy at Hastings and once again proved decisive. It enabled Hereward, with 1,000 horse soldiers and 600 other armed men, to outflank the enemy and attack their camp from the rear 'where he came upon them almost unarmed. Being wholly unable to defend themselves they were routed.'

There is nothing romantic or fabulous in this account, which is quite unlike the other descriptions of marvellous exploits against impossible odds. It is a straightforward battle report and, interestingly, it also suggests that Hereward had become well acquainted with the Norman mode of fighting, one in which the horse played a significant role. It further suggests a more modern and innovative approach to warfare than that of his countrymen at Hastings. He would appear to be not simply a hit-and-run guerrilla fighter but a battlefield commander able to deploy a considerable force of infantry and cavalry.

These foreign military experiences were the prelude and the preparation for his moment of history, his return to Lincolnshire, his revenge upon those who had wronged his family and his final stand against the Normans. One expects the *De Gestis* to be unambiguous in stressing motives of honour to explain his return to aid his homeland and particularly to help his kinsmen at Bourne in their hour of need. However, the strange mixture of what could only be fiction with what could easily be truth produced the suggestion that some dispute over payment for his mercenary services first prompted his departure. Much as General Harward tries to persuade us, it is difficult to see Hereward as a totally unalloyed hero and this only serves to strengthen our belief in him.

CHAPTER FIVE

The Avenger

What eventually made Hereward decide to return to his family home may be clouded by other factors but the version given in *De Gestis*, albeit gilded, seems to contain the essential and obvious motive. The Bevis interpretation speaks of 'a strong desire to visit . . . his country which by then was subject to the rule of foreigners and almost ruined by the exactions of many. If in any place, any of his friends or neighbours were still alive, he felt he would like to help them.'

This sounds reasonable and so does the unobtrusive manner of his arrival accompanied only by his servant Martin Lightfoot. Two nephews (previously referred to as 'sons of his own uncle'), Siward the White and Siward the Red, were left behind in Flanders to take care of his wife, Torfrida. It cannot have been difficult for a man of substance to obtain a passage on a trading vessel crossing to the east coast of England and then to slip undetected into Lincolnshire and, since this was a scouting mission, it would make sense for him to try to learn what had been happening at Bourne without revealing his identity.

According to the *De Gestis*, on his return it is from a man called Pirus and his family that Hereward hears of the wrongs visited upon the neighbourhood and his own home:

What was more grievous to them than all else, they bewailed that they would be in subjection to the men who only the day before had slain the innocent young son of their lord . . . whom his father at his death had commended to his people, with his widowed mother; and he would be his heir, if his brother, Hereward, a man most vigorous and conspicuous in every kind of valour, should not return, whom while still a lad his father had driven from his face for his misdoings.

And now . . . some men with the consent of the King attacked his inheritance and took it for themselves, killing our very light, the son and heir of our lord while he was protecting his widowed mother against them, as they demanded from her his father's riches and treasures, as well as because he slew those two who had handled her discourteously. They cut off his head and set it up over the house, by way of revenge, because he had killed two Frenchmen – and there it still remains.

69

'The old church at Bourne, Lincolnshire, stands near the site of a feudal castle,' wrote Charles Kingsley, who also affirmed that the castle replaced that earlier home of Hereward's parents, the scene of his celebrated return and vengeance.

Clearly, the imagination of one or probably several scribes has been at work here to provide a dramatically apposite prelude to the heroic tale of vengeance that follows. Hereward, stunned by grief and rage, puts on his armoured tunic, breastplate and helmet and, grasping his sword firmly in his hand, makes his way to the ancestral home. His servant, also dressed for the kill, accompanies him. Hereward's temper is not improved by the sounds of laughter and music coming from the Bacchanalian scene where the interlopers, now befuddled with ale, pledge themselves 'in a draught of a spear-shaft and in wine of sorrow'. As Hereward approaches he makes a grisly discovery: a severed head fixed over the gateway is that of his younger brother.

> Taking it down, he kissed it and wrapped it up in a cloth. Then he advanced behind the door of the building to search for the guests and there by the fireside he saw them all overcome with intoxication and the soldiers reclining in women's laps. There was a jester present singing to a lute, abusing the nation of the English and in the middle of the room the man performed ungainly antics, meant in imitation of English dancing. At last the jester demanded his fee from the chief man, something belonging to the parents of the famous youth recently slain. One of the girls at the banquet not regarding

his words, answered: 'There is still surviving a famous soldier, brother of the slain youth, whose name is Hereward and well known in our country, who is in Flanders. If he were here, not one of these things would be left here by daybreak.'

At this the company bursts into mockery of the exile's name and Hereward, unable to endure any more, storms inside and ends the jester's performance with a single sword stroke, described in a passage recalling Odysseus's return to Ithaca and his slaughter of the suitors of Penelope:

Then he attacked the guests and laid low fourteen of them and their lord, some being through drink unable to rise and others being unable to go to their help as they were unarmed; this took place with the assistance of a single servant whom Hereward had set at the door of the hall, so that whoever escaped his hand, might fall into the hand of the servant. That same night the heads of the dead were fixed over the gate where that of Hereward's brother had been placed, and he gave thanks that his brother's blood was now avenged.

A more prosaic version, however, is preferred by General Harward who suggests that it was more likely that Hereward returned to Bourne accompanied by a chosen group of followers. Far from remaining incognito, Hereward was quick to establish contact with his old friends in Lincolnshire and raise a small band of men-at-arms with which to surprise the Normans while they enjoyed a banquet in his own hall at Bourne. According to the General, the wrongdoers were cut down by the battle-axes of Hereward 'and his faithful followers', then, having restored his mother, 'Earl Leofric's widow', to her home, he returned to Flanders leaving a sufficient guard to protect her and the promise of an early return bringing his wife and reinforcements. While the General finds the *De Gestis* timing for Hereward's return – the day after his brother's murder – too convenient for credibility, at the same time the reference to a younger brother as a possible inheritor of the family estates is somewhat inconvenient. This would of course call into question the position of Edwin and Morcar and increase doubts about Hereward's father being the same Leofric, Earl of Mercia.[1]

General Harward takes pains to legitimize Hereward's actions. Now he becomes the dutiful son and caring husband and restores his mother to her home, and, making sure that there is sufficient guard to protect her, he returns to Flanders to reassure his wife and bring her to England. He decides that the time has now arrived when the presence of every Englishman is required to resist the oppression of the Norman adventurers. 'It cannot be gainsaid that Hereward was strictly

'Then he attacked the guests and laid low fourteen of them. . . .'; an H.C. Selous illustration for
Charles Kingsley's novel, *Hereward the Wake*.

within his rights in resisting force by force. William had outlawed himself,
inasmuch as he had sworn at his coronation, according to the oath of St Dunstan, to
execute justice and to govern England according to the laws of Alfred and Edward.
It is certain he never had any intention to observe this most sacred oath. . . .'

The General's Hereward was never an aggressor. He merely defended his
property and people, and punished intruders. Only after every hope of justice had
faded did he visit retribution upon the Norman criminals, allowing none to escape
his avenging arm. No word can be said against the justice of his cause, nor the
means he used to punish the Normans in return for their exploitation of the
helpless Saxon peasantry.

Harward at the same time takes an opportunity to indict King William and his
scant knowledge of, or regard for, Saxon laws and customs:

The only form of government with which he had any acquaintance was the feudal system as administered on the Continent, which differed in every respect from the Saxon laws. He had promised a large share of plunder and the landed proprietorship to his followers before he set sail from Normandy. No Danish Viking or Pict cattle-lifter committed such cruel atrocities or wholesale robbery as this unscrupulous Norman barbarian, and having broken his oath to the people, he was no longer entitled to any respect but that given and taken by the sword.

This picture, it has to be said, contrasts sharply with the idyllic scene painted by Orderic Vitalis, although that chronicler may have copied a romanticized account from William of Poitiers, who had been a soldier-chaplain in the Conqueror's service and, therefore, one of the first to acknowledge the rightness of his lord's cause:

Now that the brigands had been driven off English and Normans were living peacefully together in boroughs, towns, and cities, and were inter-marrying with each other. You could see many villages or town markets filled with displays of French wares and merchandise, and observe the English, who had previously seemed contemptible to the French in their native dress, completely transformed by foreign fashions. No one dared to pillage, but everyone cultivated his own fields in safety and lived contentedly with his neighbour.

Before recording Hereward's visit to Flanders to collect his wife, *De Gestis* inserts further adventures, some of which seem to have their basis in fact. It describes how the alarm bells rang after Hereward's bloody homecoming and as almost all of the French in that area abandoned their newly acquired properties and fled, the Saxon inhabitants, greatly heartened, began to flock to his side despite fears of the inevitable reaction from King William. Not oblivious to this threat Hereward recruited 'Forty-nine of the bravest men'[2] and proceeded to cleanse the neighbourhood of Normans, administering retribution where appropriate.

Having established himself as leader of his small army, which was swollen in numbers each day by fugitives and condemned men as well as by those who had been disinherited, Hereward took a step which emphasizes that he was no mere mercenary only interested in fighting for profit. He decided to give his actions greater legitimacy than that provided by popular feeling:

He called to mind that he had never been, according to the English custom, girt with a sword and belt of a Knight. So, with two of his most eminent men, one named Wynter and the other Gaenoch, he went to the Abbot of Burgh [Peterborough], whose name was Brant, a man of very noble birth, that he might gird him with the sword and belt of a Knight after the English practice, lest, after becoming the chief and leader of many men, the inhabitants of the country should find fault with him for not being a Knight.

On the Feast of the Nativity of the Apostles Peter and Paul he obtained the honour of Knighthood at the hands of the Abbot, and for his honour a monk of Ely, Wilton by name who was also warden [?] and a friend of Hereward's father, and faithful as a brother, made his companions Knights. Thus he wanted himself and his men to be made Knights, as he had heard it had been ruled by the Frenchmen that if anyone were made Knight by a monk or clerk or by any ordained minister, he ought not to be reckoned among true Knights, but as a false Knight and born out of due time.

Hereward in opposition to this rule, desired nearly all the men that served him and were under his rule to be made Knights by the monks. . . . He had often said: 'If any man received the Knightly sword from a servant of God and a Knight of the Kingdom of heaven, I know that such a servant displays his valour in every sort of military service, as I have often found by experience.' Hence arose the custom among the monks of Ely, that if any man there would be made a Knight, he ought always on the same day to offer his naked sword upon the altar

A medieval drawing showing the girding of a knight with a sword. In this illustration Offa is receiving the sword and spurs from Warmundus (Cotton Ms).

at high mass, and receive it again from the monk that was singing the mass after the gospel, the sword being put on his bare neck with benediction.

This passage is especially interesting in that it contains one of the few examples of reported speech by Hereward himself, even if his alleged words imply a piety not always evident in his actions. It reminds us also that Abbot Brand is identified by various writers as Hereward's uncle. The significance of the knighting becomes clearer in Harward's interpretation of the next *De Gestis* episode – the challenge of Frederic de Warrenne, brother of William Warrenne, the king's son-in-law. Frederic had vowed to avenge the massacre at Bourne and himself take Hereward's head to the king, but General Harward puts another slant on the story.

He suggests that Frederic had been one of the principal Norman pillagers at Bourne and that Hereward had challenged him to mortal combat according to the 'wager of battle' under which civil and criminal disputes could be settled by trial by battle. Frederic had declined, refusing to acknowledge Hereward's knighthood since it was conferred by a spiritual lord, and Hereward had gone to Lynn and forced Frederic to face him. It seems unlikely therefore that all the rules of knightly combat were observed although the General considers a probable outcome to have been a *combat à l'outrance* between armed knights, mounted, with spear, battle-axe, and dagger, or on foot with sword and dagger, the only witnesses being the friends and esquires of both parties.

Conisbrough Castle, South Yorkshire, built on the site once held by William Warrenne, Hereward's 'implacable enemy'.

The seal of a Warrenne, Earl of Surrey, derived from a twelfth-century seal of the Counts of Vermandois.

Whatever the circumstances, all agree that the predictable result was that Hereward killed Frederic and so added to his reputation as a man of steel whose deeds matched his words. He also made another implacable enemy in the person of William Warrenne, Earl of Surrey, who was to appear in the Norman army laying siege to the Isle of Ely. No doubt the killing of Frederic Warrenne, even if surrounded by the trappings of an affair of honour, would for political reasons have been regarded as a terrorist murder and such occurrences cannot have been uncommon.

The scanty legislation attributable to William, points out David Bates, included the institution of the so-called *murdrum* fine designed to protect the Normans who came over at the Conquest and those who followed later. The relevant clause in the text known as 'the articles of William' (*Articuli Willelmi*) stated

And if any one of them is slain, his lord shall arrest the slayer within five days if he can. If not, however, he shall begin to pay me forty-six marks of silver from the property of that lord as long as it lasts out. When, however, the property of the lord fails, the whole hundred in which the murder is committed shall pay in common what remains.

This method of making the law-abiding members of an oppressed community responsible for the actions of its wilder spirits is familiar throughout history and not least in recent times. It echoes another subtle piece of Norman law enforcement that, for the purposes of exacting further financial punishment from a community, decreed that any unidentified victim of homicide should be regarded as a Norman until his killers were brought to book.

Bates surmises that the amount of space taken up with refinements to such procedures in later treatises suggests that such murders were relatively frequent. However, he notes that 'in the event of a Frenchman summoning an Englishman to defend himself on a serious criminal charge, such as perjury, murder or theft, a concession was made to English legal procedure; the Englishman was allowed to choose between ordeal by hot iron, which was used in England before 1066, or trial by combat, which was not.'

Such legislation tells us something about William's policy towards the English which was more of a velvet glove well hidden by the iron hand. While he dealt ruthlessly with resistance in the name of law and order, he offered a kind of olive branch by setting up procedures for resolving peacefully areas of dispute between conquered and conquerors. Yet despite these efforts to achieve a *rapprochement*, the overall impact of the Conquest on the English ruling classes was, in Bates's phrase, an unmitigated catastrophe. Deprived of their lands and inheritance, many chose exile rather than life under Norman rule.

The Conqueror's respect for legality and continuity was more apparent than real. His attempts at settling the country after Hastings were token, paying little more than lip-service to the promises made at his coronation. His priority was not to ease the transition of Saxon society into a new era but to satisfy the need and greed of its conquerors. Yet the pressures that made this inevitable cannot be ignored. Following the early campaigns there must have been a steady influx of land-hungry and pugnacious Norman adventurers and we can only guess at the countless incidents of provocation and retaliation, with their brutal consequences and the transfer of land from Saxon to Norman usurper. The Domesday Book is an eloquent witness to the extent of this change of ownership although it is silent on why particular estates were transferred in this way.

The Normans were for many years an occupying power in a hostile land and the strain this imposed must have been immense. Ever aware that a vengeful knife or arrow could be waiting, they were unable to relax or sleep without a weapon near to hand, even when not engaged upon some red-handed foray of retribution or plunder. Venturing abroad alone, especially after dark, would have been as risky as it is for twentieth-century policemen to patrol some inner-city areas. Naturally, many of them being mercenaries, they expected to be rewarded in proportion to the hardships and deprivation they were asked to endure. An aspect of this self-imposed purgatory is reflected in the words of Orderic:

At this time certain Norman women, consumed by fierce lust, sent message after message to their husbands urging them to return at once, and adding that unless they did so with all speed they would take other husbands for themselves. For they dared not join their men themselves, being unaccustomed to the sea-crossing and afraid of seeking them out in England, where they were engaging in armed forays every day and blood flowed freely on both sides. The king, with so much fighting on his hands, was most anxious to keep all his knights about him, and made them a friendly offer of lands and revenues and great authority, promising them more when he had completely rid the kingdom of all his enemies. His loyal barons and stalwart fighting-men were gravely perturbed, for they saw that continual risings threatened the king and their brothers, friends, and allies, and feared that if they abandoned him they would be openly branded as traitors and cowardly deserters. On the other hand, what could honourable men do if their lascivious wives polluted their beds with adultery and brought indelible shame and dishonour on their offspring?

As a result Hugh of Grandmesnil, who was governor of the Gewissae – that is, the region round Winchester – and his brother-in-law Humphrey of Tilleul, who had held the castle of Hastings from the day of its foundation, and many others departed from the country heavy at heart, and unwilling to go because they were deserting the king whilst he was struggling in a foreign land. They returned to Normandy to oblige their wanton wives; but neither they nor their heirs were ever able to recover the fiefs which they had held and chosen to abandon.[3]

England was exhausted with tribulation after tribulation, suffering at the hands of Englishmen and foreigners alike. Fire, rapine, and daily slaughter brought destruction and disaster on the wretched people and utterly laid waste the land. Ill-fortune held victors and vanquished alike in its snare, bringing down on them war, famine, and pestilence as the omnipotent Judge thought fit.

Ruthless and powerful as he was, William had started a process which he could not stop, even if that had been his intention, and certainly in those early days he was obliged to redistribute lands to secure the Norman settlement and to recompense the followers on whom that settlement depended. His actions were those of someone reacting to events on a day-to-day basis and among them was the perverse appointment of the new Abbot of Peterborough who was to loom so large in the Hereward story.

It would seem that in this post-Hastings period of around 1069 Hereward was trying to make up for lost time by establishing himself as the rallying point for

Peterborough Cathedral, scene of Hereward's attack on the 'Golden Borough'.

resistance in the east. If his knighting by Abbot Brand is authentic, his return to Bourne certainly took place in 1069, if not earlier. The chroniclers record that Abbot Brand died in November 1069, which gave King William an opportunity to pursue his scouring of the English Church by appointing a Norman abbot as Brand's successor and at the same time do something to curb the activities of the Lincolnshire rebel.

His choice was a monk called Turold who already had gained a reputation at Malmesbury as a tyrant more addicted to power than prayer. In him William had found a warrior monk with a temper to match any local troublemaker. Such militant ecclesiastics were not unfamiliar figures in medieval times – Bishop Odo of Bayeux is a prominent example. Doubtless Turold used a cudgel or mace favoured by such churchmen because in theory they were thus able to kill without spilling blood. He was therefore the ideal figure to rule over the abbey and also to deal with the outlaws in the Fens. Abbot Turold duly set out at the head of an armed squad of Frenchmen to take over at Peterborough. The company of truculent Normans arrived at Stamford, 10 miles away, on 1 June 1070.

What the abbot learned there cannot have eased the burden of his journey. He was given a message from the frightened monks at Peterborough informing him that Hereward and his men had joined forces with the Danes who had been lurking off the English coast for months and were threatening the town and abbey. Caught between the plundering French and the ravenous wolves of Denmark whom Hereward was probably powerless to restrain, the Peterborough flock, without a shepherd for seven months, must have been in a state of high anxiety.

Turold, with some hundred and sixty armed Frenchmen, galloped to Peterborough next day but was too late to catch the raiders; he found only one ailing monk amid the smouldering ruins of the monastery. What had occurred and why it happened is obscured by time but it is sensible to go to the Peterborough Chronicle itself for the full account of how 'all manner of evils' befell the monastery from the time of Abbot Brand's death:

> Then came into England the Danes, that is to say, King Swein, son[4] of King Canute, and with him a mighty army, and the English thought he would acquire the land by battle. And a certain earl among them named Osbern and Christian the bishop and many with them came to the Isle of Ely, and Hereward with his men joined them, and they did all manner of evil things. And Hereward himself incited and invited them to come to the monastery of Burch, and take whatever was there in gold, in silver, and in other precious things, because they had heard that the abbot was dead and that King William had given the abbacy to a certain Norman monk named Turold, and because he was a very stern man and because he had already come to Stamford with his knights, therefore they made haste to go and take whatever they could find. Nor was this hidden from the monks of Burch.
>
> There was in the monastery at that time a certain sacrist named Ivar, who, upon hearing this rumour, by the advice of the monks took all that he could gather together, texts of the gospels, chasubles, copes, and similar small gear, and came to Abbot Turold at Stamford, and told him how Hereward and the Danes were coming to despoil the church.
>
> Then very early in the morning of the same day, came these aforesaid evildoers with many ships, but the monks and their men closed the gates, and

courageously began to defend from above; and a strenuous battle was there fought at the Bolhithe gate.[5] Then Hereward and his allies, seeing that they could in no wise conquer them nor force an entrance, set fire to the buildings that were next the gate, and thus entered by the aid of fire, and they burned all the offices of the monks, and the whole vill, save only the church and one house. Then the monks came unto them and entreated them not to do this great wrong; but they would not hearken to them but, armed as they were, entered the church and would have carried away the great cross, but they were not able. Albeit they took the golden crown from the head of the crucifix, with the precious stones, and the footrest under its feet, which was also of pure gold and gems, and they took two golden feretories and nine others adorned with silver and gold and gems, and twelve crosses some of gold and others of gold and silver and jewels. And even this sufficed them not, but they climbed the tower and took the great table which the monks had hidden there which was all of gold and silver and precious stones, which was wont to [stand] before the altar. No-one can tell or estimate how much gold and silver in divers sorts of ornaments, and books they took. All these things were excellent in worth, and none so good remain in all England.

Nevertheless they said they were doing this out of loyalty to the church and the Danes would guard these things better than the Frenchmen for the use of the church. And indeed Hereward was himself a man of the monks, and for that reason many believed in him. But he oft times swore in after times that he had done this of good intention, because he supposed they were conquering king William, and would themselves possess the land. Now all that was carried to Abbot Turold was saved, but all that they themselves seized was lost. So they took all things that they could gather together and put them in their ships and sailed away in haste, fearing lest the Normans could come upon them. And when they came to Ely they gave it all to the Danes, and Æthelwold the prior and Egelsin the monk and many of the older monks they had brought away with them. Then all the rest were scattered hither and thither as sheep without a shepherd, so that none remained in the monastery, save only one sick monk named Leofwin Lange who was lying in the infirmary. Thus was fulfilled what was spoken to Bishop Æthelfric: and all this took place on June 2nd, 1069.

The Peterborough scribe has a different year to that of other sources such as Orderic but confusion over dates, names and relationships is a characteristic of these records.

That same day came Abbot Turold to the monastery together with one hundred and forty[6] Normans well armed, and could not find them because they had already gone on their ships; but he found all things both within and without utterly burned, save only the church. So that city which was called the Golden Borough became the poorest of cities.

Prior Æthelwold and others of the elders were carried, as we have said, with the treasures, and were at Ely with the Danes, and because the prior was a man of wisdom and understanding, they made him a promise that if he would come with them to protect their country he should be a bishop. He pretended to them that he would gladly do so, and thereupon they gave into his keeping all their treasures, and delivered him the keys thereof.

But he secretly got for himself hammers and tools of all sorts such as he needed and kept them by him. Then on a certain day the Danes made themselves a great feast, and, as men making merry over treasure they had got with little labour, were all very joyful. While they were banqueting and carousing all day, Prior Æthelwold took his tools, and after a prayer began to open the feretory, in which he knew the arm of S. Oswald king and martyr was hidden. He appointed as watchers and scouts two faithful servants of his, one in the house where the Danes were drinking, and one halfway between, lest they should come suddenly upon him, or any inquiry should be made by them. When he had taken away all the gold and the silver, he found a wooden chest so strongly banded with iron that he utterly despaired of opening it, save by trusting in the help of God and of S. Oswald. Albeit with great labour, he removed and hid the iron bands, and revealed the inside of the chest.

He found within a receptacle wherein was hidden that most sacred and precious of all treasures, even S. Oswald's arm, together with many other relics. Then in great fear he took the holy plunder, and hid it in the straw of his bed under his head. For so he had to do in the pressing necessity of the time, but at a later date he ornamented them with gold and with silver as they had been before.

In the midst of all this, all the Danes had arisen with the intention of coming to Vespers, and he would have been caught by them in the very act, if the mercy of God and of S. Oswald had not helped him. But the Danes did not leave their places until the prior, who was flushed and heated with his labours, had washed his face in cold water, and had come into their presence. And when they beheld him they all stood up in his presence, because they all loved him as their lord and father, and rejoiced to see him, and there was none who asked him where he had been, or what he had been doing. The next day, Æthelwold received from Hereward an order to depart, because his allies were sailing overseas and thereupon he despatched the before-mentioned servants as though to carry something to Burch, but actually he sent them with the sacred relics to Ramsey, to be kept safe there.

What is so remarkable in this dusty record is the life-breath of authenticity it exhales. One can see the 'flushed and heated' complexion of the prior as he bent to his task and share his need to splash himself hastily with cold water before facing the eyes of his captors. The description of the treasures, the feretories, those portable shrines, and other relics speak, also, of the achievement of Saxon artists which has mostly vanished from the landscape. G.M. Trevelyan reminds us that 'Most pre-Conquest churches have been rebuilt, and the wooden chalets and halls where life was spent have left neither trace nor tradition, unless it be in the architecture of some of our fine old English barns. But those halls were great places in their day. . . . The log halls of Saxon thegn and Danish jarl were decorated with carving and paint both outside and in, and hung with burnished armour . . . articles of daily use were fantastically carved by native craftsmen. The art of the English jeweller was very fine, as the "Alfred jewel" and others still remain to prove.'

The architecture of the Saxons is now thought to have been technically superior to that of the Normans, whose comparative ineptness at laying foundations forced

Saxon palace at Cheddar from the west, as it might have appeared in the tenth century AD. The Witan met at Cheddar three times and the site remained in favour after the Conquest.

The famous late
(*c*. 1020–50) Anglo-Saxon
church tower at Earls
Barton, Northamptonshire,
with its distinctive vertical
lesene-strips and blank
arcades, round-topped
below and triangular-
headed above.

them to build thick, heavy walls to carry the weight of their large buildings. These
are undeniably impressive for their sheer size and bulk, but the Saxons, many now
believe, were able to achieve a greater feeling of space and elegance. True or not,
this ability must have been translated into other spheres and it is safe to assume
that church regalia would have been at the pinnacle of this artistic output. Small
wonder, therefore, that the Peterborough scribe should have devoted so much
attention to the fate of the abbey's treasures. His account continues:

Meanwhile the two kings, William, King of England, and Swein, King of
Denmark, were reconciled, and made friends. And it was agreed between
them that whatsoever Swein had obtained whether of gold or silver should
belong to him, and he should carry it with him to his own country. So it
happened that those Danes who were at Ely took all the aforesaid treasure and
putting it into their ships returned to Denmark. But when they were in mid
ocean, there arose a mighty storm, so that some of the ships holding the
treasure were driven to Norway, some to Ireland, and some to Denmark, and
of all the treasure none came safely into Denmark save only the great table
and certain of the feretories and crucifixes. Whatsoever they had they carried
to a certain vill of the King and placed in the church there.

Ivar the Sacrist of Burch, of whom we have spoken, came in after times to
Denmark, and in the same way and with the same cunning as the Prior had
done, he got all the relics which were in the other feretories and carried them
home. Afterwards, through the negligence and drunkenness of the Danes, the
church itself was burned with all the treasures. So by God's judgment they
justly lost what they had unjustly gained.

Moreover, when Bishop Æthelric, who was in fetters at Westminster, heard
all this, he excommunicated all who had done these things. And when the
Danes had gone to Denmark, Prior Æthelwold returned with all the other
monks to his own church, where Turold was now abbot. The monks also, who
had dispersed, returned to their own place, and carried on the worship of
God, where for seven days none had been observed. When the prior had
returned home, the monks of Ramsey were minded to keep the sacred relics,
but by the grace of God they were not permitted [to do so] for Abbot Turold
threatened he would burn their monastery unless they restored what had been
entrusted to their keeping.

This fascinating window on the medieval world opens up many avenues of
conjecture. We would like to learn more, for instance, about the remarkable Prior
Æthelwold, a man of sufficient stature to command the respect of wild Danish
pirates, yet at the same time a cunning dissembler plotting the recovery of some of
the abbey's sacred relics. An intriguing tale, too, could be told by Ivar the Sacrist
of his journey deep into hostile territory to rescue what stolen treasures remained.
And the attempts by the monks of Ramsey to hang on to stolen property tell us a
great deal about inter-community relations and the covetous side of monastic life.

Equally we share Freeman's difficulty in accepting under what jurisdiction
Bishop Æthelric, lacking a diocese, could claim to excommunicate Hereward and
his companions. Certainly, from other sources we hear Hereward described as 'exile'
or 'outlaw' but never as an excommunicate. It is possible to detect here the hand of
King William himself, who knew that such an edict would have had a much
deeper effect on the minds of the fenmen if it came from a Saxon prelate, even one
languishing in a dungeon. Any such censure by Abbot Turold would have been
scorned. The onslaught on the Golden Borough cannot have enhanced Hereward's
image as a national patriot but in the turmoil of the times many may well have
been persuaded that it was better for the Church's treasures to be kept out of the
hands of Norman abbots such as Turold, who had shown himself to be no different
from other land-grabbing Norman despots. How large a threat had been posed by
the possible alliance of Hereward with the Danes is perhaps indicated by the
apparent alacrity with which William bought off the Northern raiders. Allowing
them to sail away unhindered, keeping their stolen treasures, must have been a

bitter pill and involved some loss of face. It suggests that he considered Hereward too much of a handful to be permitted additional help from overseas.

The defection of the Danish fleet did not stop a stream of desperate men coming to join Hereward's resistance movement and during this period he must have set up on the Isle of Ely what became known as the Camp of Refuge. There are stories, too, of a timber fortification whose remains in after years were long referred to as 'Hereward's Castle'.

In all of England Hereward could not have found a location better suited to the art of defensive warfare. Few places in Britain could be more easily defended. Freeman recalls:

> before the great works of drainage which have changed the course of the rivers and wholly altered the face of the country, the Isle of Ely was strictly an island. It is a tract slightly raised above the level of the surrounding waters, and at the point where the great Minster still stands it may be said to rise to the dignity of a hill. The only means of approach were the roads of Roman and earlier date, roads which, in such a country, necessarily took the form of causeways. The great Akeman Street led straight to Ely from William's newly built castle of Cambridge, while another road, of uncertain date, led from his other fortress of Huntingdon, itself connected with Cambridge by the Roman Via Devana.
>
> But the main approach was not by either of these great roads, but at a point called Aldreth, a corruption of the name of the patron saint Æthelthryth, where the ancient course of the Ouse, now shallow indeed, is crossed by a causeway and bridge. As the causeway cuts through what seems to be a British site, the camp which bears the strange name of Belsar's Hill, it can hardly fail to be itself of Roman work. It was here that the Isle was most accessible to an enemy.[7]

The summer and autumn of 1070 were full of gloomy news. Quite apart from the great famine noted by the Anglo-Saxon Chronicle and other sources,[8] there was the cynical retreat of the Danish allies, who had been bought off by King William. Company by company they withdrew to their boats which sailed south to the Thames before departing to Denmark. This may have persuaded the chief rebel in the western march, Edric the Wild, to make his submission to the king, and two years later he is named as a member of the king's army fighting successfully in Scotland.

As each possible channel of help dried up the stark realities must have loomed larger and darker for the rebels in the fenlands. Once the worst is known and men accept that their destiny is truly in their own hands with no prospect of outside aid they can more wholeheartedly commit themselves to the task ahead and face whatever may be in store with courage and resignation. This seems true of that fellowship of Saxons whose resolution grew stronger as the storm clouds gathered. It is unlikely that Hereward allowed his men to remain idle since inaction corrodes morale, and the stories of guerrilla raids on Norman bases and travellers are probably true. Some are less believable than others, although the tale of Hereward's capture of no less a person than Abbot Turold adds spice to the legend. General Harward puts this incident at soon after the abbot's arrival in Peterborough. He claims that the abbot 'had to pay thirty-six thousand marcs for his own ransom and that of the Church property'.

The purpose of such raiding was not simply to harry and disturb the enemy, keeping him in a state of uncertainty. Such self-indulgence needed to be balanced against a possible adverse effect on the steadfastness of the local population whose support was essential. It might not have remained solid were the Normans to have vented their anger in reprisals such as those perpetrated in Northumbria and Yorkshire, parts of which were devastated so cruelly that they did not recover for generations. There must have been the need to obtain cattle and provisions, as well as arms and equipment, although the fenland islands were not without their own sources of sufficiency.

William of Malmesbury, writing in the next century, beheld Thorney – still an attractive village 5 miles east of Peterborough – as 'a little paradise, delightsome a heaven itself may be deemed fen-circled yet rich in loftiest trees, where water meadows delight the eye with green, where streamlets glide unchecked through each field. Scarce a plot of ground lies there waste. Here are orchards, there vineyards. . . . Nature vies with culture and what is unknown to one is produced by the other. And what of the glorious buildings whose very size it is a wonder the ground can support amid such marshes.[9] A vast solitude is here the monks' lot that they may the more closely cling to things above . . . there is nothing speaketh save for the moment; all is holy silence. . . . Truly I call that Island a hostel of chastity, a tavern of honesty, a gymnasium of Divine philosophy.'

General Harward puts the largest number of men present at any time with Hereward at under four thousand, including his own personal following, and a considerable number of Saxon thanes, freemen and peasants, of whom he asserts one thousand were to die when the Camp of Refuge was eventually captured. 'At first their headquarters were at the monastery, where monks and warriors sat side by side in the refectory, the walls and roof being equipped like an armoury with every description of weapon and armour, so that the comrades, lay and spiritual, should be prepared for any sudden call to arms. Here he was joined by all those who had been dispossessed of their lands, and who for not surrendering themselves to Norman violence were called outlaws; here also resorted the most daring spirits of England, and the ancestors of those who at the present day hold bravery and freedom as inseparable.'

We can surmise that among the genuine patriots and dispossessed were those freebooters who always attach themselves to legitimate causes in the expectation of finding rich side-pickings from the casual looting and plundering involved. To that extent at least they matched the nature of the Conqueror's own mercenaries. The *De Gestis* identifies many of these 'daring spirits' and the roll-call of their names offers us something with which to conjure up a mind's eye picture. Thus we see 'one Wynter, a famous Knight short in stature but excessively robust and strong and Wenotus and Alutus Gurgan, notable in all valour and bravery for being tall and big they were very efficient. With them were three more nephews of Hereward, Godwin Gille so-called because not unlike Godwin the son of Guthlac who is celebrated in stories of the ancients; and Duti and Outi, twin brothers, alike in character and in person and of repute as soldiers.' They were joined by Wluricus the Black, so-called because he had stained his face with charcoal and gone unrecognized among his enemies overcoming ten of them with his single spear. His friend was Wluricas Rahere, or The Heron, who once at Wroxham Bridge saved four men (presumably Saxons) from execution and slew the executioners (presumably Norman). Also there were

> The more famous of Hereward's Knights, Godricus of Corby, nephew of the Earl of Warwick, and Tosti of Davenesse, kinsman of the same Earl, whose name he acquired in baptism, and Acere Vasus, son of a gentleman near Lincoln who owned the tower of the city [?], and Lewinus Mone, that is The Sickle, so-called because being by chance in a meadow when he was cutting the grass by himself, he was set upon by a score of labourers of the place with pitchforks and spears in their hands, and alone among them all, with nothing but his sickle he wounded many and killed some, dashing among them like a reaper and so put them all to flight.
>
> In company with those already mentioned was also one named Turbentinus, great-grandson of Earl Edwin and Lefwinus Prat, that is The Crafty, because though often captured by his enemies he had cunningly escaped, many times killing his guards. With them were others most experienced in warfare: Leofric the Deacon, and Villicus of Drayton, and Turkillys and Utlamhe, that is The Outlaw, Hereward's cook Hogor, his kinsman Winter and Liveret, two men of mark, and Radenaldus, steward of Ramsey; these were standard bearers. So too were Wluricus The Black and Wluricus The White, Wluricas Grugam, Ylardus, Godwinus Gille, Outi, with those named before, and those two splendid men – Siward The White and Siward The Red, Hereward's nephews. There were also other very famous

Knights, Godricus of Corby, Hugo the Norman, a priest, and Ylardus his brother, Leofric the Deacon, Tosti of Rothwell and Godwinus of Rothwell, Osbernus, Alsinus, Lefwinus Prat, Hurchillus and Villicus of Drayton. All of these were the most renowned and splendid Knights in the Kingdom.

This list, with its apparent repetitions and confusions of identity, has about it an 'Uncle Tom Cobley and all . . .' ring yet we cannot say that it is completely without foundation and we ask ourselves whether 'Leofric the Deacon' is that same Leofric the Deacon, priest at Bourne, from whose earlier memoir *De Gestis* is supposedly derived.

CHAPTER SIX

The Guerrilla Leader

As William the Conqueror tightened his mailed grip on the land of the Saxons most men, as William Fuller was to write six centuries later, 'betook themselves to patience which taught many a noble hand to work, foot to travel, tongue to entreat'.[1] Others attempted to resist in whatever way they could. Perhaps those in remote forest dwellings, far from main highways, were able to carry on life much as before with only rumours of bloodshed and cruelty to disturb their dreams. They lived in a fool's paradise because the Conqueror's acquisitive arm was long and in time it reached into every vill and hamlet.

Those who had suffered at the hands of the invaders, the dispossessed and desperate, looked for retribution by allying themselves with the independent spirits who still preserved some rags of freedom and were willing to fight to retain them. It was such men who gathered around Hereward's standard, making their way across country by various routes that avoided the Norman castles and keeps. These grim fortifications were to dominate the surrounding countryside and become the rivets by which the fetters of Norman rule were rammed into place. Hereward was not the only voice of defiance and the widespread devastation of entire communities that marked the decade following 1066 is testimony that Saxon independence died hard. But who was left to rally opposition?

For a time hope was pinned on the youthful figure of Edgar the Ætheling, grandson of Edward the Confessor's half-brother Edmund Ironside and therefore a legitimate claimant by blood to the throne of England. He was probably still a boy of twelve when the Confessor died and because of his tender years and lack of military experience he had been passed over when Harold was chosen to rule the country. But now that Harold was dead, hearts and minds turned towards the Ætheling. He had been one of those unwilling Saxon ornaments paraded at Court when William returned triumphantly to Normandy six months after Hastings and, like the Mercians, Edwin and Morcar, and the pride of Northumbria, Siward's son Waltheof, he had found the wine of Norman hospitality as bitter as the prospect of life as a subordinate under the Conqueror's heel.

Orderic Vitalis has given us a fascinating glimpse of this strange interlude when

William celebrated Easter at the Abbey of Holy Trinity at Fécamp, together with a great gathering of prelates, abbots and lords and nobles who were

> . . . eyeing curiously the long-haired denizens of England, wondering at the splendid garments, interwoven and encrusted with gold, worn by the king and his court, and praising the gold and silver vessels, and horns of wild oxen decorated with gold at both ends. Indeed the French noted many such things, fitting the magnificence of a king, and, because they had not met them before, spread abroad accounts of them when they returned home.

William used the occasion not merely to show off his achievements but as a method of demonstrating enticingly what rewards were still to be gained, thus ensuring there was no shortage of eager recruits ready to cross the Channel and share in whatever profitable enterprises might lie ahead. The experience must have sickened those Saxons with independent spirits

During 1069 forces evidently loyal to the Ætheling had with Danish help enjoyed spectacular success in Northumbria where Waltheof earned lasting fame, reputedly slaying with his own axe a hundred Normans. In the west, too, men fought bitterly and not without effect, but one by one each insurrection was crushed and those who survived often faced the customary Norman retribution of being maimed or blinded.

The Ætheling fled first to Scotland (where his sister, Margaret, became the wife of King Malcolm), then to the Continent where he was to lead an unenviable existence as a vassal of William who offered him terms, including a modest landholding and a pension of a pound of silver a day. He lived at the Norman Court 'quiet, contented and despised' in the words of Freeman, who considered that he was the one man who might on sentimental grounds have become the focus of loyalty for the whole nation. He then dismisses him as 'utterly unfit to command'.

This is perhaps a harsh judgement on a stripling whom fate denied the years of training with which he might have equipped himself to challenge the most formidable military genius of the day. As if to compensate for what might be perceived as his failure to win back the crown of his grandfather, Edmund Ironside,[2] Edgar 'spent his early years of adulthood in search of a cause, a knight-errant *par excellence*, with a lance for hire'.[3] His warrior-like career saw him in many lands espousing many different causes, a sad Don Quixote figure who eventually retired to spend his days in quiet contemplation on his Hertfordshire estate. He was still living there in 1125, an old man of seventy-two, if a reference by William of Malmesbury is to be believed.

As Freeman also points out, the Saxons, whose own fighting resources had suffered a grievous reversal, were opposed by an enemy who had carried the martial discipline of the age to its highest pitch. The one élite Saxon corps that might have withstood them, the housecarls, had been eliminated at Hastings field and 'that noble army which had been called into being by Cnut and brought to perfection by Harold, the army which had overthrown Macbeth and Gruffydd and Hardrada, had died, man by man, around the fallen King on Senlac. There was no longer an English force of which men said in other lands that any one man therein was a match for any two elsewhere.'

Freeman's words paint a tempting picture of what might have been but do not blind us to the fatal infirmity of an England divided by its own internal rivalries. William's genius was less to divide and conquer than to exploit the dissensions already apparent or which always threatened to surface. As Freeman demonstrates, the Saxons now found themselves no longer in the straightforward position of defending their own possessions against invaders such as the Welsh or Norwegians.

Opposition to the Normans had perforce to take on the form of revolts against an established government and attempts to regain isolated pieces of territory lacking any regular government at all. Men had to challenge those holding power in their own districts and their communication with others fighting a similar battle elsewhere in the country appears to have been deficient.

If the various uprisings in the west and north and along the Welsh border could have been co-ordinated there might have been a greater chance of success, but instead William could deal with them piecemeal and before long, as loyalties became confused and diluted, we read that in engagements such as the relief of Montacute the so-called Norman army was in fact a mixture of Norman knights and English levies. Orderic Vitalis tells how Bishop Geoffrey of Coutances led the men of London, Winchester and Salisbury against the insurgents of Somerset and Dorset who, in turn, might have called upon the assistance of their neighbours in Cornwall and Devon but apparently did not.

Once these other fires of resistance had been extinguished full attention could be turned eastwards and it is a measure of Hereward's standing and his potential nuisance value that King William decided eventually to take personal command of the operation to flush out the hero of the fenlands. Most commentators agree that William looked on the fenland revolt as serious enough to demand all his cunning and energy to put down. He summoned both land troops and a fleet, which by then may well have been largely manned by English sailors. This decision has encouraged the view that Hereward was a greater threat to Norman domination than perhaps he could ever have been or, possibly, even considered.

Above all things Hereward was a realist and the terrain on which he chose to fight tells us much about him. The passive rather than active role of the Fens in English history is stressed by H.C. Darby.[4] It was always a place of refuge, rather

February at Queens Holme, that stretch of the Ouse that separates Aldreth and Willingham.

than a cradle for freedom and discontent: 'It presented possibilities of defence that were utilised during phases of national upheaval, a very different thing from dictating a political creed to its people. Stated thus, the problem of fenland rebellion is not a social one with an economic background, but a military one with a topographical background.'

The three phases in the stories of fenland rebellions identified by Darby commence with Ely being taken over by a recalcitrant group who proceed to fortify the island. From this protected and well-provisioned base they inflict damage and harassment out of all proportion to their number. Local knowledge of devious paths and winding channels gives them an advantage over invaders who are deterred by sodden trails or precarious watercourses. A period of lawlessness and amphibious guerrilla warfare follows as more and more people flock to Ely from all over the country. They find resources enough to keep them for some time and so, comparatively safe from attack, and being within striking distance of the settlements along the borders of the surrounding upland, they carry out a campaign of raiding and pillaging. Other islands such as Ramsey are also plundered and occupied and even places as far away as Norwich and Bury St Edmunds suffer.

De Gestis provides an eye-witness account of life in the Camp of Refuge from a captured Norman knight called Dada who is honourably treated by the rebels and then allowed to return to his companions, having promised to report honestly to King William on all that he has seen. Darby, however, puts the words into the mouth of one of Hereward's supporters:

> In our isle men are not troubling themselves; the ploughman has not taken his hand from the plough, nor has the hunter cast aside his arrow, nor does the fowler desist from taking birds. And yet something more. If you wish to hear what I have known and seen, I will reveal all to you. The isle is within itself plentifully endowed; it is supplied with various kinds of herbage and, for its richer soil, surpasses the rest of England. Most delightful for its charming fields and pastures, it is also remarkable for its beasts of chase and is in no ordinary way fertile in flocks and herds. Its woods and vineyards are not worthy of equal praise, but it is beset by great meres and fens as though by a strong wall.

Overhead Kingsley's 'arch of heaven', and below, the everlasting mystery of the deep fen – a fenland scene at the Lode, near Reach, Cambridgeshire.

Whatever its source, the report would have been a two-edged propaganda coup for Hereward. While doubtless designed to persuade the Normans that what they had undertaken was not going to be easy, it could also have convinced them that the rewards would amply justify their efforts.

The second phase of a Fenland rebellion is signalled when, ultimately, the royal army invests and blockades the region; and the encounters that ensue are most intense around the two southerly approaches to the isle, at Aldreth and Soham respectively. Such a conflict might last months, or even years, causing great devastation of the surrounding countryside. The twelfth-century rebellion of Geoffrey de Mandeville, for instance, resulted in much wasting of the countryside around. The writer of the *Historia Eliensis* is loud in complaint:

> For the space of twenty or even thirty miles neither ox nor plough was to be seen; barely could the smallest bushel of grain be bought for two hundred pence. The people, by hundreds and thousands, were perishing for want of bread, and their corpses lay unburied in the fields, a prey to beasts and to fowls of the air. Not for ages past had there been such tribulation. . . .

Such damage would have been especially serious in the fenland for it indicated that the whole network of sewers and channels was disturbed, and the drainage arrangements must have suffered enormously. At last, and usually attributed to the treachery of someone within the isle, the forces of the king gain an entrance into Ely and its defenders flee.

The rebellion over, there follows in Darby's scenario the final phase, a period of anxiety on the part of the royal authorities. The island is kept semi-fortified lest it should be seized again. Within a few decades normality returns until the memory of violence passes into tradition.

Darby's projection summarizes the bare outline of the Hereward rebellion which had a lasting impact on the national memory. Its cycle of events was to be broadly repeated four times: in 1139 and 1142, during the turmoil of Stephen's reign; when the barons held out against King John in 1216; and, in 1265, during the reign of Henry III.

The Normans, being such energetic and acquisitive speculators were more likely to be encouraged by the prospect of booty than discouraged by the difficulties of traversing a swamp, and the calibre of the troops now approaching would be no surprise to the defenders. Hereward's own experience in Flanders and the accounts of those of his followers who had survived the bloodlettings at Hastings, York and other bitter confrontations, will have told him much. We today have some idea of the Norman fighting machine from such sources as the Bayeux Tapestry and are familiar with the mounted knight with his hauberk or mail shirt of hundreds of interlinked iron rings or occasionally of overlapping metal, horn, or leather scales fastened to an undergarment.

The hauberk resembled a half-sleeved night-shirt, falling to the knee and slit fore and aft so that its skirts could hang down on either side of the saddle. The arms would have been covered by leather strapping. A hauberk protected torso, thighs and upper arms and could be extended by a coif or mail hood to cover the neck and head. Some may have felt that this was sufficient protection but usually, if we believe the Bayeux Tapestry, the head was also covered by a conical iron helm with its extension to protect the nose, not always effectively – 'Thorstein Midlang cut at Bue across his nose, so that the nose-piece was cut in two and he got a great wound.'

The nasal guard was broad enough to make identification difficult, which explains the tradition that at Hastings Duke William, in the heat of battle, had to lift his helm to stifle a rumour that he had fallen. The tapestry apparently shows him doing so while the ubiquitous Count Eustace of Boulogne, sporting a moustache (which may have been added later)[5] points excitedly to indicate to the wavering troops that their leader is alive and still in the saddle.

Corpses shown being stripped in the tapestry appear to be naked under their hauberks which either speaks volumes for their hardihood or, as Vesey Norman insists, is the result of a nineteenth-century restoration.[6] He argues, reasonably enough, that it is most unlikely that mail could be thus worn since its weight would rub the edge of the rings harshly against the skin and in any case an undergarment is shown at the wrists of most of the living figures. A sensible deduction suggests that padded leather or cloth placed under the armour would have absorbed blows and perhaps reduced bruising.

A knight's weapons included a long, straight sword, with a broad blade suitable for slashing, and an 8 foot ash lance or spear which was probably used to stab by thrusting. Longer spears tucked under the arm or 'couched' in the manner of jousting knights may have been employed, although the evidence is that these belonged to a later age. The sword scabbard was of wood covered in leather and lined with wool or fur which kept the blade naturally oiled.

The Normans' kite-shaped leather shield on its wooden frame was strengthened with metal and carried various designs such as dragons, lions and crosses. Heraldic devices would appear at a later date. Saxon arms and equipment were not dissimilar except that in addition they used round shields and, most famously, the dreaded Viking war axe with its 10 inch curved cutting edge which the tapestry artists may have used to distinguish Saxon from Norman. It was mounted on a thick wooden haft about 3 feet in length and when delivered two-handed could no doubt cut a devastating swathe. A possible disadvantage may have been that its use made it difficult (and risky) to maintain the close order required by the Saxon

This late Saxon sword was found at Mileham, Norfolk, in 1945. Its total length was 860 mm.

'shield wall'. And during his back swing the axeman must have exposed his undefended torso to a lance thrust.

The tapestry's evocative picture cannot give a true impression of the terrifying charge of Norman cavalry which was said to be an irresistible force whose impact 'might make a hole in the walls of Babylon', to quote the Byzantine princess, Anna Comnena, who presumably saw western knights in action during the First Crusade (1096–99). To what extent Norman cavalry had progressed towards this state by the year 1066 is debatable. They probably charged, not in line abreast but in groups, each led by the pennon of their feudal lord. Undoubtedly, the need to counter Saracen horsemen had led to the development of horse-breeding and cavalry warfare in Europe; the Normans had brought such skills to a fine pitch, something that the island English, unaccustomed to facing mounted foes in large-scale battles, were unable to match. However, the significance of cavalry in deciding the outcome of the Norman invasion may have been overestimated. In all the great battles of the following century in England and Normandy the greater proportion of the forces engaged dismounted and fought on foot – 'in precisely the old-fashioned Saxon manner so much condemned as the real cause of the English defeat at Hastings'.[7]

While the lance may not have developed into the ultimate battering ram until a

The Temple Pyx, an English twelfth-century bronze showing three armoured knights.

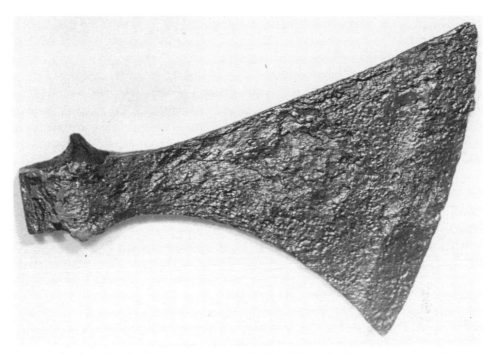

A Viking battleaxe found at Surlingham, Norfolk, in 1935. The axehead measured 175 mm from blade to socket and its cutting edge 117 mm. Such blades were sometimes richly ornamented with carved figures, animals etc. (for example, the famous Mammen axe of North Jutland).

century later, the sight of a host of mounted warriors, with or without it, approaching at speed with unfriendly intent always had a salutary effect. Ironically, by the Civil War the lance had lengthened into the foot-soldier's pike which, when used en masse in the 'hedgehog' formation, proved effective against charging cavalry. The Normans had bred a tough armour-carrying destrier or charger and exploited the aggressive instinct of full stallions, whose mass greatly increased the shock effect of a charge in close order over short distances. Such horses had to be strong enough to carry the weight of rider, armour and weapons although it is a popular fallacy to identify them with the heavy horse of our own day, the shires and Percherons that can still sometimes be seen at agricultural shows.

Experts such as Charles Chenevix Trench[8] use the tapestry as evidence and maintain that its horses resemble light- or medium-weight hunters which gallop into action, something a cart-horse could hardly do. If they are suddenly stopped, or killed, they tumble head over heels, an indication of the speed at which they were travelling. The likely weight of the knight's armour must remain a subject for conjecture until archaeologists discover intact an early medieval hauberk. Indian mail shirts of the eighteenth century weighed 25–30 lb and Chenevix Trench points out that hauberks worn at Hastings can hardly have weighed less. The tapestry shows two hauberks, slung on poles thrust through the sleeves, being carried by no fewer than three servants.

Chenevix Trench suggests that eleventh-century saddles probably weighed less than the 40 lb saddles of the late Middle Ages, some of which still survive, because they did not have to carry so much. He subscribes to the view that in those days men were smaller and lighter than they are now, averaging perhaps 10 stone. By adding a few pounds for lance, sword and shield, he calculates that in the eleventh, twelfth and thirteenth centuries (before the development of plate-armour), the knight's charger carried about 16 stone (102 kilos). He confirms that in 1914 a British cavalry horse carried between $17\frac{1}{2}$ and 18 stone, assuming that the rider himself weighed 11 stone. German and French cavalry horses carried more. Upon this evidence he therefore concludes that, until plate-armour came into fashion, the medieval charger need have been no larger or heavier than the cavalry horse of the twentieth century, 'which averaged about 15.2 hands in height and 1,000 lb in weight'.

A different interpretation is offered by Miklós Jankovich.[9] In his view, the tapestry's war-horses do resemble Clydesdales but of a miniature variety, less hirsute about the heels, and 'galloping in a way no Clydesdale could ever move'. Riding such heavy horses[10] in full armour cannot have been a comfortable experience and Jankovich suggests that on a destrier it would have been sheer torture. Trotting in full armour by the hour was in fact the first punishment in the severe disciplinary code of the Teutonic Order. The medieval knight would have chosen to travel on a palfrey, a lighter horse with a comfortable gait, and to delay switching to his war-horse until the latest possible moment – hence 'getting on one's high horse'. Jankovich refers to the order by Emperor Frederick I which declared that if a strange knight approached the camp unarmed and shieldless on a palfrey (*in palafrido*), then he was to be peaceably received, but if he rode up with slung shield on his fighting stallion (*in dextrario*), then he was to be attacked.

The rider would sit with a long straight leg to withstand the shock of impact – 'The knight rode not merely "long", but straight-legged, feet well forward, toes pointing down. With legs braced against the stirrup-irons, buttocks pressed hard back against the cantle, he was locked in position in moments of stress or urgency', says Chenevix-Trench – and the tapestry shows the typical medieval saddle with the high, wide pommel rising in front of the rider's stomach. This was far from comfortable and carried some risk of injury. King William himself was alleged to have suffered just such a mischance in 1087 at Mantes when his horse stumbled throwing his bulky frame forward on to the tall iron pommel causing internal injuries from which William died some weeks later.[11]

In open battle before the advent of the longbow or the development of more powerful crossbows,[12] this armoured wave of knights must have been almost unstoppable, which indicates the endurance of the Saxon shield-wall during those long hours at Hastings. However, cavalry required open and solid ground to ride down opponents and the Fens could never have provided such a battlefield, a factor which would have been much on King William's mind as he planned his campaign. The Norman high command directing the fenland operation would have included many seasoned campaigners and we find, in the words of General Harward, that 'opposed to the English were William Warrenne, Earl of Surrey, Taillebois, Count of Spalding, William Malet, whose death at Ely is recorded, and other Norman chiefs. Lastly, William himself, with his whole army, hoists his standard on the Castle of Cambridge and assumes command.'

Freeman appears to accept that William Warrenne took a leading part in the siege and suggests that avenging his slaughtered brother, Frederick, was his prime motivation. He finds special interest in Malet and Ivo Taillebois

who has become one of the most prominent figures in the legendary history, and who appears in the Survey as the owner of large estates in the neighbouring land of Holland. Romance endows him with the marriage and heritage of the mythical Lucy, the long-lived and often-wedded daughter of Earl Ælfgar, and therefore, according to one version, the niece of Hereward himself. . . .

Legend describes Ivo, possibly with truth, as a bitter enemy of the monks of Crowland; it is more certain that the Priory of Spalding counted him among its benefactors. And an incidental passage of the Survey may lead us to think that the one Norman who must ever claim most interest in the eyes of Englishmen was among the assailants of the last stronghold of independent England. William Malet, who had borne the body of Harold to his first burial and who had been the prisoner of the Danes after the taking of York, had escaped or had been redeemed from his captivity, and now came to fight and die in the marshes of Ely.

The events of that ill-fated year 1071 are succinctly described by the Anglo-Saxon Chronicle and Florence of Worcester expands them a little further:

Earls Edwin and Morkar, because king William sought to put them in confinement, escaped secretly from his court, and for some time continued in rebellion against him; but when they saw that their enterprise had not turned out successfully, Edwin determined to go to Malcolm, king of the Scots, but was killed on the journey, in an ambush laid by his own people. But Morkar, and Aegelwine, bishop of Durham, Siward, surnamed Barn, and Hereward, a most valiant man, with many others, took ship, and went to the isle of Ely, desiring to winter there. When the king heard of this, he blocked up every outlet on the eastern side of the island by his sailors, and commanded a bridge of two miles in length to be constructed on the western side. And when they saw that they were thus shut in, they gave up resistance, and all except the valiant Hereward, who made his escape through the fens, with a few others, surrendered to the king; who at once sent bishop Aegelwine to Abingdon, where he was placed in confinement, and died the same winter. As for the earl and the rest, who were scattered throughout England, he placed some in confinement, and permitted some to go free, with the loss of their hands or eyes.

This skims over the detail of what was a lengthy and bitter struggle but confirms that among Hereward's companions were three notable national figures: Aegelwine, Bishop of Durham, Siward Barn and Earl Morcar himself. General Harward's summary, taken from *De Gestis*, seizes the opportunity to extol once again the virtues of his hero. He becomes the life and soul of the camp; now destroying the enemy's approaches, next sallying forth against the strongest advance position; or on other occasions disguising himself as a potter or a fisherman, and penetrating into the heart of William's Court to discover all his plans. Hereward's strategy and military genius become those of Wellington in the lines of Torres Vedras, adopting a strictly defensive policy in the presence of a numerically superior foe but ready to strike a shattering blow when the opportunity occurred.

Hereward undertakes the most difficult enterprises and always with success. Ever alert, cheerful and courageous, his forethought and sagacity provided not only men, arms and training, but food, boats and horses were ready when required. Astute in forming a well-laid plan, he was in his element when 'driving back at the sword's point the flower of the Norman chivalry'.

Although the comparison with Wellington's campaign, which eventually led to his 1814 victory, might be considered fanciful, Freeman and other historians concur that this broad narrative is authentic. William employed a two-pronged strategy, attacking the isle on both sides, deploying his ships to the east to establish a blockade and prevent further help coming from Norway or Denmark. The main land assault was in the west via the bridge or causeway at Aldreth. The legendary accounts, confused as they are about the chronology of events and the precise identity of those taking part, are, in Freeman's judgement, trustworthy as far as the geography is concerned, being written by men who knew the countryside well:

They thus enable us more exactly to fix the position of the operations which our soberer authorities point to more vaguely. The castle of Cambridge was, as might be expected, the royal headquarters; but the energy of William carried him to every point at which his presence could be needed. We find him in one tale directing his naval operations against the eastern part of the Isle from Brandon, a town on the Little Ouse, the stream whose bed has in later times received the waters of its greater namesake. Elsewhere we hear of attacks made by water from Reche, a point to the south-east of the Isle on the famous Devil's Dyke, and commanding a stream called Rechelode, which joins with the Grant or Cam a little above its junction with the old Ouse.

Most writers focus on the causeway which William had constructed at the accessible point of Aldreth to take the assault troops safely across the marshes on to the Isle of Ely. *De Gestis* relates that he first moved all his army to Alrehede where it was not so wholly surrounded with waters and swamp. Stones were brought by boat from Cottenham, a village in the direction of Cambridge, commanding a tributary of the old Ouse. These were used along with tree trunks bound together and placed upon hides and sheepskins inflated with air 'so that the weight of men going over it might be better borne'.

Once the causeway was completed, 'a great multitude of men' rushed eagerly

An aerial view looking north towards Aldreth and Haddenham (top); it shows the line of the ancient trackway crossing the river and leading to the causeway.

forward, desperate to lay their hands on the gold and silver which was reputed to be hidden on the isle. Tales of abundant wealth would have bolstered the Norman propaganda effort to keep the troops together throughout the campaign and stiffen resolve when it came to actual combat. The result of this impetuosity was apparently disastrous. The men whose haste had taken them to the front of the rush were drowned when the causeway collapsed into the marsh taking them with it, and, *De Gestis* continues, 'although hardly a man pursued them, they perished in great numbers in the waters and in the swamp; and those that perished, up to this very day, are drawn from the depths of those waters, in rotten armour. This we have sometimes ourselves seen.'

Several more attempts were made to enter the isle by the causeway, and between them Hereward, using his various disguises, managed to enter the enemy camp to spy on their preparations. The most wonderful tale relates how, on the advice of Ivo, King William enlisted the aid of a witch who was placed in a wooden tower erected at the end of the causeway from where she was to overcome the resistance of the English by her spells:

> When she had got up she spoke out for a long time against the Isle and its inhabitants, denouncing destruction and uttering charms for their overthrow and at the end of her talking and incantations the witch turned her back upon them in derision. After she had gone through this disgusting ceremony three times as she had proposed, behold, the men who were hidden all around in the swamp, on the right and left, among the reeds and rough briars of the swamp set the reeds on fire and by the help of the wind the smoke and flames spread in the direction of and up to the Norman camp. Extending some two furlongs the fire rushing hither and thither among them formed a horrible spectacle in the marsh, and the roar of the flames with the crackling twigs of brushwood and willows made a terrible noise. Stupefied and very alarmed, the Normans fled, each man for himself, but they could not go far through the desert parts of the swamp in that watery road, and they found great difficulty keeping to the path. Very many were suddenly swallowed up and others drowned in the same waters and overwhelmed with arrows, for in the fire their javelins were no good against the groups of men who came out cautiously and secretly from the Isle to repel them. Among them that woman of infamous art, hysterical with fear, fell down head first from her lofty frame and broke her neck.

Such marvellous yarns may well contain crumbs of fact and the image of the witch mooning derisively at the enemy has a ribald authenticity. Shadowy figures emerging from the smoke to fire their arrows at a trapped and immobilized enemy is also a compelling picture even for a sceptical historian such as Freeman, who comments: 'What amount of truth there may be in each particular story it is impossible to guess, but the places spoken of quite fall in with the more general description of the Chroniclers, and we can have little doubt that the main struggle took place on the Ouse by the approach of Aldreth, and that many a gallant feat of arms was done on its dreary banks by the last champions of England.'

While one can understand how heavily armoured soldiers could find that a morass such as existed in the fenlands was no place to fight, it being all too easy to sink in the bog and perish ignominiously as the chroniclers relate, many have found it hard to conceive how it was possible, in the same watery terrain, to employ fire as an effective weapon. And yet, as ever in this investigation, it is dangerous to make assumptions too readily. The answer may lie in the nature of peat, of which the Fens are largely formed. Anyone who has lived in that part of England can confirm that peat is easily set on fire by burning grasses on a dried-up dyke side or by a bonfire of unwanted straw in the corner of a field. When ignited, it is, say those who know, very difficult to bring under control. Indeed, according to A.K. Astbury, 'Once fire has taken hold it can spread through the peat for hundreds of feet. . . . Such fires are also long-lived; even when tackled with all the resources of a modern fire service a peat fire can burn for days; unattended, or because isolated only partly attended, a fire could burn for years.'[13] He cites the case of the peat in Conington Fen which caught fire in 1871 and burned for several weeks; at night the brilliant display from the hillocks of flame which burst from the surface of the burning soil could be seen clearly by rail travellers on the Great Northern.

Firemen called to such an outbreak may know its approximate position but cannot always locate it until the heat comes up and strikes them. Those unlucky enough to walk over the affected spot can fall up to the waist in burning peat and many a fireman has suffered a badly burned leg when blazing peat fell into the tops of his boots. Astbury affirms that in one way at least peat fires are fundamentally different from all other fires: they cannot be smothered. Burning fibres have to be separated almost particle by particle and mixed with water, so it is useless to soak burning peat in the expectation that the fire will be extinguished. The fire will merely continue to burn and to spread underneath the solid crust of waterlogged peat above it.

Directing water on to a peat fire usually causes a minor explosion, after which the firemen have to wash the burning peat away right down to the mineral soil beneath. Often it is necessary to dig a surrounding trench which, if taken down to mineral soil and filled with water, will contain and isolate the outbreak.

Given this information it is not difficult to imagine someone as resourceful as Hereward creating the kind of havoc envisaged by Drake and his fire ships at the time of the Spanish Armada or Britain's coastline defenders, if rumour be true, during the threat of German invasion in the Second World War. Certainly by desperate means the defenders at Ely managed to extend their struggle for perhaps a year. The timespan has been much exaggerated by the writers of legend who sometimes link it with the unrelated rebellion of Ralph of Norfolk, that son of Ralph the Staller, a name, according to *De Gestis*, also attached to the grandfather of Hereward.

The end and final defeat seems to have come suddenly and unexpectedly. *De Gestis* even suggests that it occurred while Hereward was absent on a foraging expedition. Freeman interprets the various accounts as indicating that a weak link in the chain of defence was Earl Morcar himself. He and his companions may have been disheartened at finding themselves surrounded and this could have led to Morcar falling for the false promises and inducements held out by King William. Legend wrongly brings both Edwin and Morcar into the isle, and allows both of them to escape, but Freeman suggests it is correct in blaming the downfall of the isle on the treachery of the abbot and monks, whose patriotism failed them when William seized all the lands of the monastery beyond the borders of the isle itself.

Tradition says that most of the defenders fell into William's hands and were dealt with according to his customary rule. None was executed but as Freeman writes: 'At Ely, as at Alençon, the Conqueror felt no scruple against inflicting punishments which to our notions might seem more frightful than death itself. Some were shut up in the horrible prison-houses of those days; others were allowed to go free after their eyes had been put out or their hands cut off. Morkere himself, to judge from the English accounts, surrendered himself to the King's mercy.'

According to the Norman version, he did so on a promise of being received to the king's peace, a promise broken by William through fear of the dangers that might befall the realm if Morcar were allowed to remain at large. 'In either case,' says Freeman, 'he was put into ward, but as he was entrusted to the keeping of Roger of Beaumont, it may be that the dungeons and fetters of which we hear are only a figure of speech. He remained a prisoner in Normandy all the rest of the days of the Conqueror, and obtained but a single moment of freedom at his death.'

Florence of Worcester provides the epitaph: 'Morcar was released by royal decree as William lay dying but his bloated corpse was scarcely crammed into its coffin[14] before the king's son William Rufus hastened to England, taking with him Wulnoth (brother of King Harold who had been kept in confinement since boyhood) and Morcar. And as soon as he arrived in Winchester, he put them into custody as before.'

CHAPTER SEVEN

Betrayal

The popular explanation for the downfall of the Isle of Ely is that of the alleged betrayal by the monks themselves who, in any case, cannot have been regarded as the most reliable of allies in the long term. The picture of the Camp of Refuge we gain from various accounts is of Hereward's men-at-arms and Abbot Thurstan's men of God feasting together on the isle's bountiful produce, discussing the day's events and toasting success against the Normans. Thus Freeman writes: 'And if legend is allowed to count for anything, none of the warlike guests of Saint Æthelryth showed greater zeal in the common cause than the monastic indwellers of her island. Monks and warriors sat side by side in the refectory, the chief leaders being honoured with a place at the table of the Abbot, while weapons of war hung from the walls and the roof, that the comrades, lay and spiritual alike, might at once spring to their harness at any call of sudden need.'

Such comradeship may have been only skin-deep. The abbot and his brotherhood were uneasily aware of a growing moral dilemma. Five winters had passed since the tragi-drama of Hastings and fresh grass grew where the noblest Saxon blood was shed. Now the monks found themselves in open revolt against a ruling monarch who had long since been crowned at Westminster by an Archbishop of York, the same Ældred who had officiated at Harold's coronation nine months earlier. Their partners were a band of renegades and rebels – 'Hereward's gang' as the Anglo-Saxon Chronicle describes them – who needed to carry out armed robbery on a regular basis in order to maintain themselves and, presumably, pay for any provisions supplied by local residents. Nor could the monastic community have entirely forgotten Hereward's role in the sacking of Peterborough. While the monks shared his distaste for French interference in religious as in other matters, the fact remained that a monastery was still part of the Mother Church whether run by Norman or Saxon. Had not William claimed the authority of Rome herself in asserting his rights to the English throne and had not his men carried the papal banner into battle?

Much anxious soul-searching must have occurred but William eventually made up their minds for them. A devoted follower of the Church, perhaps more pragmatic than pious, the Conqueror was not blind to the psychological opportunities that the situation offered. And being a practical military man, he did not ignore them. *De Gestis* tells us that the king recognized that all efforts to take the Isle of Ely by storm were proving fruitless and expensive. Quite apart from the mounting casualty lists, there were the price of feeding and sheltering an army on active service, the cost of the engineering work in building earthworks across the marshes – Florence of Worcester refers to a causeway 2 miles long – and the continuing risk of desertions and erosion of morale.

He therefore produced his trump card, announcing his intention to divide among his more senior lieutenants the lands of Ely church that lay outside the isle itself, together with the property of the monks. This meant that, instead of risking their lives in the fenland morasses and mists, the besiegers could simply mount guard to prevent escape, cut off supply lines and spend their time more agreeably in claiming for themselves the rich church lands that lay beyond the isle.

The effect was immediate. The monks of Ely, alarmed by this development, adopted what *De Gestis* describes as 'a more prudent plan in their undertakings'. As a euphemism for treachery it stands unchallenged. *De Gestis* relates that Abbot Thurstan went in disguise with the ornaments and treasure of the church and asked the king for conditions of peace, and the restoration of all the church lands. This was done secretly to avoid Hereward finding out. The messengers were received by the king, and arrangements were made for his men to be admitted, presumably by safe pathways, to the isle when Hereward and his men were away foraging, so that the affair 'might be managed without bloodshed and grievous slaughter. But one of the monks Alwinus the son of Orgar, went to him [Hereward] to tell him that they (the Abbot and the Monks) had already received the King and made a covenant with him.'

Other chronicles differ over this. Florence, for example, speaks of crafty messengers going to and fro between William and Morcar and proposing treacherous terms, Morcar trading Ely for his own pardon and safety – 'for the besieged could have held out almost indefinitely thanks to the inaccessibility of the place'. Others emphasize that William had cut off the defenders by land and sea without suggesting that such a blockade could have also been maintained indefinitely. Whatever the truth, it would seem that Hereward, faced with a *fait accompli*, could do little to prevent the Normans forcing their way along the Aldreth causeway and so gaining a decisive foothold in the isle. The fate of the defenders was sealed. In Kingsley's phrase, 'the church had provided for herself by sacrificing the children beneath her fostering window'.

We can readily comprehend why William's ploy could have so swiftly undermined the resolve of the religious community. The seizure of all the abbey lands beyond the Isle of Ely struck at the roots of monastic life. Pillaging by North Sea rovers down the years, terrible though it was, could not have been more unnerving. A burned church could be rebuilt; stolen regalia might be replaced; but ownership of land, so arbitrarily usurped, threatened the monastery's very existence. Land was the key to power and influence for the Church just as it was for the rest of mankind. As Edward Miller has shown,[1] the accumulation of demesne lands was the principal method by which the Old English abbots had extended their lordship: 'The care the Confessor took to define the rights which Abbot Wulfric enjoyed over all his men, wherever they might live and wherever they might work, is testimony to the ever-widening circle of dependants established around the periphery of the demesne lands of the abbey.'

The character and needs of a monastic community shaped the organization which prevailed on the estate of Ely Abbey before and after 1066. A religious community was a place of refuge for the poor and hungry but that community itself also needed to feed off the surrounding countryside. Being immobile, it could not move about the estate consuming the produce of manors as could a layman or even a bishop. Its numbers were considerable and growing. Ely had fifty monks early in the twelfth century and later this had increased to seventy, and the number of servants roughly equalled that of monks. In order to feed and clothe this sizeable flock the abbots had to decide which of their farms would have to provide the needs of the church throughout the year, and the choice usually fell upon the more fertile and fruitful lands and villages. These no doubt were the very estates that William had earmarked as rewards for his most devoted aides. In the exploitation of the abbey's demesnes the units of this system of food farms were one week's supply of food for the abbey, and altogether thirty-three manors contributed fifty-six of these units. The manors of the Isle of Ely were specifically held in reserve in case deliveries should not be made from manors burdened with a farm.

This large reservation for such a contingency was fortuitous for the siege defenders, who do not appear to have been in danger of being starved into submission. Nor, indeed, does such a fate seem to have threatened Hereward and his companions when later they were hunted as outlaws in the forests of Northamptonshire, which suggests that the sympathy and help of the rural population were readily given. Apart from the manors of the isle, however, a considerable number of manors elsewhere were not called upon to contribute food farms. Miller suggests that perhaps such manors, upwards of thirty in total, may well have been farmed for a cash payment, or payments both in cash and kind. Some rents, for example, were paid in the form of honey and vast numbers of eels were delivered by the fenland manors. In 1086 such manors produced some 95,000 eels and many years earlier King Edgar had given the abbey a yearly rent of 10,000 eels from Outwell.

Hatfield was valued as a source of timber and the abbot's saltpans in the marshlands of Norfolk were a useful asset to the abbey's domestic economy.

Doddington in the isle had a stock of over a hundred cattle and twenty-four mares in 1086. Miller infers from this that Doddington was a breeding and dairy centre of more than manorial importance. The Domesday Book tells us that there were nearly 2,000 pigs on the demesne manors of Ely and the sheep flocks providing wool and manure were probably another important commercial asset. In 1086 the demesne manors had flocks totalling 9,000. Oliver Rackham's estimate of 2 million sheep in England at Domesday is quoted by Richard Muir in his fascinating picture of the English countryside in the eleventh century.[2]

Clearly, the monks of Ely Abbey had much to lose, but attributing simply selfish motives to their surrender is perhaps unfair. It would be more charitable to assume that, as godly men, their prime motivation was to prevent bloodshed if that were possible. In addition, the statistics of land and stock indicate that the welfare of a wide community outside its walls was largely dependent upon the abbey's good management.

This community was composed of the humbler Saxon whose life was doubtless hard and frugal whoever controlled his destiny. He left behind no records and does not figure prominently in the chronicles of great events so we can only guess at how he viewed the struggle between armies of fighting men disturbing his slumbers and trampling his crops. Since in this eastern region he would probably have been of Anglo-Danish stock it is reasonable to conclude that his sympathies, active or passive, would have been with the defenders of Ely and later with the partisans in the woods of the Bruneswald. Yet when the abbot, to whom he owed his livelihood, decided to treat with King William he was doubtless obliged to bite his tongue and stand in silent acquiescence 'like an ox at the furrow', as Kipling put it.

Miller records that the abbots claimed to exercise rights over some three and a half thousand freemen, sokemen, villeins and other bondsmen of lower degree. But distinguishing the lines separating these classes is not a simple matter. The varying degrees of dependence had been distorted and possibly not even understood in the maelstrom of the Conquest. As Miller points out, economically freemen and sokemen often stood no higher than their villein neighbours and sometimes the villein may have occupied a loftier social rung than the freeman, despite the latter's superior status in the eyes of the law. 'The classes standing closest to the demesne were villeins, borders, cotters and servi. There are servi on 80% of the abbey's manors in 1066. They are found on every manor in Essex and Hertfordshire; after that they are most ubiquitous in Norfolk and Suffolk; they are absent only in Huntingdonshire. Only six out of eighty-six demesne manors were without villeins at that date; only two without bordars or cottars; and there was not a single manor without representatives of at least one of these classes.' This may indicate the effects upon social organization of the constant demands which the monastery made of its estate.

Local history and legend are less concerned with such practicalities and relate with unconcealed satisfaction that the monks of Ely were justly punished for their treason. There can be no doubt that they did submit and that by so doing they sabotaged the defence of the isle. Freeman relates a curious tale of William's arrival at Ely when he entered the minster but did not dare to draw near to the shrine of the virgin patroness of the spot, because 'he was too well aware of the wrongs which he and his had done to the patrimony of Saint Æthelthryth; so, like the humble publican, he stood afar off, and offered a mark of gold on the altar'.

An undignified episode followed. While the king was in the church, the monks, apparently (and mystifyingly) unaware of his presence, were dining in the refectory when their ill-timed meal was interrupted by Gilbert of Clare, who sardonically inquired, since the king himself was actually present in the minster, whether they might not choose to dine at some other time? 'They left the board and rushed into the church,' writes Freeman, 'but the King was gone. His work had been done even in that short visit. He had marked out the site for a castle within the monastic precinct, and he had already given orders for its building by the work of men from the three shires of Cambridge, Huntingdon and Bedford. Aldreth too, the key of the Island, was to receive a garrison of foreigners faithful to the King.' Meanwhile the embarrassed monks trailed after William to Witchford, a short distance from Ely on the road to Aldreth.

The scene enacted at Witchford completed the monks' discomfiture. Having gained an audience with their monarch, no doubt after a suitable delay, they were forced to pay a fine of 700 marks of silver to purchase his peace which, as Freeman comments, was 'no bad interest for the one mark of gold which the King had offered Saint Æthelthryth'. However monkish chagrin was not ended. When the money was collected and brought to his officers in Cambridge it was found to be of light weight through some fraud of the moneyers and William threatened to withdraw his forgiveness.

If this grim man possessed a sense of humour he must have been chuckling now for, after this show of Olympian displeasure, he graciously allowed the monks to purchase his forbearance 'by a further fine of three hundred marks, the raising of which involved the loss of ornaments yet more holy and precious than those which had been already sacrificed', records Freeman. Various stories suggest that the situation would have appealed to William whose cruel jesting was illustrated at a council at Winchester in 1069 'where he demonstrated the perpetual security of a grant of property by making as if to thrust a knife into the palm of a quizzical abbot'.[3] Violent play-acting of this kind is perhaps a tyrant's method of displaying authority and can easily overstep the mark.

Even so, the monks appear to have escaped the incarceration or maiming that awaited those other defenders who were not killed in the final battle for Ely or had not escaped with Hereward to carry on the struggle elsewhere. Kingsley has a graphic, if imaginative, description of a boatload of blinded and maimed Ely defenders being rowed to Crowland Abbey, there to offer prayers for their souls to St Guthlac. The fate of Abbot Thurstan himself was at least discussed in William's councils, says Freeman, but in the end he was allowed to retain his office till his death six years later[4] when another raid was made on the precious things of the monastery.

The next abbot, Theodwine, a Norman monk from Jumièges, managed to recover some of the lost goods and, after Theodwine's death three years later, the monastery was administered for a time by a monk named Godfrey. In his time a final settlement of the rights and property of the abbey was made. The next abbot, Simeon, brother of Bishop Walkelin of Winchester, began the building of a new church, Freeman records, and of that church 'the massive and stately transepts still remain, a worthy portion of that wonderful pile which, raised soon after Simeon's day to cathedral rank, came gradually in vastness of scale and variety of style to surpass all the existing episcopal churches of England'.

Looking westwards from the spire of today's Ely Cathedral it would be possible to see on the skyline fingers of that ancient forest of Bruneswald into which Hereward the rebel disappeared after the surrender of Ely. With his escape from the isle, says Freeman, the certain history of Hereward ends, 'but legend goes on to tell how he still led the life of an outlaw, how he still remained the terror of the Normans, and from the wood by his supposed ancestral home at Bourne harried at pleasure . . . as far as the distant town of Warwick'.

Freeman's source is *De Gestis* which relates how Hereward sought refuge in the Bruneswald where the forces of nine shires were brought against him, although seven only are mentioned: Lincoln, Holland, Northampton, Cambridge, Leicester, Huntingdon and Warwick. Logically Bedford, which supplied labourers to build the castle at Ely, would have been another especially as its northern villages such as Odell, Chellington and Sharnbrook could well be on the fringe of the vanished Bruneswald.

It is difficult for us to comprehend how this countryside could have provided sufficient cover for a combat group of perhaps 200 men for any appreciable period of time since today Britain has proportionately less forest cover – around 9 per cent – than any other European country apart from Ireland. However, in the eleventh century forest still covered about a third of the land, says General Harward, and the process of forest clearance was given great impetus by the Normans and much land was adapted for cultivation in the generation following the Conquest.

The General's estimate of forest cover is generous and Richard Muir concludes that the Domesday survey – which admittedly measures woodland in terms of how many pigs could be fattened on its acorns and beech nuts in the autumn – depicts a

From the roof of today's Ely Cathedral one can look westward to where the ancient forest stood that once harboured Hereward's outlaws.

countryside which was not heavily wooded: 'Only a loose estimate of the wooded area can be made, expressed, as follows, by Oliver Rackham: "England was not well wooded even by the standards of the twentieth century, let alone eleventh-century Europe. It had a proportion of woodland between those of modern France (20 per cent of the land) and modern Denmark (9 per cent)."'

The appearance of these Domesday woodlands would have differed from those we know today in several important respects, not least the type of trees which formed them. The first thing we would notice is the absence of foreign conifers, the woods being deciduous with, as Muir suggests, just native yew, holly, juniper and box to provide winter greenery. Chestnut, a Roman introduction, could be found in a few Domesday woods, but there were no sycamores yet. These, like larch, silver fir and spruce were still to be introduced.

According to Muir, research from Epping Forest indicates that the lime-

Once the heart of the Bruneswald, the road that runs south from Leighton Bromswold to Newton Bromswold.

dominated early Saxon forest was gradually being replaced by hazel, birch and oak: 'Then beech gained a strong foothold in the forest with a late appearance and expansion of hornbeam helping to produce the modern oak, birch, beech and hornbeam composition. At the time of Domesday here the lime was still common though declining, hornbeam was not yet evident and beech had only begun to secure a foothold.'

Muir's view, in turn, is at variance with those of that doyen of silviculturists, Herbert L. Edlin, who considered that the native broad-leaved trees – hazel, alder, oak, elm and lime – reached us from the Continent in about 6000 BC. He also put the appearance of beech and hornbeam in the south-east at about 2500 BC.[5] Edlin, however, would have agreed that woods referred to in Domesday were working woods.

Muir believes that many produced more income than equivalent areas of ploughland and offers this beguiling portrait of a typical woodland scene fit for Titania herself: '. . . tall oak, ash or elm standards towered above a coppiced underwood of elm, ash, hazel or lime. Such woodland vistas are rarely seen today but are always attractive. The underwood provides ample cover for wildlife as the coppiced "stools" begin to sprout a new crop of leafy poles, while after coppicing the light streaming down through gaps in the canopy of standards allows orchids, bluebells, primroses and oxlips to produce a flush of spring colour.'[6]

Although Rackham asserts that it would not have been possible in Norman England to penetrate into woodland further than 4 miles without encountering some habitation, such forests would still have offered Hereward corridors for traversing the country from coast to coast much as the jungle paths enabled communist terrorists to move up and down the central Malaysian highlands almost unhindered in the Malayan Emergency of the 1950s. Such corridors of tree cover, while not continuous, were close enough to ensure a reasonably safe passage from one forested area to another under cover of darkness especially as the hamlets scattered throughout the woodlands and elsewhere would have been populated by sympathizers.

This woodland was much more than a place in which to hide. It supplied the timber for dwellings, permanent and temporary, provided fuel and furniture as well as farming tools and weapons of war. It also offered pasture and such food as acorns, beech mast and a variety of berries. For much of the year it supported herds of pigs and cattle and the herdsmen's lodges and sheds would have provided overnight accommodation for men on the run.

Sir Frank Stenton describes[7] how the modern forest of Wyre on the Shropshire/Worcestershire border represents the once great tract of woodland which, under the name of Weogorena leag, had extended in the ninth century for many miles along the west of the Severn, over against Worcester.

In King Alfred's time a thick belt of wooded country connected the district afterwards known as the New Forest with the swine-pastures of western Kent. In the tenth century the forest of Sherwood in Nottinghamshire stretched for at least seven miles to the north of what became its medieval boundary. The primitive English forest can rarely, if ever, have been a continuous expanse of heavy timber. Every royal forest of the middle ages included hamlets, if not villages, of pre-Conquest origin, and it is often impossible to gather from the modern appearance of a tract of country whether it had been a region of primary settlement or of forest colonisation.

Today's investigator must use his or her imagination extensively since clues on the ground are sparse. Even Stenton had to admit that no part of England was less suggestive of an ancient forest 'than the district once known as Bruneswald, in west Huntingdonshire and east Northamptonshire (its position is indicated by the place-names Newton Bromswold in Northamptonshire and Leighton Bromswold in Huntingdonshire [today's Cambridgeshire])', most of whose villages are mentioned in Domesday Book. Even so the well-recorded tradition of Hereward's life as an outlaw in Bruneswald shows, Stenton argued, that a large amount of unbroken woodland still existed in this country at the date of the Norman Conquest.

The Bruneswald has all but vanished, but its name survives at Leighton Bromswold, Cambridgeshire.

Some fragments of woodland can still be seen at the heart of what was once the forest of Bruneswald near Newton Bromswold, Northamptonshire.

Hereward's life as a rebel in the Bruneswald was to give rise to countless stories in the coming years which can be seen as the source of the legend of the medieval outlaw personified by Robin Hood. Unfortunately, although the *De Gestis* is full of detail we are now back in the province of speculation and fiction and few facts remain to tell us what really happened to Hereward in later life. We can perhaps agree with Freeman that he continued to make life difficult for the Normans in the eastern shires and the Abbey of Peterborough, under its Norman abbot, was very likely to have been the focus of his special hatred. The alleged capture of Turold is said, by some, to have occurred in this period and the abbot redeemed himself only by paying a substantial ransom. Freeman, understandably, finds the reported figure of £30,000 an incredible one and suggests that tales of a second raid on the monastery are simply a misplacement of the earlier one moved by the licence of legend out of its proper place.

Nothing is absolutely certain about Hereward and nobody can be sure how long he was able to continue guerrilla warfare from his base in the Bruneswald. According to some versions he eventually made his peace with King William and this seems likely since an early demise at the hands of his Norman pursuers would surely have been more widely recorded or would have survived in traditional folklore. Incidental confirmation to support this view could be the subsequent references to him in Domesday, the Ingulph account of his burial at Crowland and the recorded survival of his daughter (by Torfrida) who handed on the paternal estate at Bourne to her husband, Hugh of Evermue.

How the transformation from hunted terrorist to loyal subject was achieved is where various sources part company. For instance, General Harward's ability to interpret even the darkest moments favourably for his famous ancestor again does not fail him. In his book Hereward is not a supplicant asking for peace but a free warrior bargaining from a position of strength.

He describes how the war was carried into the counties of Cambridge, Huntingdon, Northampton, Leicester and Warwick, and how 'no force could be raised able to cope with Hereward's strength and strategy'. At length he was able to capture Ivo de Taillebois upon whom William had conferred large estates, and 'an opportunity was afforded Hereward to make peace with William, as he had now other plans in view, and further resistance was absolutely futile, as William's authority prevailed from the Grampians to the southern coast'. Accordingly negotiations were started and these resulted in the restitution of Hereward's lands, and his acknowledgement of William's lawful authority.

Since this is the first occasion on which Hereward is said to have submitted it requires careful explanation and the General is equal to the task. His argument is that Hereward's surrender was in strict accordance with the laws of honour, and in the best interests of the Saxons. His followers, though numerous, were badly armed and much weakened by exposure and privation, while the Norman strength increased daily. As a recognized landholder, Hereward would be in a better position to save his people from famine and extermination. Subsequent history shows that he did not care to retain the lands as an under-tenant except Pebwith (Pebworth), at Marston Jabbet, of which he may have obtained the fee.

His action, therefore, was in accordance with military usage and no less patriotic than his previous resistance. Harward even glosses over his hero's apparent infidelity by the convenient assumption that Torfrida was no longer alive: 'Hereward, who seems to have found time for everything, had fallen in love a second time with a Saxon lady of large estates and wealth, named Ælfthryth. His first wife Torfrida was probably dead, as Freeman suggests in his *History of the Norman Conquest*. Nothing more is heard of her after she entered the convent, nor is there any mention of her taking holy vows. Hereward seems to have been free to marry again, and according to the rhymer, the lady was yet more eager.'

Hereward's exploits, perhaps already the subject of ballads, had reached the ears of Ælfthryth in Worcestershire, where 'she appears to have been a ward or tenant of good Bishop Wulfstan'. The General points out that in 1086 Hereward held a knight's fee in land at Evenlode, in Worcestershire, under the bishop, which may have been a portion of Ælfthryth's estate, or may have been given by Wulfstan.

This Saxon prelate had been installed as bishop by Edward the Confessor and 'was no doubt a personal friend of Leofric; he fought against William at Senlac, but afterwards swore allegiance to him, when he perceived that resistance was unavailing, and only tended to prolong civil dissension. He would in his heart have desired to aid Hereward, and Wulfstan may not only have aided his reconciliation to the King but have provided him with a wife and an estate.' Further corroboration was that the bishop was born at Long Itchington, in Warwickshire, and must have been acquainted with Hereward's family.

General Harward concludes that there was every reason to believe that Hereward's marriage with Ælfthryth was a happy one, and 'more suitable to both of them than Hereward's previous marriage to a foreign lady though both his wives appear to have possessed admirable charms and the highest qualifications. Hereward's chief family appears to have sprung from his second marriage, and this must have been a further source of mutual happiness. . . . Hereward, though now past his early manhood, was well entitled to enjoy the love and happiness which is especially the reward of the brave. At length, therefore, he obtained well-earned rest, a truce from incessant warfare, a loving wife of his own nation, and the restoration of a considerable part of his own estates.'

The General, a sentimentalist after all, would of course have favoured such a version since it provides richer soil for his genealogical tree (even if, ironically, it also provides us with a possible link with his *bête noire*, the Wake family). But this happy ending and the convenient replacement of one wife with a more acceptable Saxon spouse who is not only beautiful but wealthy and on reasonably friendly terms with the Conqueror, may seem perhaps a shade too convenient to many. *De Gestis* is more censorious:

> In the interval Hereward's wife, Turfrida, had begun to turn away from him, because he had at that time very often received messengers from a lady most powerful from her wealth (she was the wife of Earl Dolfinus), asking for licence from the King, which he could obtain for the mere asking as she had heard from the King's own mouth, if he were peaceably disposed and were willing to give him his adherence. For this purpose, and charmed with the beauty of the lady, Hereward gave his consent, because there was no one more beautiful or comely in the realm than she and hardly any one more eminent in wealth. Whereupon Hereward sent messengers to the King and demanded the lady aforesaid, declaring that he was willing to be reconciled with the King's Majesty. The King received the messengers graciously and appointed a day for him, agreeing to what he had demanded, adding that he had for a long time been wishing to receive him into his favour. But the real wife of Hereward, whom we have mentioned, by reason of this went to Crowland and

chose the better life, taking the veil of a nun. On this account many evils happened to Hereward, because she was very wise and helpful in giving him advice when emergencies arose. Afterwards, as he himself often admitted, many things happened to him not so fortunately as in the time of his success.

Freeman suggests that the writer of *De Gestis* has combined two separate stories about the wife or wives of Hereward that had been preserved by Gaimar and Ingulph. Although independent, they may not necessarily be contradictory, as 'Torfrida may have died before Ælfthryth made her proposals to Hereward. But the notion of Torfrida going into a monastery to make way for Ælfthryth is plainly another form of the story in Ingulph which makes, not herself but her mother, do so. The description of (the lady) . . . as wife of Earl Dolfin is a more baffling confusion or tradition. Dolfin was a renowned Northumbrian name, but no Earl so called is recorded.'

Torfrida, if earlier tales in *De Gestis* contain any truth, seems to have been much too spirited to capitulate as lamely as we are asked to believe and, with Freeman, we must tend towards the view that she had indeed died before the new alliance took place. Writers of fiction, of course, might prefer the alternative version which provides much more dramatic colour and gives the shadowy figure of Hereward all-too-human frailties.

The transition from terrorist to respected member of the community is not an impossible one as we have seen in our own century, but *De Gestis* makes clear that it can be a difficult phase. Hereward's reputation seems to have provoked challenges from a succession of young bloods – much as ageing gunfighters are frequently being pushed into unwanted confrontations in the mythology of the Western – and Hereward's distaste echoes their weary reluctance.

His eventual acceptance at the king's Court provides the opportunity for a last warlike display and Harward records that 'the King himself went to see Hereward's soldiers . . . and he was greatly delighted with them and praised them with compliments on their handsome appearance and height, and added that they were all bound to be very eminent in warfare'. This may perhaps explain the suggestion that Hereward, as Edric the Wild, was recruited to the king's armies in subsequent conflicts.

Freeman interprets Hereward's reconciliation as an example of William practising a similar policy to that adopted earlier in his reign towards other Englishmen whose power and influence he dreaded. 'William on his first voyage to Normandy took with him the chief Earls and Prelates of England, and we shall presently see Eadric of Herefordshire, now reconciled with William, accompany the King in his expedition against Scotland. It was another instance of the same policy when William . . . took Hereward with him among the Englishmen who helped to win back the revolted County of Maine.'

This reconciliation did not stifle old grudges still harboured by many Normans and *De Gestis* describes how Hereward's enemies, among them Earl Warrenne and Ivo Taillebois, tried to poison the king's mind against him with false reports of subversive activities. Accordingly Hereward was arrested and thrown into prison at Bedford in the custody of one Robert de Horepol who, however, appears to have been a sympathetic gaoler. Hereward's loyal followers, learning that their leader was to be taken in chains to Buckingham, ambushed the cavalcade and freed him.

Robert de Horepol then interceded with the king so persuasively on Hereward's behalf that William was satisfied that the allegations against him were malicious inventions, restored Hereward's lands and the famous warrior 'lived afterwards for many years, faithfully serving King William, and wholly devoted to his neighbours and friends. And so at last he rested in peace and upon his soul may God have mercy. Amen.'

Writing some seventy years after Hereward's supposed interment at Crowland, Geoffrey Gaimar produced his more tragic version of the hero's last days. The French poet relates how the king's peace could not make him safe against the violence and treachery of lesser men. Many writers have repeated Gaimar's description with embellishments of their own but it is in Freeman's massive treatise, the definitive work on the Conquest, that the scene comes vividly to life:

> He still remained exposed to the hatred of men of the conquering race, men perhaps who had suffered from his prowess, men at all events whose deeds were as lawless as any of his own during his days of outlawry. He had to keep watch within and without his house, and to plant guards when he was at his meals. Once his chaplain Æthelward, on whom this duty fell, slumbered at his post. A band of Normans now attacked Hereward. He armed himself in

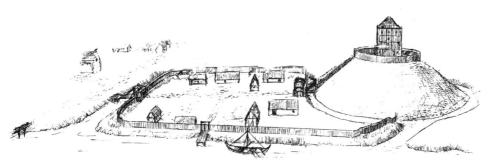

An artist's impression of the eleventh-century fortification by the Great Ouse at Bedford where Hereward was sent to be imprisoned. This developed into a stone castle, demolished after a siege in the thirteenth century, and only the castle mound remains.

haste; his spear was broken, his sword was broken; he was driven to use his shield as a weapon; fifteen Frenchmen lay dead by his single arm, when four of their party got behind him and smote him in the back. This stroke brought him to his knees.

A Breton knight, Ralph of Dol . . . now rushed on him, but Hereward, by a last effort, once more wielded his buckler with deadly effect, and the Englishman and the Breton fell dead together. Another Norman, Asselin by name, now gave the last stroke; he cut off the head of the English hero, and swore by God and his might that so valiant a man he had never seen, and that, if there had been three more in the land like him, the Frenchmen would have been slain or driven out of England.

Such is the tale, a tale worth the telling; but all that certain history can say is that a Hereward, most likely the hero of Ely, appears in Domesday as a holder of lands in the shires of Worcester and Warwick under Norman lords.

CHAPTER EIGHT

The Legend

Historical characters inevitably sustain personality changes when they become the subject of fiction. Shakespeare's kings may welcome their literary immortality even at the expense of probity, while others, less fortunate in their authors, might complain. If records are available to confirm or contradict fiction, such adapting of the truth is of no deep consequence; where records are sparse, however, a fabrication will readily supplant reality and such is the case with Hereward.

His survival, even if only as a shadowy figure, owes more to the invention of story-tellers than to the integrity of historians and each at times has masqueraded as the other to confuse the trail still more. He could not have been first choice as a subject for eulogy among contemporary Norman writers who would have considered him a member of the conquered ruling class and a potential rallying point for the dispossessed and discontented.

This acclaim was established by long-forgotten minstrels and doubtless also by those kindred spirits to the Irish *seanchai*, the old hearth-side story-tellers or wandering tale-bearers who begged their way from parish to parish.[1] Their vanished songs and stories seem to have ensured that Hereward was preserved in folk-memory until such Victorians as Charles Kingsley breathed more life into the legend and it is to Kingsley that we owe much of our awareness of the Saxon hero.

Kingsley was fortunate to be writing at a time when the historical novel was enormously popular. Book-loving Victorian children could devour with unimpaired appetite the solid fare provided by writers such as Sir Walter Scott and Charlotte Yonge. The Waverley novels were regarded in many households as a treat, not a task, and far from being driven to read them, children 'were allowed, as reward and privilege after lessons were done, to indulge in one of those enchanting volumes'.[2]

Kingsley's own motivation in writing about Hereward has been the focus of much debate. However, most writers, whether of fiction or history, at least agree about Hereward's importance as the progenitor of a traditional outlaw figure, one who exercised so powerful a fascination for the common man during the Middle Ages that he found his way into literature.

Modern writers Jack Lindsay[3] and Maurice Keen see Hereward as the first of the

The Victorian view of the Saxon hero – illustration from *Hereward the Brave* by Julia Corner (Groombridge and Sons, 1896).

English outlaws, the lineal ancestor of Robin Hood and all those other folk heroes who were to frolic in the greenwood during the coming centuries. Hereward, like Fulk Fitzwarin, combines in his historical and his legendary roles various themes that would have struck a chord in the hearts of his countrymen down the centuries. He was exiled and banished, if not excommunicated, only to return to avenge the wrongs inflicted on his family. He was dispossessed but undefeated and became an outlaw with a price on his head. The episode of Hereward disguised as a potter not only looks back, as Jack Lindsay and General Harward show, to the tales of Alfred entering the Danish camp, but even more strongly forward to those of Robin Hood and his stratagems. It becomes the basis of one of the earliest ballads and reappears in the stories told of Eustace the Monk.

Returning exile and avenging hero are, as we know, recurring elements of classical drama. But the exile–outlaw figure and the woodland refuge are matters whose appeal is peculiarly, if not exclusively, English. The cross-fertilization with European folk literature is well attested and so Fulk Fitzwarin's fortress at Whittington becomes, in French romance, Blauncheville in Blauncheland.

Many such clues support the view that Hereward was, indeed, the parent of the English medieval outlaw cult that linked legend and real life. Taking the *De Gestis* account on one hand and the tales of Fulk Fitzwarin, as recounted by Keen, on the other, the parallels suggest themselves endlessly.

Hereward's youthful revolt against authority is echoed by Fulk's lifelong feud with King John, as is his rough handling of French courtiers by the story of John being whipped for breaking a chessboard over Fulk's head. Hereward took refuge in Flanders while Fulk fled to Brittany; both spent much time with their companions living in forests (the Bruneswald near Bourne has its cousin in Fulk's Babbyng forest near his home in Blauncheville[4]), eluding pursuers and preying on their enemies; Hereward's conquest of a bear with human intelligence is upstaged by Fulk's adventure in Carthage where he overcame a dragon monster, said to be half-human, which fed upon human flesh; and both were practised rescuers of princesses from repugnant marriages, although Fulk's exploits are set in more exotic lands than Cornwall and Ireland.

The violence at times is almost identical. Hereward's vengeance on the despoilers of Bourne, which left fourteen Norman heads grinning from the battlements, is given an elaborate twist in the account of Fulk's punishment of Piers de Bruville who had taken Fulk's name to cover his own banditry. Piers is forced to behead every one of his followers before he suffers the same fate. Fulk overcomes a black giant in Ireland and takes his axe back to Blauncheville as a trophy, thus emulating Hereward's defeat of the 'wicked and haughty' Ulcus Ferreus whose famous sword he kept as his prize. The line between truth and fancy becomes blurred but the similarities remain constant in tales of rescues, disguises and stratagems.

All this rich material was given another dimension in Norman-dominated England by the imposition of Draconian forest laws which, apart from putting a vast area of the countryside out of bounds for most of the population, allowed deer to destroy crops without being curbed and huntsmen to gallop unpunished over cultivated land. This became a powerful spur to the stories of woodland outlaws and to public resentment so that any tale, real or imagined, showing how the laws were evaded and foresters outwitted, would receive an appreciative audience. Something of this covert approval survives in our own half-grudging admiration for the poacher in his battle with the gamekeeper.

The greenwood was, therefore, as essential to the mythology of the medieval outlaw as the prairie was to be to the nineteenth-century Western gunfighter. Analogies can be drawn between them and when we look at the documentary evidence about such men as Wyatt Earp and Jesse James who lived, in historical terms, only yesterday, we can, perhaps, learn how quickly in the saga of Hereward fact and fable could have become interchangeable.

Lindsay pursues the woodland theme in another direction when discussing the epithet of *Silvaticus* or Forestman attached by later legends to Edric the Wild, but this perhaps stretches the point since Edric's revolt seems to have remained located in the marshes of Wales. Keen elevates the greenwood to rank as 'the fourth matter of importance' deemed worthy of a poet's attention in the days of medieval romance.[5] The stories of Robin Hood and his outlaws do possess the same childhood fascination as those of King Arthur and Merlin and are also much more familiar to us than the tales of Roland and Oliver, or of Brut the legendary Trojan who, having rid the land of giants, founded the kingdom of Britain.

It is not, of course, surprising that the greenwood should form the backdrop to so much medieval romance. The shady depths of the thick forest which covered large parts of the country was the natural setting for the kind of adventures that Arthur's knights encounter. The credulity of audiences in the Middle Ages encouraged the colonization of dark woods and wild places by enchanted harts, dwarves, elves and strange knights covered from head to toe in armour of bizarre hue. Such tales told how Saxon saints, living as hermits in the Fens, had elfish sprites as their companions and foresters saw among the trees mysterious torchlit processions. Small wonder that when Shakespeare came to write *A Midsummer Night's Dream* his magical spirits found their natural habitat in the woodland glades. In *As You Like It* the Forest of Arden provided a refuge for a banished duke – 'are not these woods more free from peril than the envious court?'

Hereward's place in this specialized world has some ambiguity since he does not quite conform either to the Robin Hood milieu nor, despite the attempts of the writer of some parts of *De Gestis*, to the environment of silken dalliance and courtly chivalry as exemplified by the Round Table. There is a chasm between these worlds which Keen explores when he insists that the tales of Robin Hood and his band of outlaws belonged to the forest in a special sense, whereas in the courtly romances the woodland was reduced to stage-prop, albeit a useful and engaging one.

Such romantic tales invariably opened in Court or castle and remained firmly attached to the life that was led there, but to Robin Hood and Little John and Gamelyn the forest background was indispensable. In contrast, it offered no sanctuary to Arthur and his knights. It was instead, says Keen, a perilous place within which lay an unknown world where the rule of law did not run and where wicked men found a refuge. But to Robin Hood, an outlaw whom society had placed outside the law's protection, it afforded asylum from tyranny and corruption, a protection against evil lords and their contemptible underlings.

By putting Arthur and Robin Hood at opposite poles of society – the one synonymous with chivalrous aristocracy, the other a yeoman shielding the poor against that aristocracy now degraded – there is a sense in which Keen mirrors the arm's-length confrontation of Hereward and William I. It is not illogical to suggest that the reason such contrasting champions never came face to face in the medieval story, although sallying forth in the same forests, is that they were the heroes of different story-tellers.

Keen argues entertainingly that Robin Hood, the people's hero, did not excite the imagination of writers of courtly romance whose audience was the high-born and the wealthy. While they were as eager as any to use popular myth, that great paint box of material into which all medieval story-tellers dipped their brushes when a narrative required embellishing, the Robin Hood legend was too close to the soil for the delicate sensibilities of their listeners.

The ballads about him were created, not by courtly poets but by the same men who sang of Hereward and the Bruneswald in the twelfth century – 'obscure minstrels whose names are one and all forgotten, and only a fragment of whose repertoire remains to bear witness to the tastes and ideas of their peasant listeners'. What survives is, however, enough to show Keen what the average peasant thought of that baggage train of corrupt officials which 'hung about the loins of their masters, and what they would have liked to do to them'.

Class hatred is a convenient, if sometimes misleading, label that may even encourage the notion that Hereward, as the forefather of Robin Hood, might be viewed in some way as a kind of eleventh-century Che Guevara. Such an idea, while intriguing since it makes Hereward an activist in social evolution, if not revolution, is some distance from reality since it is clearly dangerous to interpret his actions in terms of later social and political values. What it does do, however, is help us to develop our character outline of Hereward, and part of the fleshing-out of this sketch is a recognition of the barbaric side of his personality.

The separation of fact from fiction is as difficult with Robin Hood as it is with Hereward, and Professor J.C. Holt has shown that by the thirteenth century the name itself began to be attached to living persons. Various figures called Robynhood, Robert Hod or Hobbehod appear on contemporary documents, and the wooded area in South Yorkshire known as Barnsdale seems to be especially linked to such characters. A striking feature of the Robin Hood stories is the atmosphere of violence that pervades them all. We can safely assume that the Robin Hood of medieval legend is a much truer picture of Hereward than the anodyne nursery tale version.

'In the ballads,' says Keen, 'we are up against a full-blooded medieval brigand, who, even if his conduct is redeemed by a courtly generosity to the poor and deserving, is a brigand nevertheless and can be called by no other name.' Keen is, of course, echoing here the description found in Orderic Vitalis – 'Now that the brigands had been driven off English and Normans were living peacefully together in boroughs, towns and cities.' Keen sees Robin (and, by implication, Hereward also) as a desperate man driven to desperate and violent remedies: 'Revelling in the blood of one's enemies is now an outmoded pleasure, but to the middle ages it appeared natural and almost justifiable. There is nothing sinister, therefore, in the violence of the outlaw ballads, but ruthless it certainly is.'

Thus the story of Hereward's homecoming and his slaughter of the fourteen

Normans would have raised no contemporary eyebrows. Certainly, in such robust accounts neither man nor child was spared. Little John and Much the Miller's son, when coming upon the monk who had betrayed Robin to the sheriff, having dealt summarily with the monk, showed no scruples about silencing for ever the boy witness riding with him. More grisly still, when Robin slays Guy of Gisborne he also has to cut off his head, stick it on his bow's end and with a knife so disfigure the face that none 'on woman born, could tell whose head it was'.

This barbarism, horrifying to us, simply reflects the violence of the days when the ballads were composed. The Middle Ages were rough times, and their woods and fens concealed threats to the traveller more tangible than that offered by sprites and goblins. Should the arm of the law become enfeebled or too short to impose the king's authority everywhere, wild places could easily become a refuge for desperate and unfortunate men of all sorts.

Modern society in looking back across the millennium at such lawlessness may not be so well placed to take the moral high ground. Today's violence is often casual and not necessarily linked to notorious danger spots, and we can well believe that the savage tone of the outlaw ballads is probably true to life, revealing their authors as realists whose forests were peopled not with phantoms but with all-too-human thugs who, perhaps, had more legitimate excuse for brutality than their latter-day successors. This is especially true if the violence of the outlaws was directed at a cruelly unjust social system and expressed a popular outrage that seethed below the surface for generations and could not be articulated in other ways.

It is not the violence in such stories that challenges belief. Where the characters depicted grow larger than life is not in their savagery but in their occasional saintliness. Redressing wrongs, easing the peasants' burden and confounding injustice cover the outlaws' deeds in a cloak of Arthurian chivalry that has no statutory place in the real world of highway robbery. Keen insists that no robber ever could have lived as did the Robin Hood of legends. Unlike Hereward, he is an ideal, not an actual figure who wandered with Lancelot and Gawain in a never-never land of legend.

The process of weaving historical personages into myth inevitably means that they become altered and the story-teller's own beliefs may determine how they are changed. Kingsley is one among many myth-makers to face this charge and the process is not without its benefits. Keen believes that the value of popular legend is that it can tell the historian what his archives so often conceal – 'what it was that men really believed in and what they really desired. It is this that makes the violent tone of the outlaw legends so striking.'

That violence is explained in Keen's argument by the popular imagination of an age with an exaggerated respect for authority, choosing to personify its aspirations in the stories of men who had the courage to defy the law. Might this, he asks, have been a consequence of literacy being the preserve of a small educated class, so that the written records conceal the revolutionary ideas which were surging beneath the upper crust of the social world? 'The outlaws of legend, if they undeniably belong to the world of mortal men, have equally undeniably been enlarged and romanticised to more than life-size in the minds of the people who heard and loved the ballads which recounted their deeds. Indeed, though their activities are corporeal enough, their stories do not have quite the ring of true history.'

We suspect that 'true history' is a chimera. We must settle for a compromise, basing our assumptions and deductions on the inherited fruits of scholarship, common sense and an awareness of humanity. What might be described as historical myth can play a role when writers use it to advocate a partial version of history, a criticism levelled at Charles Kingsley for his *Hereward the Wake: Last of the English* – its very title was enough to enrage opponents such as General Harward who pointedly called his own book *Hereward, the Saxon Hero*. We

Hereward wooing Torfrida – an H.C. Selous illustration for Charles Kingsley's novel.

Charles Kingsley breathed more life into the Hereward legend and to him we owe much of our awareness of the Saxon hero.

encounter here something of the 'secular scripture' mentioned in Michael Young's paper on Kingsley's novel[6] whose text, he asserts, is dedicated to proving the inevitability of Britain's rise through history to the status of pre-eminent world power and to confirm the supremacy of the Anglo-Saxon civilization.

In Young's eyes the book's conclusion begins the history of England as a unified nation and appears to 'predict the greater cohesion of the Victorian Empire, the fulfilment of the historical process that leads inexorably . . . from fragmented tribal organisation to the unity of the Nation'. Kingsley, the clergyman, was unashamedly Protestant and patriotic and offered his opinions on a variety of contemporary issues from social reform to education in the unmistakable style of the muscular Christian.

Young correctly says that Hereward's rebellion against religion and family authority enabled Kingsley to make his 'anachronistic insertion of contemporary Anglican values' (and, incidentally, display his anti-popery). Young seems to be on less solid ground when he suggests that Kingsley, sensing that the young Hereward's rebellion against religious and family authority was becoming an embarrassment to the text, avoids this danger by placing Hereward in the forest, physically isolated outside settled society, and closer to nature. The text, he argues, now supports the inevitable historical process, the fusion of Anglo-Dane with Norman and the creation of the 'New English' by costuming him 'in the cultural cliché of the outlaw identity, with all the romance trappings of the "merry greenwood" and feasts of venison'.

Kingsley, of course, invented neither the outlaw nor the greenwood element in the Hereward story. The evidence that Hereward lived in the Bruneswald is ancient and Kingsley would have been at fault, both as historian and novelist, had he omitted it. Kingsley's text also stands indicted by Young of trivializing the outlaw's status and placing it at the centre of a particular institutional structure rooted in hierarchical society: 'Hard knocks in good humour, strict rules, fair play, and equal justice for high and low; this was the old outlaw spirit, which has descended to their inlawed descendants; and makes, to this day, the life and marrow of an English public school.'

This analogy is particularly interesting if we remember that any piece of popular adventure fiction written in England around 1865 would stand a fair chance of including some of Dr Arnold's self-righteous virtues – Thomas Hughes's *Tom Brown's Schooldays* had appeared only a few years earlier. In fact Kingsley was a great friend of Hughes, had read his book in manuscript and encouraged him to have it published. Young's summation, that ultimately Kingsley's novel 'is not the stuff of history, but that of dreams', will come as no surprise and probably Kingsley himself would not have entirely disagreed despite his protestation that he had 'followed facts as strictly as I could, altering none which I found, and inventing little more than was needed to give the story coherence, or to illustrate the manners of the time. . . .'

Charles Kingsley, whatever his critics say about his imaginative powers, cannot be indicted for sentimentality. In his novel the 'merry greenwood', although merry enough in the summer, '. . . was a sad place enough, when the autumn fog crawled round the gorse, and dripped off the hollies, and choked alike the breath and the eyesight; when the air sickened with the graveyard smell of rotting leaves, and the rain-water stood in the clay holes over the poached and sloppy lawns'. In winter, too, it was merry enough in friendly farmhouses or while the bright sharp frosts lasted, 'but it was doleful enough in those same farm-houses in the howling wet weather, when wind and rain lashed in through the unglazed window and ill-made roof, and there were coughs and colds and rheumatisms . . .'. There is nothing like a runny nose to lend verisimilitude.

Kingsley wrote for a wide audience and his novel achieved popularity when first published in serial form in *Good Words* and then as a book in 1866. It is probably his best-known work after *Water Babies* and *Westward Ho!* Its appearance was probably timed to coincide with the anniversary of Hastings, although Kingsley's biographer, Brenda Colloms,[7] makes no reference to this. Kingsley, she reminds us, was at all times the preacher and the lecturer, though one with a gift for story-telling. It follows that his explanation for Hereward's eventual downfall is disarmingly simplistic: 'But the grace of God had gone away from Hereward, as it goes away from all men who are unfaithful to their wives.'

Opinions of Kingsley as historian or writer may vary but his book has become the single, most widely known work on Hereward and must now be regarded by most people as their chief and perhaps only introduction to the subject. Its timing prevented Hereward from being swept into the maw of G.A. Henty who in the next decade began his series of historical yarns that 'took all history for his province'. Hereward would have been a natural subject and his absence from the pantheon of Henty heroes is a matter of some surprise. It is interesting to speculate that Henty might have ignored the bloody Gaimar version of Hereward's end, an ending that Shakespeare, had he been moved to use the tale (which must have been known to him), would surely have made memorable. The body count of sixteen would not have deterred him and he would have appreciated the piquancy of that final tableau in which the four knights who steal behind Hereward and thrust their spears into his back include his own son-in-law, Hugh de Evermue.

Kingsley allows Winter, the faithful retainer, to share this final scene but not inside the ancestral home. Scorning to die 'like a wolf in a cave' the pair rush outside to face impossible odds. The scene is repeated in substance in juvenile books such as Arnold's Bright Story Readers but in a recent version[8] the casualty list is reduced to more acceptable levels with a mere seven Normans being killed by Hereward's own hand. Common to all, however, is the last defiant gesture of throwing his shield with sufficient force to break the neck of the luckless Breton, Raoul de Dol, and the final accolade 'If there had been three more such men. . . .'

Kingsley always considered *Hypatia* to be his best historical novel and in both this and *Hereward the Wake* his admiration for the Danes (and the Teutons) is evident. As Brenda Colloms points out, 'The Danes are almost as much the heroes of his book as the Saxons – "the free Norsemen, among whom there was not a single serf". Hereward himself . . . is an anti-hero, handsome, self-willed, rebellious, who becomes an outlaw rather than obey his devout mother and become a monk. . . . In Flanders he marries a Flemish princess, Torfrida, who is strangely like Kingsley's other heroines (almost an eleventh-century Fanny Grenfell): "Pure she was all the while, generous, and noble-hearted; with a deep and sincere longing – as one soul in ten thousand has – after knowledge for its own sake; but ambitious exceedingly, and that not of monastic sanctity."'

Kingsley's interest in Hereward reflected that Victorian nostalgia for a pre-industrial England, that medieval dream that can be detected in the works of Ruskin and William Morris and finds expression in the allegorical paintings of Burne–Jones. But it was also a natural product of his boyhood spent partly in the Fens – his father, a churchman like him, was for a time rector of Barnack, near Stamford, and there the young Charles lived from the age of six to eleven. His

The Great Ouse near Offord Cluny, Cambridgeshire, where the landscape begins to assume a fenland character.

biographer describes how the fen country appealed strongly to the impressionable boy and later he was to testify to this in lectures and essays, but above all in *Hereward the Wake*. The book is memorable for its pictures of landscape and seascape that meant so much to Kingsley and are integral to the story of Hereward:

> They have a beauty of their own, these great fens even now, when they are dyked and drained, tilled and fenced – a beauty as of the sea, of boundless expanse and freedom. Much more had they that beauty when they were still, for the most part, as God had made them, or rather was making them even then. The low rolling uplands were clothed in primeval forest; oak and ash, beech and elm, with here and there perhaps a group of ancient pines, ragged and decayed, and fast dying out in England even then; though lingering still in the forests of the Scottish highlands.
>
> Between the forests were open wolds, dotted with white sheep and golden gorse; rolling plains of rich though ragged turf, whether cleared by the hand of man or by the wild fires which often swept over the hills. . . .

133

Wide waters and wider skies form the timeless panorama of the Fens. Reflections at Morley's Holt, Cambridgeshire.

For always, from the foot of the wolds, the green flat stretched away, illimitable, to a horizon where, from the roundness of the earth, the distant trees and islands were hulled down like ships at sea. The firm horse-fen lay, bright green, along the foot of the wold; beyond it, the browner peat, or deep fen; and among that dark velvet alder beds, long lines of reed-rond, emerald in spring and golden under the autumn sun; shining 'eas' or river-reaches; broad meres dotted with a million fowl, while the cattle waded along their edges after the rich sedge-grass, or wallowed in the mere through the summer's day. Here and there, too, upon the far horizon, rose a tall line of ashen trees, marking some island of firm rich soil. In some of them, as at Ramsey and Crowland, the huge ashes had disappeared before the axes of the monks; and a minster tower rose over the fen, and orchards, cornfields, pastures, with here and there a tree left standing for shade.

But the preacher in Kingsley was always at his side, pulling the poet's sleeve to remind him that such idylls have their shadows:

134

Overhead the arch of heaven spread more ample than elsewhere, as over the open sea; and that vastness gave, and still gives, such cloudlands, such sunrises, such sunsets, as can be seen nowhere else within these isles . . . that fair land, like all things on earth, had its darker aspect. The foul exhalations of autumn called up fever and ague, crippling and enervating, and tempting, almost compelling, to that wild and desperate drinking which was the Scandinavian's special sin. Dark and sad were those short autumn days, when all the distances were shut off, and the air choked with foul brown fog, and drenching rains from the eastern sea; and pleasant the bursting forth of the keen north-east wind, with all its whirling snowstorms. For though it sent men hurrying out into the storm, to drive the cattle in from the fen, and light the sheep out of the snow-wreaths, and now and then never to return, lost in mist and mire, in ice and snow; — yet all knew that after the snow would come the keen frost and bright sun and cloudless blue sky, and the fenman's

While the Fens have been largely drained and tamed since Hereward's day, some corners, such as Wicken Fen, can still suggest something of the mystery and hidden perils that confronted the besiegers of Ely.

yearly holiday when, work being impossible, all gave themselves up to play, and swarmed upon the ice on skates and sledges, to run races, township against township, or visit old friends full forty miles away; and met everywhere faces as bright and ruddy as their own, cheered by the keen wine of that dry and bracing frost.

Such was the fenland; hard, yet cheerful; rearing a race of hard and cheerful men. . . .

Fenland memories were in his mind when he wrote *Hereward* and the year following its appearance they were in full flood in a lecture he gave in Cambridge. Brenda Colloms tells us that he spoke with nostalgic affection of the Fens, and the passage she quotes contains some of the most evocative natural history prose of his time:

And yet the fancy may linger without blame, over the shining meres, the golden reed-beds, the countless water-fowl, the strange and gaudy insects, the wild nature, the mystery, the majesty — for mystery and majesty there were — which haunted the deep fens for many hundred years. Little thinks the Scotsman, whirled down by the Great Northern Railway from Peterborough to Huntingdon, what a grand place, even twenty years ago, was that Holme and Whittlesea, which is now but a black and unsightly steaming flat, from which the meres and reed-beds of the old world are gone, while the corn and roots of the new world have not as yet taken their place. But grand enough it was, that black ugly place, when backed by Caistor Hanglands and Holme Wood and the patches of the primeval forest; while dark green alders, and pale green reeds, stretched for miles round the broad lagoon. . . .

This is the voice of a lover of his country and its landscape sharing his passion with us in a vision of the Fens unsurpassed in its lyricism, a place where

the coot clanked, and the bittern boomed, and the sedge-bird, not content with its own sweet song, mocked the notes of all the birds around; while high overhead hung motionless, hawk beyond hawk, buzzard beyond buzzard, kite beyond kite, as far as eye could see. Far off, upon the silver mere, would rise a puff of smoke from a punt, invisible from its flatness and white paint. Then down the wind came the boom of the great stanchion gun; and after that sound, another sound, louder as it neared; a cry as of all the bells of Cambridge and all the hounds of Cottesmere; and overhead rushed and whirled the skein of terrified wild-fowl; screaming, piping, clacking, croaking — filling the air with the hoarse rattle of their wings, while clear above all sounded the wild whistle of the curlew and the trumpet notes of the great wild swan.

It is a powerful image made all the more poignant because it portrays a paradise lost forever. Conservationists will identify with this lament:

They are all gone now. No longer do the ruffs trample the sedge into a hard floor in their fighting rings, while the sober reeves stand round, admiring the tournament of their lovers, gay with ruffs and tippets, no two of them alike. Gone are the ruffs and reeves, spoonbills, bitterns, avocets; the very snipe, one hears, disdain to breed. Gone, too, not only from the Fens, but from the whole world, is that most exquisite of butterflies – *Lycaena dispar* – the great copper; and many a curious insect more.[9]

Kingsley the naturalist is, however, subservient to Kingsley the story-teller and the latter conjures up some graphic scenes, as when describing William's first attack upon the causeway at Aldreth:

At last the army was in motion, and Willingham field opposite was like a crawling ants' nest. Brigade after brigade moved down to the reed beds, and the assault began. And now advanced along the causeway, and along the bridge, a dark column of men, surmounted by glittering steel; knights in complete mail; footmen in leather coats and jerkins; at first orderly enough, each under the banner of his lord: but more and more mingled and crowded, as each hurried forward, eager for his selfish share of the inestimable treasures of Ely . . . men stumbled over each other, and fell off into the mire and water, calling vainly for help. . . . The front rank could not but rush on: for the pressure behind forced them forward, whether they would or not. In a moment they were wallowing waist deep; trampled on; disappearing under their struggling comrades, who disappeared in their turn. . . .

Here Kingsley is invoking the *De Gestis* account from which he also obtained the tale about Hereward slaying with his own hands his famous mare called Swallow 'so that no man of lower rank should boast that he had got Hereward's horse'. Kingsley's scene has Hereward escaping by boat with Swallow swimming along behind until 'Hereward turned, and bent over the side in the darkness. There was a strange gurgle, a splash and a swirl. . . . None spoke a word. The men were awe-stricken. There was something despairing and ill-omened in the deed. And yet there was a savage grandeur in it, which bound their savage hearts still closer to their chief. . . . And so mare Swallow's bones lie somewhere in the peat unto this day.'

The chief Victorian rival, perhaps the only one, to Kingsley's version of the saga of Hereward was the now forgotten *The Camp of Refuge* by Charles Macfarlane, which first appeared in 1844. Macfarlane produced an enormous number of books upon a variety of subjects – travel, historical works, 'stories to impart useful information', and treatises on political and social questions of the day. He died, in 1858, a poor pensioner of the Charterhouse. Out of all the 'voluminous, not luminous' works (as an unkind obituarist described them), of the industrious Scot, the only ones that have proved of any permanent worth are the *Civil and Military History of England*, which he contributed to Knight's *Pictorial History*, and three out of his novels, the Hereward book, and two similar historical stories, *A Legend of Reading Abbey*, set in the reign of Stephen, and *The Dutch in the Medway*, based on the diary of Pepys, which deals with the blockade of the Thames by the Dutch Admiral De Ruyter. Both were worthily and scrupulously researched but neither was quite so interesting as *The Camp of Refuge*.

This volume offers an altogether different picture of Hereward than that made familiar to us by Charles Kingsley. In his preface to the 1903 edition E.A. Baker asserts that this, not Kingsley's, is the true picture that stays closer to authentic history. Baker makes the surprising claim that 'Macfarlane takes no great liberties with the scant records that are extant; he invents no story, and but few characters. He simply gives us an amplified version of the authenticated facts, in the simplest language, with little heightening or romantic colouring, and no comment whatever. But his unpretentious chronicle carries a conviction that Kingsley's more imaginative story never attains. We can hardly persuade ourselves that we are not reading history, true and unadorned. Kingsley's Hereward is a memorable creation; Macfarlane's is the Hereward we must believe in.'

Macfarlane's book is certainly unpretentious, even pedestrian, but in his way Macfarlane is just as partial as Kingsley. He does omit much of the romantic decoration: what Baker calls the gathering in from miscellaneous sources of all the legends that have accumulated round 'this champion of a lost cause'. Instead, Macfarlane merely expands history and, since he does not bring Hereward upon the scene until 1070, he makes little attempt at character analysis, being content to allow the words of minor characters to fill in the details of Hereward's early life.

Thus out goes that whole Odyssey of romantic adventures and illustrious pedigree. No links are claimed with Earl Leofric of Mercia (and none, for that matter, with the Wake family); no exile is endured and therefore no encounter with a bear; no rescue of the Princess of Cornwall; no marriage with Torfrida, and indeed no Torfrida; and no visits in disguise to the enemy camp. Even so, Macfarlane's 'factual' Hereward is an altogether nobler creature and less believable. No doomed hero this, his actions are not stained by any dubious motives. So he does not lead the Danes to Peterborough and help them to plunder the Golden Borough. Instead

Macfarlane favours J.H. Round's interpretation that Hereward carried the treasures to Ely to put them beyond the reach of the rapacious Turold and that the misguided monks of Ely, without his knowledge and in spite of his intention to guard the church's property until the Saxons were restored, foolishly used the riches to bribe the treacherous Danes.

Charles Macfarlane's 'amplification' of history opens up other avenues for speculation. It enables him to place Hereward in the van of Harold's victorious army at Stamford Bridge and alongside his royal master on the journey south so that at the battle of Hastings 'his battle-axe was seen close by the battle-axes of Harold and the king's two loyal and brave brothers, Gurth and Leofwin, dealing terrible blows and cutting the steel caps and coats of mail of the Normans like chaff.' Even more remarkable, his Hereward, 'though but a stripling', inspired the townsfolk of Dover to the diplomatic incident of 1051 which led to the rift between King Edward and Earl Godwin. If our deduction of Hereward's birthdate at around 1037 is accurate, he would have been a fourteen-year-old. But at least

Crowland Abbey, Lincolnshire, the supposed last resting place of Hereward.

such a precocious involvement in the Dover adventure would explain his early identification as a troublemaker and subsequent banishment by Edward the Confessor.

Since Macfarlane has severed Hereward's link with the House of Mercia his unquestioning loyalty to Harold becomes more plausible, and it is not astonishing to find him fighting with Harold on his Welsh campaigns against Gruffydd. One argument in favour of Macfarlane's version is that it better explains how Hereward became the leader of the Ely resistance despite the presence there of apparently more legitimate candidates. A military reputation built on achievements at Stamford Bridge and Hastings would surely have weighed more heavily than tales of mercenary deeds in far-off lands across the sea.

And, finally, Macfarlane remains true to *De Gestis* in providing Hereward with a happy ending, living in comfort and peace: 'Both he and the Lady Alftrude [Ælfthryth] reached a patriarchal age, and they left a patriarchal stock behind them. They were buried with honour in Crowland Abbey, which by this time had become a holier and better governed house than it had ever been before.'

CHAPTER NINE

A Forgotten Hero?

It was on one of those bold-as-brass days of early spring when the sunshine sparkles and the wind has rediscovered a milder southerly quadrant that I made the first of many trips to the Fens in search of Hereward. To stand at the likely scenes of battle and betrayal and attempt to imagine the thoughts and feelings of the doomed brotherhood in the Camp of Refuge was a fanciful impulse but one that was impossible to resist, even though the surroundings have changed their appearance as if to draw a curtain across the stage of history and so erase the bloody events of 1071. Time has redrawn the contour map so that we may be seeing the landscape at the Roman level again, an experience that at York, for example, can only be gained by a long descent to the Minster's crypt.

If, as A.K. Astbury maintains,[1] the courses of long-forgotten rivers are remembered only by stripes of lighter soil crossing the peaty plain,[2] such opaque clues may also indicate where the Normans tried to unlock the Ely defence by boat and where they were ambushed by Hereward's men.

The evidence is elusive, tantalizing and wholly in keeping with the mood of the landscape. For centuries the Fens were regarded with superstitious fear as a province of magic and mystery and as Christianity supplanted paganism they retained this special quality. The area in fact became a blessed place – witness the number of saintly men and women revered there in the Middle Ages. In the century before Hereward the Abbé Floriancensus, describing the Fens, spoke of huge lakes, some 2 or 3 miles wide, and the islands upon which holy men, some to be canonized, established recluse cells.

The last of these great inland lakes was Whittlesey Mere,[3] now drained, its bed marked to the north, says Astbury, by Black Ham and north-western Cut, and to the south by an imaginary line from Holme Lode Farm to Old Decoy Farm. It was still shown on nineteenth-century maps of the Peterborough district. The mere, 2½ miles long by 1¾ wide, was for centuries a playground for yachtsmen, anglers and skaters. If one writer is to be believed, some combined two activities in winter when the pike were 'run down' by skaters, who followed them for miles until the fish were exhausted. Then the ice was broken and the pike netted.

That great plain stretching from the Wash towards the Midland shires and down to East Anglia was inundated after the fourth century as the Roman sea walls fell into decay and since then this has been a watercolour landscape. The sea invasion was aggravated as rivers such as the Welland, Nene and Great Ouse, meandering from the uplands, overflowed their banks and the rhythm of rivalry between sea and river has persisted. Despite being banked and dyked, dredged and diverted, half-tamed by canals and pumping stations, the water sprites and demons remain omnipresent in shaping the Fens and perhaps also those who have lived and worked there.

Here in fog-bound winter and mosquito-ridden summer was incubated the feared Fen ague, akin to malaria, whose fevered victims suffered thirst and painful, shaking limbs. Fenmen, seeking escape from the damp and pestilence became, it is said, renowned topers (Kingsley blames the drinking partly on the climate and partly as a dark inheritance from the Scandinavian invaders) and some took opium as a palliative. Yet when the great seventeenth-century drainage plans, masterminded by the Dutch engineer Cornelius Vermuyden, were put into effect they met fierce opposition from the 'Fen Tigers', the eel-trappers, hunters and men of the marshes, who feared that their livelihoods would drain away with the waters and the mosquitoes.

Such days have passed. Tree felling and the reclamation of waterlogged land have, on the surface at least, transformed those misty lakes and marshes into a wide landscape of rich ploughland and vast skies – the 'Land of the Three-quarter Sky' under whose benign dome are cultivated vast acres of cereal and root crops. Yet a sense of impermanence is pervasive, as if the land that was once a seabed is awaiting its inevitable annexation by the ocean. Environmentalists, concerned about global warming and rising sea levels, have produced a worst-case scenario for the middle of the next century when they say a 5 metre rise in ocean levels would see the Fens once again covered by a North Sea whose waves would then break upon the beach at Cambridge.

While the sea is rising, land levels are falling and the feared combination of mountainous seas inflated by tides and severe storms becomes ever more menacing. Such apprehensions are part of local lore and they have helped to breed a characteristic fenland independence and self-reliance. An official of the National Farmers' Union tells a national newspaper, 'You have to remember this has always been a very isolated part of England. For centuries Ely was an island of monks and reed-cutters and even today that feeling of being out on a limb persists.' In the peat this is manifest. There are no villages, only isolated dwellings, perhaps clinging to a pocket of clay or silt. Communities of any size were inevitably, and prudently, restricted to the islands of firmer ground. Astbury lists other significant rarities such as graveyards, playing fields, airports, churches and factories.

With the wastage of the soil, he says, graves would in time give up their dead

The edge of Wicken Fen – a sketch of 1882 by R. Farrer showing reeds being gathered.

and bowling greens or football pitches would wrinkle up with the shrinkage, their surfaces destroyed by cracks and depressions. Airfield runways, unless given costly foundations, would collapse under the pounding of aircraft landing and taking off and large buildings would also require expensive foundations. 'I know of only five churches in the peat fens not built on islands, and not one is on peat,' writes Astbury. 'The church at Little Ouse is on a vein of gravel which also underlies Church Farm and then peters out a short distance to the east. It is in effect on an island, although an island which has never been so recognised.'

More curious, perhaps, is Astbury's assertion that there are no springs in the peat. Most wells marked on large-scale maps, he alleges, are nothing more than sunken rainwater tanks filled by the piped run off from a house roof and all mains water comes from the higher ground.

Thus, while the landscape has altered, man's capacity to disfigure it has been curbed. With a little imagination it is still possible, at Aldreth for example, to look towards Ely and visualize, instead of today's vale of farmland, the lagoons and reed beds that might have confronted the Conqueror himself as he considered the risky task of uprooting that troublesome Saxon briar patch.

Approaching Aldreth it is necessary first to reach Haddenham, poised 120 feet above sea level, and at once the locale's military significance becomes evident. After

The ring of Belsar's Hill, site of an ancient fortification, can be seen clearly from the air. The track running through it leads *(left)* to the Aldreth causeway.

miles of typical level fenland the horizon suddenly rises like some recumbent animal getting lazily to its feet. It comes as a growing shock to realize that Haddenham is on a *hill*, a veritable mountain in these parts, and as you leave Earith and ascend the A1123 it is apparent that the hill is, in fact, part of that greensand ridge that disappears north of ancient Belsar's Hill – marked as a fort near Willingham on Ordnance Survey maps – leaving a gap through which flows the Old West River Ouse.

The ridge rises again at Aldreth, runs north-east towards Haddenham before turning east to Wilburton and Stretham and then northwards again to Ely, providing that passageway of high ground above the deepest marshes that a besieger would seek. The landscape remains a persuasive witness, for between the river and Aldreth is the suggested site of William's causeway and it makes sound military sense for him to have chosen it.

E.A. Freeman walked the country between Cambridge and Ely in the summer of 1870 with Professor C.C. Babington, a Victorian antiquary, after which he came to his conclusion that no part of Britain could be more easily defended. The main approach, he says, was 'at a point called Aldreth, a corruption of the name of the patron saint Æthelthryth, where the ancient course of the Ouse, now shallow indeed, is crossed by a causeway and bridge. . . . In the *Gesta Herwardi* the place is called Abrehede . . . in the Ely History it is Alrehethe. . . . The bridge, when I was there, looked very much as if it had been broken down by Hereward and not mended since.'

In Freeman's sketch-map the Aldreth causeway extends an eleventh-century route from Camboritum (Cambridge) past Haddenham to connect with another 'Soham' causeway that stretched eastwards below Witchford to Ely. In his book, Trevor Bevis shows Aldreth causeway as a logical link between a bridle way at Belsar's Hill and Aldreth village just north of the Old West River. He cites Bentham, writing about the Normans' forward position, stating that 'The camp that was occupied by the Conqueror's army when he besieged the Isle of Ely is still visible at the south end of Aldrey Causeway within the manor of Wiveingham (Willingham) and is corruptly called Belsar's Hills.'

There is much to recommend Bevis's suggestion that William's forces would have advanced from Cambridge, where a castle had been erected, along a route that passed by Impington and Histon on its way to Cottenham where the materials of stones, timber and hides for laying down a causeway would have been assembled. A tributary stream at Cottenham runs north to the Old West River and could have offered the means of transporting heavy loads by boat. Having established a bridgehead at Aldreth, the Normans, following the Bevis map, would have pressed on to Haddenham on the high ground, following today's minor road, and then swung right along the ridge top to Stretham, negotiating another depression near Thetford to gain entry into the Isle of Ely itself.

Standing on Aldreth hill and recalling Astbury's comment about bodies being preserved in death as in life by the iron tannate waters of the peat, I wondered whether below me under the ploughland lay buried the bones of the men who fought to gain entry into Hereward's domain. A cuckoo flew overhead, its bell-like song mocking such futile speculation. And speculation it must remain until it is considered feasible or worthwhile to arrange an organized dig.

The preservative qualities of peat might encourage the hope that at some future date the Fens could yield much of interest to the archaeologist. Around Ely, however, the situation is less promising. Because of the extensive drainage over the centuries the peat itself is retreating. Newly drained peat, it is said, sinks by the height of a man in the life of a man and, unprotected by water, peat dries out, decomposes and even without the help of the abrasive spring winds – 'the Fen blow' – eventually disappears.

A depreciation rate of an inch a year is supported by the evidence of Holmes Fen Post on the edge of what was Whittlesey. This iron pillar from the Great Exhibition was driven into the peat in 1851, its base resting on the hard clay bottom and its top level with the peat surface. Today its top stands more than 13

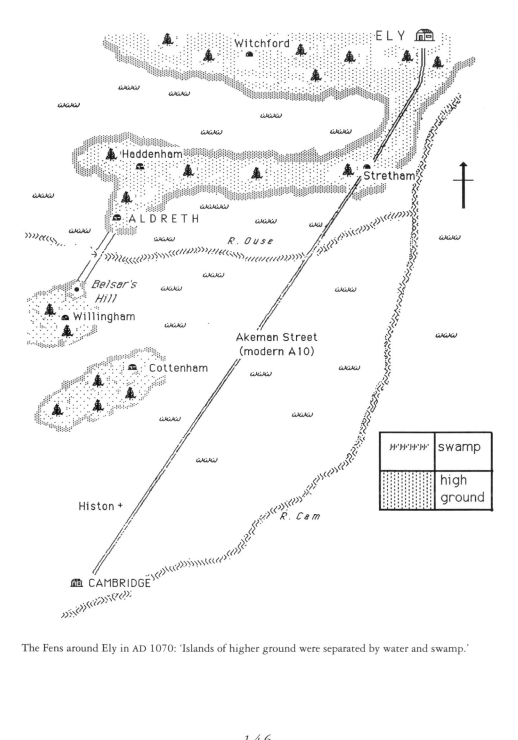

The Fens around Ely in AD 1070: 'Islands of higher ground were separated by water and swamp.'

feet above ground, which suggests an annual loss of 1.09 inches and you can feel the ground below 'give' underfoot. Much of the Fens is therefore sinking except where the peat is by chance preserved beneath railway embankments or alongside rivers that may flood and offer the peat a renewal of life.

Astbury is an entertaining interpreter of the landscape language that can tell us more of this absorbing story. Obvious clues for the motorist are those curious hump-backed (known locally as 'cock-up') bridges that seem such oddities in a flat landscape. Astbury explains them by describing how the slow sinking of all road levels in the peat fens causes a sharp drop on either side of the bridges which rest on piles of up to 40 feet driven straight down on to the firmer clay floor. The load-bearing qualities of peat are about a quarter those of other soils and, where it was not possible to sink piles or build on concrete rafts that float on the peat surface, houses may exhibit tell-tale signs of instability. Settlement causes dangerous leaning and doors and windows become lozenge-shaped. Where the brick centre chimney happens to be on piles the outer walls sink at a greater rate and the house, in Astbury's phrase, tends to 'hang about the chimney'. If surrounding soil has

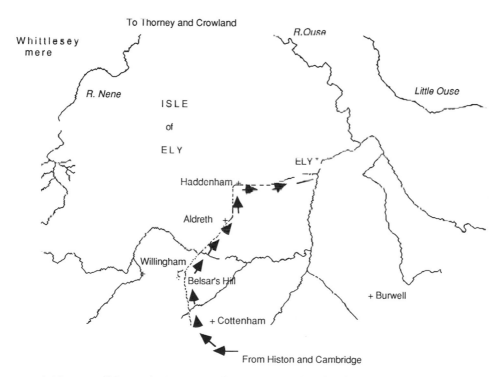

Probable route of Norman besiegers into Ely via Belsar's Hill and Aldreth causeway.

The 13 ft post at Holmes Fen, near Ramsey. Its height bears witness to the land shrinkage since it was sunk up to its top in 1851.

sunk houses can seem taller than intended and their front door steps, of necessity, may have been lengthened, and in some cases cellars have become ground-floor rooms.

In such a shifting environment it may well be that any archaeological treasures have already surfaced down the centuries and been lost for ever. The Fens contrast sharply with some other wild places such as the New Forest where even the treeline and deer paths have scarcely altered in a thousand years so that a modern investigator was able with confidence to identify the very spot from which an assassin launched the arrow that killed William II on 2 August 1100.[4]

Even so, the ephemeral fenland landscape is not entirely without encouragement for the archaeologist. Alison Taylor, Cambridgeshire's County Archaeologist, tells me that while there are no specific sites or finds that can be related to Hereward, she favours the view that William used Belsar's Hill as a base camp for his assault on Ely and she kindly provided a computer print-out of the discoveries of 'Late Saxon weapons' in the area. These are many and varied (see Appendix A), but include only one specifically from Aldreth. This was a fragmentary iron sword, minus the hilt, found in the Old West River a short distance downstream from Aldreth High Bridge. Old river beds would provide a more permanent resting place for such artefacts.

Without the hilt accurate dating becomes difficult but the blade's broad central 'blood groove' makes the Viking or early medieval period seem likely. Other finds closer to Ely have been made, notably those of five tenth- or eleventh-century spearheads and an axe-head discovered in the Cam about seventy years ago. The archaeologists' view is that probably all these came from Braham dock on the city's south approach nearer Stuntney, another suggested location for William's causeway. Stuntney, 2 miles from Ely, would have been a logical choice from a military view and the nearby 'Alderforth' farm has been offered by some as further proof, being a corruption of Aldreth.

Professor Gordon, the Wake historian, refers to an 'Alderbrook' farm on his sketch map which is shown between Braham dock and Braham farm where an earthwork has, not surprisingly, been dubbed 'Hereward's fort'. Freeman's view that Aldreth to the west was the location for the Normans' causeway followed the early chroniclers' version in the twelfth-century *Liber Eliensis* and *De Gestis Herwardi* which, of course, included the handed-down testimonies of people who took part in the siege. *De Gestis* mentions a causeway of 4 furlongs (half a mile) which would appear to be more realistic than Florence's 2 mile construction.

For these reasons we must favour Aldreth as the most likely site for the final confrontation between the Saxon beseiged and their Norman attackers, but there may have been, in fact, no less than three possible access points. Another westward passage at Earith was certainly used in later times, although the distance of 10 miles from Ely seems to rule this choice out. A causeway at Stuntney would have enabled the monks to reach their great grange there, as H.C. Darby has pointed out.[5] Horses drawing wainloads of provisions and material would have required much firmer footing.

Some of the Ely chronicles appear to suggest that the Aldreth causeway was not laid down until the twelfth century but this could well refer to extensive rebuilding that was carried out during the reign of Stephen. Causeways, like bridges, were costly to maintain and failure to do so led to angry exchanges. Darby cites the example of one bishop of Ely who so neglected the upkeep of the Aldreth causeway that it was out of commission for sixteen years. He then had the gall to establish a ferry at which 'he took toll of a half penny from every horseman and a farthing from every foot-passenger, his receipts being so large that he sometimes let the ferry at farm for as much as 20s. a year'.

Wherever the Ely defenders made their last stand it is reasonable to suppose that the final assault came from more than one direction and many such a last-ditch defiance may have occurred. If the accounts of the siege are to be believed it would seem that hundreds of attackers and their armour and weapons could have been engulfed by the fenland mire and never recovered so a quantity of such material may still await discovery near the site of the causeways at Aldreth and Stuntney and elsewhere.

Trevor Bevis, the
Fenland historian.

The documented finds would be only a fraction of what must have lain buried following the prolonged conflict. Trevor Bevis told me an intriguing tale of an encounter with a fen roder who claimed to have found over the years a quantity of armour and weapons in the ditches between Reach and Upwell. Part of his job was to maintain the ditches in good order and he would have been in an ideal position to make such discoveries. However, he was at first strangely reluctant to show Bevis his hoard which he kept locked in a garden shed but eventually agreed to fetch a few samples. This he did and emptied a sack on to the kitchen table. As the contents spilled out Bevis stared in amazement at a motley collection of Roman, Saxon and Norman spears, swords, axes and shield fragments such as he had never seen before or since.

Alas, the roder could not be persuaded to pass on his trophies to a museum nor was he shaken from his determination that after his death his sons would return the contents of the shed to the surrounding ditches and fields, there to await rediscovery at some future date. If the roder was not romancing his hoard might go some way to illuminating the Hereward legend but, of course, he had not recorded the precise location of his finds. After such battles captured weapons, especially if damaged, could have been dumped or buried near the scene of victory, although it is arguable that they may just as likely have been regarded as booty that would fetch a price when times were hard.

Today, visitors seeking more tangible clues to Hereward are likely to be disappointed. Even at Bourne, his ancestral home, one finds little awareness of him. The library assistant was polite but possessed only vague knowledge of his fame and knew nothing of the nearby 'Morkery' woods whose name, up until the last century at least, confirmed a link with Earl Morcar. Even the proposed Bourne heritage museum had no plans to celebrate the district's most famous inhabitant, although a special room was to be devoted to a twentieth-century hero, Raymond Mays, creator of the BRM racing car.

Northwards along the road to Folkingham, where Gilbert de Gand had his castle, stands a Robin Hood inn. It is unlikely that the Hereward connection was considered when the inn received its name. Bourne was also the birthplace of William Cecil, the Elizabethan statesman, but he has suffered similar neglect. Although travel posters speak of this as 'Hereward Country', in the official tourist information leaflet on South Lincolnshire's famous people Cecil rates twenty-four lines to Hereward's nineteen. They concede pride of place to Mays, Lady Thatcher and England's fattest man, the 52 stone Daniel Lambert, yet all these are eclipsed by a 32-line eulogy for Charles Frederick Worth, a nineteenth-century dressmaker to Empress Eugenie of France.

Even Ely seems to have forgotten its Saxon defender, preferring instead an 'Oliver Cromwell' House to accommodate a tourist office. The American couple ahead of me, uninterested in Cromwell, expressed surprise at the lack of Hereward memorabilia and wondered why he had never received the ultimate accolade and been made the subject of a Hollywood film. All is not silence, however. A local radio station bears the name of Hereward and at Ely Museum a semi-permanent display explores the phenomenon of Hereward by looking at how he has been represented in different eras and by various media. Finally, the Countryside Commission has a 43 mile Hereward Way long-distance footpath (Fenland section) from Peterborough to Ely providing 'a unique walking experience . . . in some of the lowest land in England'.

So the search for Hereward continues. It started with some preconceived ideas that gradually began to change. The gilded warrior-hero of *De Gestis* dissolved into the mists of legend as pieces of the puzzle came together momentarily, making sense briefly only to crumble away again. That Hereward was a fighting man and an exceptional military commander seems beyond dispute. He was, however, neither superhuman nor supernatural. He had his human frailties that moved even his most famous apologist, Charles Kingsley, to moralistic censure while at the same time helping to make him more real.

We can argue about what it was that drove his parents to seek his banishment and to what extent he was involved in the political manoeuvring of the Godwins and the Conqueror. His links with Flanders and such figures as Gilbert de Ghent

151

and Baldwin seem too oft repeated in so many accounts to be merely coincidental.

What was the true explanation of his apparent faithlessness to Torfrida and why did he not return to defend his native land in 1066? Was his association with William's father-in-law close enough to be uncomfortable, even incriminating? Students may debate such questions endlessly, but what remains is the realization that in Hereward the new nation of England found its first authentic hero, the one man who seems to have defied the Conqueror and who has become enshrined through the Robin Hood legendary cycle as the epitome of Saxon independence. 'If there had been three more such men the Normans would never have conquered Saxon England' is the accolade that rings down the years and has been echoed ever since from the old chroniclers to men as disparate as Freeman, Stenton and Kingsley. If nothing else, Hereward is a worthy icon to represent the idea of freedom and resistance against oppression.

Late Saxon Weapons from the Ely Area

This listing of archaeological finds, with comments, recorded at the Cambridgeshire County Council archaeological department is of 'late Saxon weapons' discovered in the area covered by the events of the battle for Ely, 1070–1.

Date	Place	Description
1985	Chippenham	Spear. Other finds include an Anglo-Saxon spearhead.
1984	Soham High St	Spear, iron. Anglo-Saxon socketed spearhead with leaf-shaped blade.
1985	Aldreth	Sword, iron. A fragmentary iron sword, lacking the hilt, was found in the Old West River, a short distance downstream from Aldreth High Bridge. Without the hilt accurate dating is impossible but the broad central 'blood groove' of the blade suggests a date in the Viking or early medieval periods.
1985	Ely	A throwing axe of 'fransisca' type is displayed in a tea shop in Ely. Found on Back Hill.
1979	Soham	Spear. Anglo-Saxon spear found at Angle Farm.
1968	Soham	Spearhead, Anglo-Saxon, found by Mr Ralph Peacock in 1968. Stray find.
1924	Ely	Five spearheads and an axe head of tenth- or eleventh-century date were found 'in the River Cam' about 1924. At least one spearhead and probably all the finds, were found at Braham Dock. It is unlikely that these objects were lost accidentally and the presence of these finds, together with similar finds at Dimock's Cote, Wicken and Quanea support the view that this is the place where William I finally defeated Hereward in 1070 (*sic*) and captured Ely. Five good examples, one of which is an unusually fine weapon. The form is evidently based upon the Carolingian 'Knebellanz', but the silver ornamentation on the socket seems to be of British workmanship. Dr Jan Petersen of Stavanger suggested a date of 900. The damascening of the blade is found on a wide range of forms.

1932	Ely, Roller's Lode	Axe, spearhead, scramasax, pottery. A number of weapons of eleventh-century date were found in Roller's Lode, Quanea, about 1932. The weapons are an axe, a spearhead and a small scramasax, all much damaged. It is conjectured that the weapons may be connected with 'the ravaging of the "wild fens" by the Danes . . . in AD 1010', or that they were lost in William the Conqueror's campaign against Hereward in 1070. The site was excavated the following year and a 'remarkable pot' with stamped ornamentation and sagging base was found. Its date is uncertain; the paste is late Anglo-Saxon, its ornamentation Merovingian and its base Mediterranean in origin. 'Perhaps it should be placed in the last century of Anglo-Saxon freedom.' A group of weapons (found in 1930) was discovered at one of the points where the dyke cuts into the bed of an old river. 'The axe belongs to Petersen's type L (Jan Petersen: *De Norske Vikingsherd*).'
1932	Ely, Roller's Lode	Pottery, animal bone, worked wood (stake), water management system. 'The old river bed had been at some period obstructed by a line of stakes driven into its bed at intervals of slightly over 2ft apart . . . in an attempt to block the passage; it might even be suggested that they had been obtained in a hurry, for one was a piece of squared timber with a mortise hole in it evidently dragged from some building. Lying beside one of these piles was a remarkable pot . . . all these things may be of 11th-century date; and in this connection it should not be forgotten that William I is said to have blocked the river in his investment of the Isle of Ely.'
1971	Stetchworth/ Woodditton	Spear. An Anglo-Saxon spearhead was found in a rabbit hole in the inner edge of the ditch of the Devil's Dyke; Nigel Wheeler, 1971.
1962	Soham	Spearhead. Anglo-Saxon spearhead found in Dawn (Down?) field, 1962.
1938	Ely	Spearhead. Found in the river 'near Ely'. It has a very wide socket and was probably a horseman's lance-head. The edges of the blade are welded to the body of the weapon with a ribband of damascening such as is probably often present in weapons of the tenth and eleventh centuries but is hidden by rust.
1938	Wicken	Anglo-Saxon scramasax, knife, skeleton, from the vicinity of Wicken Fen. With damascening (different pattern on either side of blade) instead of brass inlay. Found together with a small knife on a skeleton (probably but not certainly towards the Upware side of Wicken Fen).
1938	Sutton	Burial, spear. Stray find. Burial of a man with Anglo-Saxon spear found on the high ground above the Fen between Sutton and Earith. No precise location.
1990	Haddenham	Emergency excavations took place in December 1989, after the discovery of burials during preparation for an extension to the car park of the Three Kings public house. There was a double burial – the male

accompanied by a spear, knife, shield boss and buckle (iron), the female by 27 amber and 7 glass and silver beads, a bronze brooch, tweezers and a spindle whorl. A larger area was cleared but only fragments of human remains were noted (representing nine identifiable individuals).

pre-1940 Wicken Spearhead, scramasax, nails, axe found in dredging of River Cam at Dimock's Cote. Late Viking spearhead (*c.* 1000), scramasax (*c.* 800), other spearheads, clunch-nails etc. of Viking type. Iron axehead found at Dimock's Cote at time of construction of new bridge. Spearhead and scramasax also found at same spot at different times. All finds appear to be contemporary and may have been lost in an incident in the Viking wars.

Family Matters: The Genealogical Argument

About the parentage and standing of Hereward the *De Gestis Herwardi Saxonis* is unequivocal: 'Of the nations of the English many very mighty men are recorded, and Hereward the Outlaw is esteemed most distinguished and a famous Knight. . . . His father was Leofric of Bourne, grandson of Earl Radulf surnamed Scabre (Scalre); his mother was Aediva, great-great-grand-daughter of Duke Oslac, most nobly descended by both parents.'

Many have tended to dismiss this genealogy as legend and one can sympathize with the frustration behind E.A. Freeman's comment, 'At this moment we hear for the first time of one whose mythical fame outshines all the names of his generation, and of whom the few historical notices make us wish that details could be filled in from other sources than legend.'

To find himself suddenly faced by this 'renowned but shadowy' figure, who could not be satisfactorily authenticated, was no doubt irksome for someone engaged in mapping the grand panorama of the Norman Conquest and yet, as a historian of detail as well as landscape, he could not ignore Hereward or, at best sweep him neatly into a footnote as others have done. 'With no name', writes Freeman, 'has fiction been more busy. One tale, the wildest of all, has made the famous outlaw the son of the great Earl Leofric. Romancers probably did not stop to think that this was to make him a brother of Ælfgar, an uncle of Eadwine and Morkere, an uncle by marriage of King Gruffydd and of King Harold. In truth, nothing whatever is known of his parentage; there is no more evidence for making him the son of an unknown Leofric of Bourne than there is for making him a son of the renowned Earl of the Mercians.'

Freeman acknowledges that both the voice of legend and the witness of the Domesday Book agree in connecting Hereward with Lincolnshire while the survey also has him as a landowner in Warwickshire and preserves another fact with which the legendary versions of his life have been especially busy. This concerns the evidence that before his fenland exploits he had fled the country, although the date and cause of this flight and whether he had incurred the wrath of King Edward or Harold is uncertain.

Freeman is, however, a reluctant sceptic and cannot resist this muted panegyric: 'We know enough of Hereward to make us earnestly long to know more. There is no doubt that he defended the last shelter of English freedom against the might of William. His heart failed him not when the hearts of the noblest of the land quaked within them. Our most patriotic Latin annalist (Florence) adorns his name with the standing epithet with which he adorns the name of Harold (*Herewardus vir strenuissimus, strenuus Dux Haroldus*), and our native Chronicler records his deeds in words which seem borrowed from the earlier record of the deeds of Alfred.'

Professor Freeman's decent interment of the Saxon hero with at least partial military honours remained largely unchallenged for twenty-five years until the publication of a volume of history in 1896 by the London publishers Elliot Stock of Paternoster Row. This was a book, bursting with research and here and there glowing with indignation, called *Hereward; The Saxon Patriot*. To describe it as an ambitious volume would be something of an understatement since it is self-styled *A History of his {Hereward's} Life and Character, with a Record of his Ancestors and Descendants, AD 445 to AD 1896*. It claimed that, although his pedigree was naturally incomplete, it was by no means impossible to trace an outline of the movements and vicissitudes of the family of Hereward from a very early period.

The reference to descendants gives a clue to part of the book's *raison d'être* since it was written by Lieut.-General Thomas Netherton Harward, who confessed that his attempt to determine which families have a right to trace their descent from Hereward was not without some personal interest 'as we ourselves claim him as our illustrious ancestor'.

The General clearly resented pretenders to this dynasty, especially 'some of the noble lords who desire to trace their ancestry to the great Saxon patriot . . . [and] . . . evidently imagine that he was a spontaneous creation'. Commencing with a confident etymological analysis of the name Hereward,[1] General Harward assured his readers that the name represented a military officer, holding large and important functions in war, and corresponding rank and position. He found the spelling proof that the word came straight from Germany without touch from Dane or Jute and had no difficulty in carrying speculation back to a remote period when a Harvard may have come with a band of Northmen to the Low Countries, and so into Germany. He reminds us of the Norse saga which refers to the mythical hero Thorvard and that the name is of Gothic origin and of great antiquity. We may boggle at his next speculative leap when he describes Chariovalda or Harivaldi, the Batavian prince mentioned by Tacitus, as the oldest and most famous of the family mentioned in history. Having gone this far, why stop? Indeed, he points out that Har, or Haro, was an ancient name of Woden and that the Norman cry for justice, 'Haro', still used in the Channel Islands, is probably an appeal to an old Celtic god.

A logical conclusion to the General's argument was to elevate Hereward to Valhalla,[2] but coming closer to his own time he returns to safer ground when discussing a link between Hereward and Heornvard, a Saxon term for a sword guardian:

> The sword has always been held to be an emblem of justice, as well as the scales. At Queen Victoria's coronation the Duke of Wellington, carrying the sword, fulfilled the ancient Saxon office of Heornvard, or Hereward, the warden of the sword. The rank of Heretoga was sometimes accorded to a Saxon earl, or earldorman, corresponding to *herzog* in German, finally translated *dux* in Latin, *duke* in English. It had a political and territorial signification. The Hereward, or sword-guardian, may have been an officer in charge of Woden's Wagon, which always accompanied a Teutonic army, with judicial as well as military functions.'[3]

General Harward refused to be fettered by facts for long and was soon speeding off again after another alluring hare, conjecturing that Hereward may, however, have been descended from Ariovistus, the warlike chief of the Suevi, who around 56 BC were among the most formidable of the barbarian tribes of northern Europe.[4] The General recognizes many shared character traits such as fearlessness, skill in arms, and contempt for his enemy and conjectures that Ariovistus might be translated into Hereward via Herefurst.

The temptation to link Hereward with a character such as Ariovistus was clearly irresistible and the General relates how the latter rejected a summons to attend Caesar, suggesting that the representative of imperial Rome should attend him instead. A resourceful and skilful soldier, just as

Hereward, he not only created panic in Caesar's army, but communicated with leading patricians at Rome. He then told Caesar that, although his death was desired at Rome, he would be his friend, and be responsible for the good government of Gaul. Although eventually defeated by Caesar, Ariovistus was indeed a worthy ancestor for Hereward. For the General, the logical outcome of his deductions meant that the alleged confrontation and dialogue between local hero and imperial conqueror was satisfyingly repeated a thousand years later by Hereward and the Norman Duke William.

While parallels in the lives of Hereward and Ariovistus may be detected, such apparently fanciful attempts to enrich the Hereward pedigree do not assist the General's contention that Hereward was, indeed, the son of Leofric, Earl of Mercia, and therefore related to the noblest in the land. His leadership of the last Saxon resistance to William the Conqueror would thus have been endorsed by rank and position and not merely prowess.

General Harward was not readily diverted from his habit of defying historical convention and scepticism. His diligence in hunting down Hereward's ancestors throws on the subject a great deal of light, not all of which need be artificial though unfortunately he fails to back his arguments with sources. Leaving mythological speculation behind, he focuses on the arrival [possibly in the fifth century], of a Saxon leader named Hereward who landed in England at the old Roman port near Pevensey, and with his followers marched through the forest of Andredes-weald, until he arrived on the northern slope of the Surrey hills. There he established his first settlement, known as Herewardesleag, and afterwards as Harwardsley, abbreviated to Horley, now a town of 21,000 inhabitants in Surrey.

Horley evidently started life ambitiously since Saxon settlements known as tithings had to number no less than ten families, and Horley comprised a hundred, so it is not unfair to assume that a like number of families would have accompanied their chief to England and settled there. The position was on the route to London but as years passed its proximity to the coast and marauding sea-rovers persuaded such settlers in Britain to spread inland. Harward identifies a second settlement by a clan of the same name being formed in Oxfordshire on the borders of Warwickshire, 16 miles south-west of Weedon, and mentions further movements by them in this and neighbouring counties.

Harward states that in the days of Edward the Confessor Hereward held lands at Merstone, Marston Jabbet in Warwickshire, and Barnard and Ladbroke in the same county, besides a knight's fee at Evenlode, in Worcestershire (his estates in Lincolnshire are attested by the Domesday Book itself). The position was strategically well chosen, being near the Watling Street but a few miles off the direct road. It does not appear ever to have become a place of as much note as the Surrey settlement, but it established the family in Mercia, in which province 'they at once took an influential part, until they occupied the almost regal position of earls. As a matter of fact, the chief of the party led by Hereward had, according to Teutonic usage, held the authority and power of an under-king over his own tribe.'

On the Ordnance Survey map one can draw a straight line to connect Ladbroke and Barnard Gate and there is a certain point where the line runs directly down the main street at the Warwickshire Horley. If one accepts General Harward's theory, this thrusting and acquisitive Hereward family or clan would have conformed to the traditions of aristocratic Teutonic society in which the heads of clans or tribes chose land for their families and followers to occupy and pass on to their descendants as a freehold.

Anglo-Saxon landowners were by now firmly wedded to the soil and from this they developed the territorial boundaries' system which divided England into shires and hundreds for the purpose of administration and justice and which in time, with the additional establishment of ecclesiastical authority, led to the development of counties and parishes. By 1066 many of today's villages already existed, in the south and Midlands especially, and cultivation was boosted by the growth of monasteries particularly in the fenlands around Ely. The landowner owed allegiance to the chief under whom he had arrived in Britain, and it was logical for that chieftain to rule as king of his region.

While the focus of history directs our attention to the successive waves of immigrants, usually uninvited, who descended on Britain's shores from Scandinavia and northern Europe, it remains true that a substantial proportion of the population must have been of the old stock. Indeed, some writers suggest that remnants of the original Britons still lingered in the Fens at the time of Hereward and later.

The nineteenth-century antiquarian Thomas Wright[5] believed that the old Roman and mixed population of the towns still occupied their former houses under the Saxon lord but that the Saxons themselves were loath to occupy the Roman houses, preferring to build abodes for themselves of timber, thatch and plaster. Archaeological research supports his description of a typical Saxon settlement, such as may have been formed by the Hereward clan, grouped for defence around a fortified mound established on the nearest hill.

Thatched dwellings of timber and plaster, or wattle and daub, would be lined with animal skins and furs, their floors carpeted with rushes. Freemen, employing serf labour, worked the land and bargained with their neighbours for wool, homespun, or cattle, corn, or cheese. Barter was common although a mixed currency in Roman, British and Saxon coin, of leather, copper, tin and silver, was in use. Apart from working the land and chopping timber or cutting turf for fuel, men could relax in the exercise of arms, a bout at quarter-staff, shooting at a mark with long- or crossbow, training a hawk or hound for the pursuit of game, all carried out on land that was public property in the days before the forest laws were extended by the Normans, making these activities illegal on land no longer allowed to them.

The quarter staff was a favourite old English weapon, being a stout pole of between 5 and 8 feet in length which Dr Johnson described as 'A staff of defence, so called, I believe, from the manner of using it; one hand being placed at the middle, and the other equally between the end and the middle.' When attacking the latter hand shifted from one quarter of the staff to the other, giving the weapon a rapid circular motion, which brought the ends to bear on the adversary at unexpected points.[6]

The use of the crossbow at this time is debatable. Some writers put its introduction into England at not long before the beginning of the thirteenth century while others suggest that crossbowmen may have been included in William's army at Hastings. One history of archery[7] cites the tradition that Hengist and Horsa, when they invaded Britain in AD 457, were accompanied by soldiers armed with crossbows. The Domesday Book states 'Heppo the crossbowman has 2 ploughs.' Certainly the crossbow is an ancient weapon used by the Romans and originated in China where in the sixth century BC Sun Tzû in his treatise *Art of War* mentioned the use of powerful crossbows for shooting fire arrows at the enemy.

Thomas Wright's pastoral picture of Saxon society portrays justice being administered under the nearest large tree in patriarchal fashion by the tribal chief who also saw to the defences and inspected and bought arms or implements for husbandry or defence. 'Truly a simple but not a distasteful life to lead in time of peace. In war the tribe had to fight for hearth and home, or for their lord's quarrel; women and children listened with bated breath for news from the wars, and sometimes trembled, not without reason.'

The chief, if of sufficient standing, might be required to attend a *witangemote*, the traditional assembly or council of eminent men and ecclesiastics summoned to give their sovereign counsel. There he would renew acquaintance with earl, bishop, abbot and other functionaries, and give account of his estates, the number of men-at-arms at his command and so on. Education such as it was came perhaps from an occasional visit by an itinerant cleric, but no doubt if a son showed sufficient fondness and aptitude for his letters, in preference to more strenuous pursuits, he may have had the opportunity to follow a scholar's path at the nearest monastery.

This advantage appears to have been given to another of Hereward's supposed forebears identified by General Harward. Bede records that a Hereward or Herewald was ordained Bishop of Sherborne in AD 736 and the General identifies this dignitary as the boy sent from the Surrey clan to study under Abbot Hadrian at Canterbury and the man who became adviser to Ethelhard, successor to Ina, King of the West Saxons. Thus he establishes a centuries-old link with the highest in the land which lends credibility to the family's subsequent eminence. The General follows the *De Gestis Herwardi* version of the Hereward pedigree which offers further logical support for elevating their status.

His argument is that the Hereward family settled in Oxfordshire had raised themselves to prominence in the kingdom of Mercia before Egbert united the Saxon kingdoms under one crown. He produced a genealogical tree to suggest a direct line of descent from Leofric, Earl of Leicester, down to Hereward at the time of the Norman Conquest.

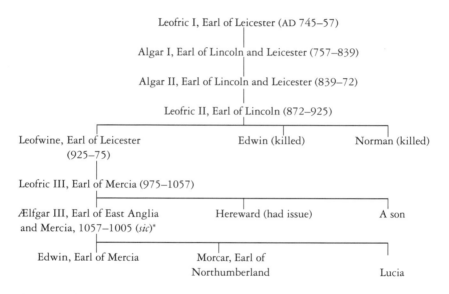

Leofric I, Earl of Leicester (AD 745–57)

Algar I, Earl of Lincoln and Leicester (757–839)

Algar II, Earl of Lincoln and Leicester (839–72)

Leofric II, Earl of Lincoln (872–925)

Leofwine, Earl of Leicester (925–75)   Edwin (killed)   Norman (killed)

Leofric III, Earl of Mercia (975–1057)

Ælfgar III, Earl of East Anglia and Mercia, 1057–1005 (*sic*)*   Hereward (had issue)   A son

Edwin, Earl of Mercia   Morcar, Earl of Northumberland   Lucia

* An error. The General presumably meant 1062. The dates given appear to refer to the title-holding periods although the 82-year tenure of Leofric III is also his lifespan which may also be true of others in the tree.

The novelist Charles Kingsley, like his contemporaries the historians Thomas Wright and Sir Henry Ellis, would appear to have shared General Harward's conviction that Hereward was indeed the son of Earl Leofric III of Mercia and Godiva (the same lady who rode naked through Coventry) and he takes some pains to explain why such an important fact should have remained unrecorded.

Kingsley maintains that to the Normans the English nobility were barbarians without a name or a race: 'They were dead and gone, too; and who cared for the pedigree of a dead man whose lands had passed to another?' He points out that nothing is known of Marlesweyn, who appears again and again in the chronicles, and all but nothing about Edric the Wild, a great chieftain in his day. Even the mighty Earl Godwin had become within three generations a 'herdsman's son' and 'as for Leofric, we know that he was the son (according to Florence of Worcester) of Leofwin . . . and had two brothers, one Norman, killed by Canute [Cnut] . . . the other Edric Edwin, killed by the Welsh. . . . But we know no more'.[8]

Thomas Wright's history can be seen as the inspiration for Kingsley's novel. In 1846, thirty years before it appeared, this learned antiquarian, sometimes criticized for inaccuracy, had published his *England in the Middle Ages* that included a chapter entitled *Adventures of Hereward the Saxon*, based largely on the *De Gestis Herwardi*. The warmth of Kingsley's regard can be gauged from his *Hereward*'s dedication to Wright which runs:

> My Dear Wright, Thus does Hereward, the hero of your youth, reappear at last in a guise fitted for a modern drawing-room. To you is due whatever new renown he may win for himself in that new field. You first disinterred him, long ago, when scarcely a hand or foot of him was left standing out from beneath the dust of ages. You taught me, since then, how to furbish his rusty harness, botch his bursten saddle, and send him forth once more, upon the ghost of his gallant mare. Truly he should feel obliged to you; and though we cannot believe that the last infirmity of noble minds endures beyond the grave, or that any touch of his old vanity still stains the spirit of the mighty Wake; yet we will please ourselves – why should we not? – with the fancy that he is as grateful to you as I am this day.

While General Harward finds much to admire in Wright's work he is less than enthusiastic about Kingsley, acidly observing that he wrote probably as much unintelligible nonsense as any author of his day: 'His utter incapacity as a professor of history was clearly exposed by various critics, in the notices which appeared of his book.' Harward is referring here in particular to the *Saturday Review* critic who hammered Kingsley for his 'mad escapade as Professor of English History in twisting the hero of these pages, the renowned Hereward, into a peg on which to hang a Northampton family named Wake or Jones'.

The General hints darkly at some collusion between Kingsley and the Wakes to establish the family connection, pointing out that the novelist refers to Hereward throughout his book as the Wake, 'for which he was most liberally remunerated'. Whoever said ancestor worship was boring? The Wakes were one of many claimants to be contemptuously dismissed by Harward as upstarts. This may seem a little harsh since the Wake family traces its ancestry back eight centuries in an unbroken line to a Norman baron. Harward, however, based his own family claim on much deeper roots:

> Leofric, the first chief recorded in the annals of Croyland and Coventry, was Earl of Leicester in AD 745; his son Algar was created Earl of Lincoln (*note: Leofric and Algar are both names of Old Norse or Scandinavian origin, and at the end of the eighth century Norse and Danish families had settled in the country of the Lindiswaras, with whom the ancestors of Hereward had married. Lincoln was always the chief town of the five great cities of the Danelagh. The last Earl Algar {Ælfgar}, in the reign of Edward the Confessor, was made Earl of the entire Anglo-Danish province of East Anglia in his father's lifetime*) and the Earldom of Hereford was also conferred upon their descendants, until Leofric III became lord of the marches and Earl of Chester, with a residence at Hedoinc, now Hawarden, Castle, and ultimately Earl of Mercia, 975–1057.

While accepting that many authorities would not agree that Hereward's father, Leofric, Lord of Bourne, in Lincolnshire, and the Earl of Mercia were one and the same, he argues that the evidence in favour of this contention recorded in Domesday is so strong that he had no hesitation in adopting it. The lands in Surrey, Sussex, and Oxfordshire, to which the Herewards gave their name, he cites as sufficient proof that the family of this name were leaders of the Saxons in England at least as far back as the time of Ethelbald, King of Mercia, and most probably the lands were named after Hereward at the first foundation of the South Saxon kingdom about the end of the fifth century.

Hereward's direct descent from the Earls of Mercia, including in their control the earldoms of

Chester, Leicester, Lincoln, Hereford, and East Anglia, the General traces from his birth-place at Bourne, which Domesday shows became at one time the property of Morcar, grandson of Leofric, Earl of Mercia, and the same authority proves that Hereward held lands in Warwickshire and Lincolnshire, which were at one time the property of Ælfgar III (son of Leofric and thus Hereward's reputed brother), and of Edwin, elder son of Ælfgar (and so Hereward's nephew). These are substantial claims and the General defends them stoutly:

> To any reasonable mind this evidence must be conclusive as to the consanguinity of Hereward with the family of the last Earls of Mercia. It is the combined effect of this evidence, not in one instance only, but in three corroborating links, which affords the strongest confirmation of the assumption; and while the connection in estates in one instance might have been only a coincidence, the three distinct cases point distinctly and incontrovertibly to the fact of a family relationship. Evidence has also been given as to the relationship of Leofric and Ælfgar to Ralph, Earl of Hereford, and through him to the reigning house of England, and there appears no reason to dispute this fact, or to doubt the kinship of the Mercian Earls to Edward the Confessor.

In evolving his ingenious genealogical sketch the General claimed to have drawn upon a variety of sources including Domesday Book, the Harleian MSS, general and county histories, Palgrave's *Saxon Commonwealth*, various charters and deeds, authorities on the heraldry of Worcestershire, Warwickshire and Norfolk, a family pedigree drawn out by Sir T. Phillips, FSA, a trustee of the British Museum, for the Rev. J. Harward, MA, of Hartlebury, monastic records, manuscripts and seals in the British Museum. Attempting to prove or disprove descent from a pre-Conquest figure could occupy a lifetime's study at the end of which the results would not be conclusive given the fragmentary and contentious nature of the 'evidence'. Such an exercise has a doomed futility that echoes the Jarndyce case in Dickens's *Bleak House*.

Yet, while Harward's book includes much greater detail than need concern us here, if we do not dismiss his reasoning out of hand we are able to fill in much more of the story of Hereward and explain with some confidence the reason for his appearance and its impact on his contemporaries. Looking at the family tree it is significant that five of the six first earls of this line have names with a distinct Danish termination, *ric* or *gar*, perhaps suggesting that the family, of Saxon origin, had consistently intermarried with Danes. This would have obtained for them the goodwill of Osburga, wife of Ethelwulf, and, later on, of the powerful Duke Oslac and of King Cnut. It also helps explain the readiness with which Hereward tried to enlist the support of the Danes in his struggle to cast aside the Norman yoke.

Hereward, then, was of Saxon descent modified by Danish alliances, and General Harward concludes that he can only be described as Anglo-Saxon. Kingsley's reasonable alternative was *Anglo-Danish*. As to his descendants Harward is even more informative, but for our purposes it is the generations closest to Hereward that might throw light upon the man. He is said to have married twice, but the General finds no record of his family by his second wife, Ælfthryth, until the time of Henry II, and 'except that his only daughter by his first wife, Torfrida, married a Norman lord, Hugh de Evermue, of Deeping, Lincolnshire', we have no knowledge of his descendants for a hundred years, when two families are found in Warwickshire and Norfolk bearing the name of Hereward. But the connection with the Saxon hero is completely established by the record of the *Historia Ecclesia Eliensis*, that Hereward, husband of Wilburga, of Terrington (Taunton), Norfolk, in the reign of Henry II, granted a carucate of land in Torrington to the church at Len (Lynn), and directed that prayers should be said for the souls of Hereward, his father, and of Hereward, 'the exile', his grandfather. 'The date of the latter's death is uncertain, but the three generations are completely established, and Hereward must have left male issue, probably more than one son, as Herewards were established at Pebwith (subsequently Pebworth and Bedworth), in Warwickshire, as well as in Norfolk in the time of Henry III.'

General Harward's confident assumptions have to be admired, especially in the face of judgements such as this by L.G. Pine,[9] editor for many years of *Burke's Peerage*: 'The genealogical moral, and one which many writers of family legends have found it impossible to draw, is that, with a very few exceptions, no one can genuinely claim a pre-Conquest pedigree.' The evidence of the Domesday survey that only a small proportion of the landowners bore English or Danish names, the former native ruling class having largely disappeared, either slain in battle or replaced by William's companions, led him to that conclusion. He further points out that even the loftiest nobles of pre-Conquest England possess only meagre pedigrees of not more than six generations which makes it impossible to trace a pedigree from one of them.

Pine conceded that Hereward the Wake has been claimed at different times as ancestor of the Wakes, baronets; of the Howards (the dukes of Norfolk); and of the Harwards.

The problem cannot be solved, yet every now and then someone comes along with a claim based, not always accurately, on the possession of a Saxon surname and asserts his descent from the pre-Conquest English.

King Harold II, who fell at Hastings in 1066, had seven children. We know what happened to one daughter, Gytha, who married Wladimir of Novogorod, son of Uselovod, Tsar of Russia, and who figures in many of the Russian pedigrees. But of the remaining six – Hakon, Godwin, Edmund, Magnus, Gunhild and Ulf (whose name may have been Harold) – we know nothing beyond the fact that two of Harold's sons made a Viking-like descent on the Somersetshire coast near Bristol in 1068–9. This noble line which had produced a king of England then vanishes from history. What happened to the Godwinsons? We simply do not know. And if a family of this magnitude is lost to view, how can someone assume, merely on the strength of possessing an Old English name as surname, that his family is traceable to ancient Saxon times?

What a pity that General Harward was not alive to respond. The letters pages of *The Times* and the *Daily Telegraph* would have become incandescent as he sprang to defend the Harwards and some idea of the kind of verbal grapeshot that might have ensued can be gained by his wholesale decimation of all other claimants to the Hereward line. Hareward, Harewood, Harwood, Haywood, Horwode, Whorwode, Whorwood, Hayward, Haward, Howard, Temple, and Wake – all falter, he declared, with claims that are 'badly founded and inadmissible', and are tumbled down much as the Norman defenders of York are said to have fallen to the axe of Waltheof 'hewing their heads off one and one, as they came out by the wicket[gate]'.[10] Such names are dismissed as being nearly all subsequent to the Norman Conquest, and are not only doubtful claimants of the lineage of Hereward but it is impossible to prove they even belonged to the same family. Harward's arguments occupy many pages and he conveniently divides the claimants, apart from the last two listed, into two classes. Each is derived from offices held under the Norman forest laws or agricultural system: the names ending in *wode* or *wood* coming under the first category; those ending in *ward* being offices of husbandry.

He discovers confirmation of this in the registered armorial bearings of Harwood of Hagbourne and Streatley, one of the most ancient and respectable of these families whose arms feature three stags' heads. These, he maintains, are clearly the bearings of an officer possessing power and privilege under the forest laws. The forest officers – wardens, verdurers, foresters, etc. – were nearly all of Norman extraction. Those of the highest rank could kill game, as well as having the right to maim dogs or cattle found in the preserve, while poachers caught red-handed suffered death.

Further clues are found in the crest of the same family, which is: 'On a wreath, a stag's head caboshed, gules, having in its mouth an oak bough proper, acorned, or'. Here is literally the *wood* typified by the oak bough and acorn, in addition to the forest-warder's emblem of the red stag's head, seen full face (caboshed).

'Hayward', on the other hand, is an ancient name, dating back almost to the Norman Conquest, and indicating an officer appointed in each town, under the Norman laws, ostensibly to check the waste or injury of hedges, in which the under-tenants had certain rights under the Saxon common law of hedge-bote, wood-bote, wood-geld. The appointment of this officer was a further exaction upon the Saxon peasants, who had to pay either bribes for permission to cut helves or staves, or fines for trespass.

None of the names, argues the General, can be traced to a period before the Conquest but they represent relics of the oppressive and vexatious Norman laws which for so many years curtailed the liberties of the English people. He comes down heavily on the Howards:

As hereditary Earls Marshal of England successive Dukes of Norfolk have had exceptional opportunities of verifying their pedigree; and enriched with great wealth and high rank by the Crown . . . they should have been most careful to avoid assuming honours to which they had a doubtful right, or tampering with their own pedigree or with those of others.

No weaker claim, or one supported by more unreliable evidence than that to the kinship of Hereward by the Duke of Norfolk as stated in the last editions of *Burke's Peerage*, has ever been advanced. In earlier days Dugdale[11] refused to support this claim, although employed, as he states, to 'manifest the greatness' of the Howards. He had not, however, the full courage of his opinions, for while avoiding any reference to the absolutely false statement that 'Howard' and 'Hereward' are one and the same name, he attributed his failure to trace a pedigree to Hereward solely to an alleged default of heirs male! Dugdale, after most careful research – for his character for accuracy is unimpeachable – was satisfied that the Chief Justice Sir W. Howard, 1308, was the best ancestor the Howards could possibly produce.

As a final rebuff General Harward produces a shaft worthy of Stephen Potter: 'There is one reason strongly in favour of the presumption that the name, whether "le Howard" or "Haward", or "Hayward", was of Norman origin. The difference between the Saxon and the Latin races is still sufficiently marked not to be easily mistaken. The numerous portraits of the Howard family show no indication of Saxon origin, the men being dark in complexion, with a profusion of dark hair; the Saxon characteristic being a smooth cheek with very small beard.'

No such cavil impedes the aspirations of the Wake family who according to repute all had distinct Saxon features, light-coloured hair and eyes and *nez retroussé*, but this cuts no ice with General Harward. Having dismissed the claims of the Temples as too frivolous to be seriously entertained he writes that 'The last and weakest, not to say most ludicrous, claim we have to mention, is that of Wake, of Courteen Hall, Northampton . . . as to the affix of "le Wake" to Hereward, on which nickname the Wakes found their claim to consanguinity, it was never heard of until the fifteenth century, when John of Peterborough used it for the first time.[12] It is not mentioned in any of those records from which we derive our only historical facts regarding Hereward, neither by Florence Wigorn, nor in the *De Gestis Herwardi*, nor by the "Rhymers Gaimar",[13] or Ingulph.'

He offers another explanation for the origin of 'le Wake' or Wake-dog applying it to a totally different person. When Fulk, Count of Anjou, was at war with Count Herbert of Maine (1015–36), the latter was so persistent in his night attacks that even the dogs were kept awake by his frequent sallies, and Fulk's men-at-arms got no sleep. So Count Herbert was called the wake or wake-dog.

This interpretation of the 'Wake' derivation is preferred by Freeman and has corroboration from similar tales related by Orderic Vitalis; and some critics allege that the Wakes seem to have started naming their sons Hereward only after the publication of Charles Kingsley's novel, the plot of which revived interest in the Hereward legend. This is unfair since the fourth son of the 10th baronet was christened Herwald Craufurd and was born in 1828, nearly forty years before Kingsley's romance appeared. The 11th baronet named his first two boys Hereward (who died in infancy in 1846) and Herewald, who became the 12th baronet. Eldest sons in the family have borne the name Hereward ever since. But the Wake family can afford to be philosophical. It does, after all, trace its ancestry back through twenty-nine generations, without break or taint of illegitimacy, or even descent on the female line, to the reign of King Stephen, the Conqueror's grandson. And the 14th and present baronet, Sir Hereward, has seen the family history published by his local government authority. This impressive volume[14] reveals that the Wake family has produced many individuals who played important roles in national life, including military and naval leaders, politicians, one Archbishop of Canterbury, and, most famous of all, Joan of Kent, wife of the Black Prince and mother of Richard II. She was the same Fair Maid of Kent whose dropped garter was picked up by King Edward III and, according to one account, led him to rebuke the jesting bystanders famously with the words, '*Honi soi qui mal y pense*', which then became the motto of the Order of the Garter.

The author of the Wake family history, Professor Peter Gordon, confirms that the first member to be named after Hereward was Herwald Craufurd Wake, fourth son of the 10th baronet, born in 1828.

The rivalry between the Wakes and the Harwards in claiming descent from Hereward is an intriguing study in itself but in fact both claims might be justified. The Harward link would appear to stem from Hereward's second marriage to the Saxon lady Ælfthryth and although Professor Gordon does not claim a known link between the legendary Hereward and the Wake family, there appears to be one connection involving Hereward's first wife, Torfrida, that is at least worthy of consideration.

Professor Gordon confirms that the founder of the Wake line was one Geoffrey Wac, a Norman born during the eleventh century who probably died about 1150. His son, Hugh, married Emma, daughter of Baldwin fitzGilbert, founder of Bourne Abbey, a connection echoed in this reference in W.F. Rawnsley's guide to Lincolnshire:[15]

> In Deeping Fen between Bourne, Spalding, Crowland and Market Deeping there is about fifty square miles of fine fat land and Marrat tells us that as early as the reign of Edward the Confessor, Egelric, the Bishop of Durham, who, having been once a monk at Peterborough, knew the value of the land, in order to develop the district, made a cord road of timber and gravel all the way from Deeping to Spalding. The province then belonged to the Lords of Brunne or Bourne. In Norman times Richard De Rulos, Chamberlain of the Conqueror, married the daughter of Hugh de Evermue, Lord of Deeping. Their only daughter married Baldwin fitzGilbert, and his daughter and heiress married Hugh de Wake, who managed the forest of Kesteven for Henry III, which forest reached to the bridge at Market Deeping. Richard De Rulos, who was the father of all Lincolnshire farmers, aided by Ingulphus, Abbot of Croyland, set himself to enclose and drain the fen land, to till the soil or convert it into pasture and to breed cattle.

If the 'Hugh de Evermue' referred to here is the same person described by General Harward and various other sources as the Norman knight who became the husband of the daughter of Hereward and Torfrida we have the missing link that might establish a connection between Hereward, the Wake family and the term 'Hereward the Wake'. Assuming for a moment that Hereward and

Torfrida did have a daughter who married Hugh de Evermue we can perhaps project the following descent through the female line:

Hereward m. Torfrida
|
      daughter m. Hugh de Evermue
        |
            daughter m. Richard de Rulos
              |
                  daughter m. Baldwin fitzGilbert
                    |
                        Emma m. Hugh Wac

Hugh Wac's mother-in-law thus becomes a great-granddaughter of Hereward and Torfrida. For this hypothesis to work we would have to believe Rawnsley's statement that Hugh de Evermue and Hereward's daughter did have children and assume that Rawnsley's printer translated his Henry II as Henry III since Hugh de Wake died in 1172, long before Henry III was born. There we must leave the genealogical speculation but before doing so we can at least follow the General into one final fascinating notion.

In proving to his own satisfaction at least the Harwards' legitimate descent from Hereward through the great man's daughter by his second wife the Saxon lady, Ælfthryth, General Harward's genealogical explorations took him in spirit to many parts of the country. However, the longest and most intriguing journey was to the United States, where he finds that a descendant of Hereward was the founder of Harvard University in Massachusetts. This John Harvard (1607–38) was the son of Robert, who lived in the parish of St Saviour, Southwark, for many years. His business was probably that of a butcher or meat salesman and he died in the first plague, 1625, together with six of his family. The only survivors of this tragedy were his wife and two sons, John and Thomas:

The Harvards of Southwark were descended from an offshoot of the Herwards of Norfolk and Warwickshire, as we find John Herward, gent., was resident in the parish of St. Mary Magdalene, Southwark, and died in 1487. A colony of Danes had settled in St. Mary Overies, the old name of St. Saviour's, and the name Herward in Saxon became Harvard in Danish. It seems therefore natural that Robert Harvard should have gone back to Warwickshire to find a wife. In Shakespeare's town he married Katherine, daughter of Thomas and Margaret Rogers.

This Rogers was an alderman of Stratford-on-Avon and his house, called 'Ye ancient house', can still be seen today. On the front, under a broad oriel window, is inscribed TR 1596 AR. Robert's widow was not blessed with happiness for long for her second husband, John Ellison, or Elletson, died within a year. She then married Richard Yearwood, or Yerwood, Esq., MP for Southwark, a first cousin to Sir G. Yardley, or Yeardley, appointed Governor of Virginia in 1626. This connection appears to have had a significant influence on John Harvard's career.

After studying at Cambridge where he graduated BA in 1631, and MA in 1635 he seems to have emigrated to America in 1637 when his mother died. He had married Ann, daughter of the Rev. John Sadler, a Sussex clergyman, and, having disposed of his estate, which included the Queen's Head Inn in Southwark, he sailed for New England. In the same year he was made a freeman of the colony of Massachusetts, and in 1638 a member of the Committee for Legislation. He died of consumption on 14 September 1638.

Comments General Harward:

Harvard University, near Boston, Massachusetts, U.S.A, was founded by him with a moiety of his fortune and his library of books. He resided some time at Charleston, and is said to have preached there. His last resting-place was in the graveyard, Charleston, where a monument has been erected. At Harvard he is commemorated by an ideal bronze statue, inscribed on the plinth, 'John Harvard, Founder'. In the chapel of Emmanuel College, Cambridge, eight windows are dedicated to theologians. In the third window on the north side is John Harvard, with Lawrence Chaderton, first Master of Emmanuel, as his companion. In John Harvard's hand is a scroll with *'Populus qui creabitur laudabit Dominum.'*[16]

Much of this is confirmed by Dr Frank Stubbings, Emmanuel's honorary keeper of rare books, who points out that no contemporary portrait of Harvard survives. The stained-glass window put up in 1884 is merely an 'icon', the artist following instructions to imitate the portrait of John Milton, making the hair a little longer. Stubbings includes Harvard in his anthology of portraits of Emmanuel men[17] and explains that he was one of many Cambridge graduates who sailed to the new colony on Massachusetts Bay in the 1630s seeking a freer climate for their Puritan views, following the advancement of the High Church William Laud, first as Bishop of London and then, in 1633, as Archbishop of Canterbury.

Harvard was thus not, strictly, the founder of the famous American university, although he was its first major benefactor. His bequest of 400 volumes and half his estate, valued at about £1,700, may sound little enough but, as Dr Stubbings writes: 'It set the infant college on its feet, and the grateful community decreed that it should forever bear his name. Thomas Shepard summed up what it matters to know of him: "The man was a Scholler in his life and enlarged toward the country and the good of it in life and death."'

That Harvard University Archives have no knowledge of a possible link with Hereward is not altogether astonishing. Until the 1880s Harvard possessed little information about its own 'founder' John Harvard. As the *Boston Herald*[18] records: 'The college was on the point of observing its 250th anniversary in 1886, as much in doubt about its original benefactor as it always had been. And then Harvard – John Harvard – was rediscovered. The man who carried the astounding information to Cambridge – he made the 50 minute journey from Boston in a horse car, how impatiently may be imagined – is Charles A. Drew.'

Mr Drew and others had been campaigning for some time to start an investigation into Harvard's ancestry and, raising funds from wealthy alumni, they had engaged a noted genealogist, Henry F. Waters, to sail to England and search for facts about John Harvard in whatever archives and records he could find. All previous attempts had failed and even the distinguished antiquarian, James Savage, who went to England in 1842 chiefly to ascertain the early history of John Harvard and would have given $500 for five lines about him was unable to find anyone entitled to claim the money.

Waters was much more of a Sherlock Holmes and was not baffled by the fact that John Harvard's mother had married a second and then a third time, changing her name from Harvard to Elletson and then to Yearwood. These changes, commented the *Boston Herald* ingenuously, had been enough to throw previous searchers off the track – 'Who would look under Elletson or Yearwood for the will of Katherine Harvard? Then again, spelling was a lost art 300 years ago. . . .' Harvard clearly missed an opportunity by not recruiting the indefatigable researcher General Harward to the task and it is interesting to speculate what those distinguished academics would have made of having Hereward the Wake presented to them as the progenitor of their founding father.

The John Harvard commemoration window in Emmanuel College Chapel.

Such a paragon would adorn any family tree and perhaps even Harvard itself would not be uncomfortable at having its founder linked with the Saxon resistance hero. Whether one agrees with General Harward's arguments or not he is an engaging and persuasive advocate and certainly his own distinguished Indian Army career would have equipped him to make informed comments on the military aspects of Hereward's life.

Notes

CHAPTER 1. 1066 AND ALL THAT

1. 'Swein was the son of Earl Ulf and Cnut the Great's sister Estrith; he was first cousin of Hardacnut, the son of Cnut and Emma, but there was no blood kinship with Emma's son by her first marriage, Edward the Confessor. The Scandinavian interest in the English throne derived from Cnut, and not from the children of Emma's first marriage'; Marjorie Chibnall, editor and translator of *The Ecclesiastical History of Orderic Vitalis* (Oxford University Press, 1969).
2. R.J. Adams, *A Conquest of England* (Hodder and Stoughton, 1965).
3. The actual size of the opposing forces is debatable but a combined host of under twenty thousand for both armies is generally accepted. Compare this with the battle of Manzikat in Anatolia in 1071 where 100,000 Turkish warriors defeated a Byzantine army of equal magnitude.
4. Article in the Historical Association journal, *History*, October 1966.
5. R. Allen Brown, *The Normans and the Norman Conquest* (Constable, 1976).
6. J.H. Round, *Feudal England* (Swan Sonnenschein, London, 1895).
7. Frank Stenton, *Anglo-Saxon England* (Oxford University Press, 1943).
8. Trevor Rowley, *The Norman Heritage* (Routledge & Kegan Paul, 1983).
9. H.G. Richardson and G.O. Sayles, *Governance of Mediaeval England from the Conquest to the Magna Carta* (Edinburgh, 1963).
10. R.H.M. Dolley and D.M. Metcalf, *Anglo-Saxon Coins*, ed. R.H.M. Dolley (Methuen, 1961).
11. 'Around Bayeux 'Thor aid!' was the battle cry rather than 'Dex Aie!' (God's Aid)'; Christopher Gravett, *Hastings 1066* (Osprey, 1992).
12. The notable exceptions listed by R.H.C. Davis are Bernay (*c.* 1017–50), the nave of Mont Saint-Michel (*c.* 1040) and Jumièges (1040–67), and the chancel of the Abbaye aux Dames at Caen (1062–6).
13. Everyman Library (Dent, 1972).
14. R.W. Chambers, *On the Continuity of English Prose from Alfred to More and his School* (EETS, Oxford, 1932).

15. E.D. Laborde, *Byrhtnoth and Maldon* (1936) and E.V. Gordon, *The Battle of Maldon* (1937).

CHAPTER 2. SOURCES

1. Trevor Bevis, *Hereward and De Gestis Herwardi Saxonis* (Westrydale Press, 1981).
2. H.W.C. Davis, *A History of England*, Vol. II (Methuen, 1905).
3. Hugh Candidus, *The Peterborough Chronicle of Hugh Candidus* (Peterborough Museum Society, 1966).
4. Charles Kingsley, *Hereward the Wake: 'Last of the English'* (Macmillan, 1877).
5. The survey's administration is fully described in V.H. Galbraith, *The Making of Domesday Book* (Oxford University Press, 1961).
6. Bovata – a measure of land, usually an eighth of a carucate, equivalent of the hide in former Danish areas. Stenton refers to a normal hide of 120 arable acres in Cambridgeshire and of similar scale in other eastern shires, although smaller elsewhere, i.e. 40 acres in Wiltshire. Twelve bovates by this reckoning would be approximately 180 acres. Compare this with the Bourne holding of Earl Morcar measured in the Domesday survey at 2½ carucates, or 300 acres. 'The men of Aveland Wapentake testify that the manor of Bourne was Earl Morcar's before 1066. Now Odger has it from the King. Drogo claims it, but wrongfully.'
7. Jack Lindsay, *The Normans and Their World* (Hart-Davis, MacGibbon, 1973).
8. Prefatory note to The Anglo-Saxon Chronicle, translated by G.N. Garmonsway (Everyman Library, Dent, 1972).
9. *Chambers Biographical Dictionary* (1984).
10. *Florence of Worcester* (Llanerch Enterprises, 1989). Facsimile of the Joseph Stephenson translation first published in the Church Historians of England.
11. *The Ecclesiastical History of Orderic Vitalis*, Vol. II (Oxford University Press, 1969), edited and translated by Marjorie Chibnall who in noting that the Anglo-Saxon Chronicle and *Florence of Worcester* indicate that Edwin was killed while Morcar was still in Ely, suggests that the discrepancy could be explained if Orderic had inflated the information in William of Poitiers with part of the later legend that rapidly gathered round the last stand of Morcar, Hereward and others in Ely.

CHAPTER 3. THE OUTLAW

1. Mills's *History of the Crusades*.
2. Maurice Keen, *The Outlaw of Medieval Legend* (Routledge & Kegan Paul, 1961).

3. Benjamin Thorpe, *Ancient Laws*.
4. Harold R. Smith, *Saxon England* (Heath Cranton, 1953).
5. After the death of her husband Æthelred II the 'Unready', Emma was summoned back from Normandy to marry King Cnut and she seems to have favoured Harthacnut, the son of that union, more than her older son Edward.

CHAPTER 4. 'VALIANT HEREWARD'

1. Florence, *Florence of Worcester* (Llanerch Enterprises, 1989). Facsimile of the Joseph Stephenson translation first published in the Church Historians of England.
2. Here Florence appears to err. Harold Hardrada, and not Harold Harfagr, was the ally of Tostig.
3. J.H. Round, *Feudal England* (Swan Sonnenschein, London, 1895).
4. *The Ecclesiastical History of Orderic Vitalis* (Oxford University Press, 1969) edited and translated by Marjorie Chibnall, who points out that Orderic anticipates somewhat; Alexius Comnenus did not become emperor until 1081.
5. Arnold J. Toynbee, *A Study of History* (Oxford University Press, 1934).
6. L.R. Cryer, *A History of Folkingham (with Laughton and Stow Green)* (1991).
7. W.F. Rawnsley, *Highways and Byways of Lincolnshire* (Macmillan, 1914).
8. Stone from Folkingham Castle, now vanished, was reputedly used to build the existing Folkingham manor, a Grade II listed seventeenth-century building of stone with a Collyweston slate roof.
9. David Bates, *William the Conqueror* (George Philip, 1989).
10. The General must be referring to the sister of Edwin and Morcar (see family tree, page 160) and, therefore, according to his theory, Hereward's niece. Lucia was said to have been first married, or betrothed, to Ivo de Taillebois, the villainous Norman Lord of Spalding and Hereward's sworn enemy.
11. Doubtless a reference to the eighteenth-century copy of a sixteenth-century portrait of William as a Renaissance prince displayed in the abbey church of St Etienne of Caen.
12. *William the Conqueror, op. cit.*

CHAPTER 5. THE AVENGER

1. Unanswered, too, are questions about Hereward's apparent abundance of nephews – Edwin, Morcar and the two Siwards are subsequently joined by three more in *De Gestis*. Could the Siwards have been ciphers for Edwin and Morcar?

2. The magical figure of seven or its multiples again occurs – 14 men slaughtered single-handed at Bourne and later in another incident Hereward 'slew seven of those who attempted to seize him'. The Romans considered 7 a lucky number, perhaps because they could see seven bright objects in the sky – Sun, Moon and the five planets: Venus, Jupiter, Saturn, Mars and Mercury, which suggested the seven days of the week.

3. The evidence of Domesday Book confirms that Humphrey lost his English estates, as he held nothing in 1086; but Hugh of Grandmesnil either retained or recovered his.

4. This seems to be an error since Swein was Cnut's nephew.

5. C. Mellowes and W.T. Mellowes in their 1941 translation of the Peterborough Chronicle suggest that the Bolhithe gate was presumably at the east end of the abbey near the twentieth-century site of the Florence Saunders Nursing Home, as at this period the road through Peterborough crossed the river by a ford and passed the east end of the abbey.

6. This figure is given as 160 in other sources; it does not seem an adequate force to deal with the combined group of Danish adventurers and Saxon patriots.

7. A long mounded causeway is still to be seen running from Aldreth village across the fields towards Belsar's Hill.

8. 'So great a famine prevailed that men were forced to consume the flesh of horses, dogs, cats, and even that of human beings'; Florence of Worcester.

9. See Chapter 9 for a description of the difficulties of building in the Fens.

CHAPTER 6. THE GUERRILLA LEADER

1. Arthur Bryant, *The Medieval Foundation* (Collins, 1966).
2. Edmund Ironside succeeded his father, Aethelred the Redeless in 1016 and fought a bloody but eventually unsuccessful campaign against King Cnut. Mystery surrounds Edmund's sudden death six weeks after negotiating a treaty with Cnut.
3. Gabriel Ronay, *The Lost King of England* (Boydell Press, 1989).
4. H.C. Darby, *The Medieval Fen* (David & Charles, 1940).
5. Christopher Gravett, *Hastings 1066* (Osprey Military Campaign Series, 1992).
6. Vesey Norman, *The Medieval Soldier* (Arthur Baker, 1971).
7. R.J. Adam, *A Conquest of England* (Hodder and Stoughton, 1965).
8. Charles Chenevix Trench, *A History of Horsemanship* (Jarrold, 1970).
9. *Pferde, Reiter, Völkerstürme*; published in English as *They Rode into Europe*, translated by Anthony Dent (Harrap, 1968).
10. Jankovich quotes the researches of L.S. Ruhl, Curator of the Museum of Electoral Hesse, who weighed a complete set of armour, saddlery and

accoutrements with personal weapons from the same period and produced a total weight of 255 lb 9 oz and, assuming a 12½ stone rider, produced a total burden of 430 lb (224 kg). This is almost twice the Chenevix Trench estimate.

11. Orderic Vitalis says that the king, who was very corpulent, fell ill from exhaustion and heat and makes no reference to any injury received at Mantes. Conversely, William of Malmesbury says that he was injured internally by being thrown against the pommel of his saddle.

12. William of Poitiers, however, claims that William used crossbowmen at Hastings.

13. A.K. Astbury, *The Black Fens* (Golden Head Press, 1958).

14. In the grotesque funeral scene as described by Orderic Vitalis, William's corpse was too large for its stone coffin and the frantic efforts made to cram it into its narrow bed caused the swollen bowel to burst filling the church with a fearful stench.

CHAPTER 7.   BETRAYAL

1. Edward Miller, *The Abbey and Bishopric of Ely* (Cambridge University Press, 1951).

2. Richard Muir, *Portraits of the Past* (Michael Joseph, 1989).

3. David Bates, *William the Conqueror* (George Philip, 1989).

4. Freeman's account is slightly at odds with Edward Miller's history of Ely Abbey in which he says Thurstan's abbacy ended in 1072 and Theodwin's in 1075.

5. Herbert L. Edlin, *Wayside and Woodland Trees* (Warne, 1904).

6. Such vistas were not unknown some years ago. As a boy I lived in a cottage on the edge of a fragment of that ancient Bruneswald forest that still clung to a Bedfordshire hilltop. It was 1944 and a USAF Flying Fortress crashed into the wood on its return from a bombing mission, killing the crew. The wide swathe cut by the aeroplane as it plunged into the trees is still discernible in the undergrowth. The grim discovery of a human finger was partly ameliorated by solemnly carving a miniature cross to mark its reburial amid a clump of primroses.

7. Frank Stenton, *Anglo-Saxon England* (Oxford University Press, 1943).

CHAPTER 8.   THE LEGEND

1. William Trevor, *Oxford Book of Irish Short Stories* (Oxford University Press, 1991).

2. Marion Lochhead, a contributor to *Only Connect*, readings for children's literature (Oxford University Press, 2nd edn, 1980).
3. Jack Lindsay, *The Normans and their World* (Hart-Davis, MacGibbon, 1973).
4. It is gratifying that the name Babbinswood still survives in that of the village a mile south of today's Whittington (Blauncheville), in Shropshire.
5. The others were the matter of Britain, the matter of France, and the matter of Rome; see M. Keen, *The Outlaw of Medieval Legend* (Routledge & Kegan Paul, 1961).
6. Michael Young, *Studies in the Novel*, 17 (1985), 2, 174–88.
7. Brenda Colloms, *Charles Kingsley* (Constable, 1975).
8. Linda Hague, *Saxon Superman* (Anglia Young Books, 1989).
9. Charles Kingsley, *Prose Idylls* (Macmillan, 1874).

CHAPTER 9.   A FORGOTTEN HERO?

1. A.K. Astbury, *The Black Fens* (Golden Head Press), 1958.
2. One such marks that extinct stream up which St Withburga's body (stolen from Dereham by Brithnoth, first Abbot of Ely) was brought to Ely in 974.
3. Perhaps that 'wide sea' across which, in some accounts, Hereward escaped from Ely.
4. Duncan Grinnell-Milne, *The Killing of William Rufus* (David & Charles, 1968).
5. H.C. Darby, *The Medieval Fen* (David & Charles, 1940).

APPENDIX B.   FAMILY MATTERS: THE GENEALOGICAL ARGUMENT

1. *The Anglo Saxon Dictionary* (Bosworth and Toller, 1898) gives the following definitions: *Here-wæda* A war-hunter, hunter whose game is the enemy; *Here-word* Praise, applause; *Herewósa* One who is fierce in fight (a warrior?); *Here-wæd* War-weed, armour.
2. A semi-divine descent is not unknown in the pedigrees of kings in the Dark Ages; see e.g. King Ethelwulf's pedigree in the Anglo-Saxon Chronicle.
3. The College of Heralds, when asked to confirm the General's description of the role of sword-guardian, did not reply.
4. 'Jealous as the Germans were of military renown, they all confessed the superior valour of the Suevi . . . they esteemed it not a disgrace to have fled before a people to whose arms the immortal gods themselves were unequal'; Edward Gibbon, *The History of the Decline and Fall of the Roman Empire*, Vol. I (Folio Society, 1983).
5. Thomas Wright, *The Celt, the Roman, and the Saxon* (Arthur Hall, Virtue & Co., 1852).

6. Joseph Strutt, *Sport and Pastimes of the People of England 1801* (Firecrest Publishing, Bath, 1969).
7. E.G. Heath, *The Grey Goose Wing* (Osprey, 1971).
8. Here, again, confusion arises since General Harward identifies these tragic figures as Leofric's uncles.
9. L.G. Pine, *The Genealogist's Encyclopedia* (David & Charles, 1969).
10. From William of Malmesbury.
11. Sir W. Dugdale, Garter King at Arms.
12. A reference to John of Peterborough's Chronicle, completed in 1368.
13. Some authorities, however, put the first reference to Hereward 'the Wake' in a rhyming French chronicle written in the middle of the twelfth century by Geoffrey Gaimar.
14. Peter Gordon, *The Wakes of Northamptonshire* (Northamptonshire County Council, 1992).
15. Willingham Franklin Rawnsley, *Highways and Byways in Lincolnshire* (Macmillan, 1914).
16. 'A people which shall be created shall praise the Lord' (Psalm 102, l. 18).
17. Frank Stubbings, *Forty-nine Lives* (Cambridge University Press, 1983).
18. 20 September 1936.

Bibliography

In addition to the books and sources mentioned in the Notes the following list contains suggestions for further reading. It does not include every book or article which has been consulted.

Baker, T., *The Normans* (Cassell, 1966).

Baker, T., *Saxon England* (Cassell, 1966).

Barlow, Frank, *The Feudal Kingdom of England*, 1042–1216 (London, 1955).

Boutell, C., *Arms and Armour* (Reeves and Turner, 1893).

Brooke, Christopher, *The Saxon and Norman Kings* (Batsford, 1963).

Brooks, F.W., *The Battle of Stamford Bridge* (East Yorks. Local History Series, VI (1956)).

Christie, A.G.I., *English Medieval Embroidery* (Oxford, 1938).

Davis, H.W.C., *England Under the Normans and Angevins* (Methuen, 1924).

Hewitt, J., *Ancient Armour and Weapons* (Oxford 1860)

Klindt-Jensen, Ole, and Svenolov Ehrén, *The World of the Vikings* (Allen & Unwin, 1967).

Loyn, H.R., *Anglo-Saxon England and the Norman Conquest* (Longman, 1962).

Oman, C., *History of the Art of War in the Middle Ages* (Burt Franklin, 1924).

Poole, A.L. (ed.), *Medieval England*, 2 vols (Oxford, 1958).

Poole, R.L., *The Exchequer in the Twelfth Century* (Oxford, 1912).

Sayles, G.O., *The Medieval Foundations of England* (Methuen, 1960).

Warner, Philip, *Sieges of the Middle Ages* (Bell, 1968).

Index

Numbers in italic indicate illustrations.

Adam, R.J. 3, 97
Adela, William I's daughter 32
Aediva, Hereward's mother (*see* Godiva) 156
Aegelwine, Bishop of Durham 102
Ælfgar, Hereward's brother(?) 41, 43, 48–9, 58, 61–2, 101, 156, 160–2
Ælfgifu, Cnut's mistress 45
Ælfric 46
Ælfthryth (Alftrude), Hereward's second wife 118–20, 140, 162, 165–6
Ætheling (*see* Edgar)
Æthelred, King 43, 52
Æthelric, Bishop 81, 85
Æthelstan, King 42
Æthelthryth, St 86, 111, 144
Æthelward, Hereward's chaplain 121
Æthelwold, resourceful prior at Ely 81–5
Akeman Street 86
Alderbrook farm 149
Aldred (Ældred), Archbishop of York 54, 107
Aldreth, causeway 86, 95, 102–3, *103*, 105, 108, 111, 137, 143*ff.*, *147*
Algitha (*see* Ealdgyth)
Allen Brown, R. 7–10
Alwinus 108
Anglo-Saxon Chronicle 13, 29, 86, 101, 107
Anna Comnena 97
Arnold, Dr, of Rugby 131
Art of War, Chinese treatise (sixth century BC, Sun Tzû) 159
Asfrothr 28–9
Asselin, one of Hereward's assassins 122
Astbury, A.K. 105, 141*ff.*

Babbyng, forest 125
Babington, Professor C.C. 144
Baker, E.A. 138
Baldwin, Count of Flanders 30, 58–60, 63–4, 66, 152, 165–6
Bardney Abbey 59
Barnack, near Stamford, Lincs. 132
Barnard, Warwickshire 158
Bates, David 62, 66, 76–7
Baudri, Abbot of Bourgueil 32–3
Bayeux, town 13
Bayeux Tapestry *1*, 15, 31–2, *32*, 46, 49, 62, 65, *65*, 95*ff.*
Beaumont, Roger, castellan of 35, 106
Bedford, supplies castle builders 111–12
    Hereward imprisoned at 121, *121*
Belsar's Hill 86, *144*, 144–5, 148
Bevis, Trevor, fenland historian 17, 19, 69, 145, 150, *150*
Black Prince 165
Blauncheville 124–5
Boston Herald 167
Bothildr 28
Boulogne, Eustace, Count of *46*, 46–7, 56–7, 96
Bourne, Lincs., Hereward's home 2–3, 21, 28–9, 40–1, 59–60, 68–9, *70*, *71*, 75, 79, 89, 112, 118, 125, 151, 156, 161–2, 165
    massacre at 70–2
Braham dock, Ely 149, 153
Brand (Brant), abbot of Peterborough, Hereward's uncle 74–5, 79–80
Bruges 47, 51, 58–60, 63
Bruneswald, ancient forest 2, 25, 110, 112, *114*, 116–17, *116–17*, 125, 127, 131

Burke's Peerage 163–4
Bury St Edmunds *61*, 62, 93

Cambridge 86, 101, 103, 111–12, 136, 142, 144–5, 166–7
Camp of Refuge 86–7, 93, 107, 138, 141
castles, as instruments of Norman power 22, *23*, 53, 59, *75*, 90
Chambers, R.W. 13
Chenevix Trench, Charles 99–100
Clifford's Tower, York 22
Cnut, King 2, 39, 44–5, 57, 65, 92, 160
Colloms, Brenda 67, 131, 136
Constantinople 51, 57
Cottenham, Cambs., 103, 145
Coutances, Bishop Geoffrey 92
Crowland (Croyland) Abbey, 25, 33–4, 60, 101, 112, 118–19, 121, 134, *139*, 140, 161, 165
Cryer, L.R. 59–60, 63

Dada, Norman eyewitness at Ely 94
Darby, H.C. 92*ff.*, 149
Davis, H.W.C. 18–19, 23
Davis, R.H.C. 6–7, 11–12, 26–8
de Dol, Raoul 132
De Gestis Herwardi Saxonis 17*ff.*, *20*, 35–8, 42, 58*ff.*, 71, 73, 75, 88–9, 93, 102–3, 106, 108, 112, 117, 119–21, 124, 126, 137, 140, 145, 149, 151, 156, 160–1, 164
de Horepol, Robert, Hereward's gaoler 121
de Mandeville, Geoffrey 95
Deeping, Lincs. 162, 165
Devil's Dyke 103, 154
Dickins, Bruce 31
Doddington, Cambs. 110
Domesday Book, 3, 6, 15, 25–9, *26*, 39, 59, 77, 110, 112, 114–16, 118, 122, 156, 158, 159, 161–3
   Hereward references 28–9, *28*
Dover 47, 56–7, 139–40
Drew, Charles A. 167
Dugdale, Sir W. 164

Ealdgyth, Queen, Godwin's daughter 45, 47
Ealdgyth (Algitha), Ælfgar's daughter 48–9, 54
Earith 144, 149, 154

Edgar the Ætheling 1, 12, 51, 54, 56, 65, 90–1
Edgiva, abbess of Leominster 39
Edith the Swan-neck 38
Edlin, Herbert L. 115
Edmund Ironside 90–1
Edric the Wild 86, 120, 125, 160
Edward III 165
Edward the Confessor, King 26, 34, 38, 40, 43*ff.*, *44*, 49, 51, 55, 60, 62, 72, 90, 119, 139–40, 156, 158, 161–2, 165
Edwin (Eadwin), Earl of Mercia, 1, 35, 43, 49, 52–3, 54–6, 62–3, 71, 90, 101, 106, 156, 160, 162
Ellis, Sir Henry 160
Ely, abbey 108–10
   cathedral 112, *113*
   museum 151
Ely, Isle of 1, 4, 18, 25, 33–5, 49, 62, 66, 74, 76, 80*ff.*, 86, 93, 95, 101–3, 106*ff.*, 122, 137, 139*ff.*, 151, 153–4, 158
Emma, wife of Hugh de Wac 165–6
Emma, Queen, mother of Edward the Confessor 43, 45, 59
Emmanuel College 167–8
Ethelbald, King of Mercia 161
Ethelhard, King of West Saxons 160
Ethelwulf 162
Eustace the Monk 124
Evenlode, Worcs. 118, 158
Exeter, siege of 57

Fair Maid of Kent 165
Fécamp 91
Fen Post, Holme, Cambs. 145
fen roder, weapon finds 150
fenmen, character 142
Fens, The 92, 93–4, 95, 101, 105, 126, 132, *133–5*, 136, 141*ff.*, *143*, *146*, *148*, 159
fitzGilbert, Baldwin 165–6
fitzOsbern, William 56–7, 66
Fitzwarin, Fulk 124
Flanders 30, 39, 50*ff.*, 63–4, 66–7, 71, 73, 95, 125, 132, 151
Florence of Worcester 18, 29, 35, 39, 51, 64, 101, 106, 108, 149, 156, 160, 164
Floriancensus, Abbé 141
Folkingham, Lincs. 59–60, 151

forest, extent in England 112*ff.*
Freckenham, Suffolk 27
Freeman, E.A. 7–10, 9, 33, 60, 63–4, 85–6,
    91–2, 101–2, 105–7, 111–12, 117–18,
    120–2, 144–5, 149, 152, 156–7, 165
Fulford, Yorks., battle of 53–6
Fulk, count of Anjou 164
Fuller, William 90

Gaimar, Geoffrey 18, 25, 120–1, 132, 164
Gamelyn 42, 126
Garibaldi, Giuseppe 58
Garmonsway, G.N. 13
Gilbert of Ghent (Gand) 58–60, 63, 151
Godiva 160
Godwin, Earl 8, 10, 39, 41, 43*ff.*, 49, 52, 55,
    59, 139, 151, 160
Golden borough (*see* Peterborough)
Gordon, Professor Peter 149, 165
Gruffydd ap Llywelyn, king of the Welsh 4,
    48–9, 92, 140, 156
Guy of Gisborne 128
Gyrth (Gurth), earl, Harold's brother 48, 139
Gytha, Godwin's wife 45
Gytha, Harold's daughter 163

Haddenham, Cambs. 143–5
Hardrada, Harold, King of Norway, 51, 65, 92
Harold I, 'Harefoot', King 44–5
Harold II, King 1, 8, 15, 46–9, 53–6, 62, 90,
    92, 101, 139
    coronation 51, 107
    links with Hereward 156
    offspring 163
    visit to Normandy 31, 149
Harthacnut 44–5
Harvard, John and family 166, *168*
Harvard university, 166–7
Harward, Lt.-Gen. T.N. 39, 41, 49, 58, 63–4,
    68, 71–2, 75, 87, 101–2, 112, 118–20,
    124, 129, 157*ff.*
Hastings, battle of, 1, 3–4, 6, 10, 12, 15–16,
    25, 30–2, 38, 46, 53*ff.*, 60, 62, 66, 68,
    77–8, 90, 92, 95–7, 100–1, 107, 131,
    139–40, 159, 163
hauberk 66, 95–6, 99–100
Hawarden castle 161

Henry I 18, 59
Henry II 18, 162, 166
Henry III 14, 23, 95, 163, 165–6
Henry VIII 65
Henty, G.A. 132
Herewald, Bishop of Sherborne 160
Hereward
    appearance 37–8, 40, 64, *124, 129*
    betrayal 106–8
    birthdate 58, 139
    death 25, 34, 118, 121–2, 140
    Domesday Book entries 28–9, 118
    duel with Warrenne 75–6
    exile 38–9, 41–3, 51, 58, 60–3, 66–8
    family 41, 48–9, 60, 62–3, 101, 119,
        156*ff.*
    followers 19, 21–2, 58, 88–9, 94, 102,
        132
    Hereward's castle 86, 149
    horse, Swallow 137
    imprisoned at Bedford 121
    knighting 73–5, *74*, 79
    return and vengeance 58, 69–72, *72*, 127–8
    surrender 117–20
    Wake, derivation 29, 164*ff.*
    wives 63, 67, 69, 118–20, *129*, 132
Holt, Professor J.C. 127
Hood, Robin 2, 117, *124*, 126–8, 151–2
horses, in warfare 68, 99–100
housecarls 15, 92
Howards, the (Dukes of Norfolk) 163–4
Hugh de Evermue, Hereward's son-in-law 118,
    132, 162, 165–6
Hughes, Thomas 131

Ingulph, Abbot of Crowland 18, 33–4, 118,
    120, 164–5
Ivar, the sacrist 80, 85

Jankovich, Miklós 100
John, King 12, 95, 125
John of Peterborough 18, 164

Keen, Maurice 42, 123*ff.*
Kingsley, Charles 25, 37–8, 40, 42–3, 51, 67,
    108, 112, 123, 128*ff.*, *130*, 142, 151–2,
    160–2, 165

Leofric, Earl of Mercia (Hereward's 'father') 40–1, 43*ff.*, 58, 60–1, 71, 119, 138, 156, 158, 160–2

Leofric the Black 19, 22, 25

Leofric the Deacon 19, 21, 23, 88–9

Leofwin, Harold II's brother 48, 54, 139

Leofwin Lange, Peterborough monk 81

Leominster 39, 45

Leominster, abbess of (*see* Edgiva)

Lightfoot, Martin, Hereward's servant 58, 69

Lindsay, Jack 123–5

Little Domesday Book 26

Little John 126, 128

Lucia, sister of Edwin and Morcar 63, 101, 160

Macbeth, King of Scotland 58, 92

Macfarlane, Charles 138–40

Magoun, F.P., Jr. 13

Maine 66, 120

Maitland, F.W. 12

Malcolm, King of Scotland 51–2, 58, 91, 101

Malet, William 101

Malmesbury 33, 79

Malmesbury, William of 18, 33, 38, 55–6, 66, 87, 91

Mantes 100

Marlesweyn 160

Marston Jabbet, Warwicks. 118, 158

Matilda, wife of William I 30, 59–60

Mercia(ns) 36, 40–1, 44–5, 48–50, 52, 54–6, 60, 62–3, 71, 90, 138, 140, 156, 158, 160–2

Miller, Edward 109–10

Morcar, Earl 1, 3, 35, 43, 49–50, 52*ff.*, 62, 71, 90, 101–2, 106, 108, 151, 158, 160, 162

Morkery woods 151

Muir, Richard 110*ff.*

New Forest 116, 148

Norman, Vesey 96

Northumbria 15, 44, 48*ff.*, 60, 87, 90–1, 120, 160

Odo, Bishop of Bayeux 31, 32, 56–7, 59, 80

Order of the Garter 165

Orderic Vitalis 18, 22, 29–30, 33, 35–6, 57, 73, 77, 81, 90–2, 127, 165

Osbeorn, Siward's son 48

Oslac, Duke 156, 162

Oswald St, relics 82

Paris, Matthew 34

peat fen, distinctive character 141*ff.*

fires 105

Pebwith (Pebworth), Warwicks. 118, 163

Peterborough, abbey 18, 29, 33, 40, 74, 78, 80, 87, 107, 117, 136, 138, 141, 151, 165

cathedral 18, 79

Chronicle 17, 80*ff.*

Picot, Norman sheriff 27

Pine, L.G. 163

Poitiers, William of 6, 33, 36, 57, 62, 66, 73

Rackham, Oliver 110, 114–15

Ralph, Earl of Hereford 162

Ralph of Dol (*see* de Dol)

Ralph of Norfolk 106

Ralph the Staller (Radulf Scabre) 60, 106

Ramsey, Cambs. 83, 85, 88, 93, 134, 145

Rawnsley, W.F. 59, 165–6

Richardson, H.G. 10

Robert of Jumièges 46–7

Round, J.H. 10, 29, 139

Rowley, Trevor 10–13

Savage, James 167

Sayles, G.O. 10

Scabre (*see* Ralph the Staller)

Scaldemariland 67

Shepard, Thomas 167

Sherwood Forest 116

Siward, Earl 44–5, 47–9, 56, 58, 60, 90

Siward, Hereward's follower(s) 19, 22, 25, 28, 69, 88, 102

Smith, Harold R. 45–7

Soham, Cambs. 95, 145

Stamford Bridge, battle of 53, 55–6, 139

Stenton, Sir Frank 1, 10, 31, 33, 44, 47–9, 56, 60, 115–16, 152

Stephen, King 33, 95, 149, 165

Stevenson, W.H. 10

Stigand, Archbishop 54, 56

Stratford-on-Avon 166

Strutt, Joseph 159

Stubbings, Dr Frank 167
Stuntney, Cambs. 149
Sun Tzû 159
Swein, King of Denmark 2, 4, 57, 80, 84
Sweyn, Earl Godwin's son 39, 41, 45–8, 59

Taillebois, Ivo 101, 104, 118, 121
Taylor, Alison 148
Theodwine, Abbot of Ely 112
Thurstan, Abbot of Ely 107–8, 112
Torfrida, Hereward's first wife 63, 67, 69,
    118–20, 132, 138, 152, 162, 165–6
Tostig, Earl 39, 47*ff*., 58–9
Toynbee, Arnold J. 58
Trevelyan, G.M. 3, 83
Turold, Abbot of Peterborough 28–9, 79–81,
    85, 87, 117, 139

Ulfketill (Ulfcytel), Abbot of Crowland, assigns
    land to Hereward 29, 60

Varanger (Varangian) guard 51, 57
Vermuyden, Cornelius 142

Wace, Robert 55
Wake family of Courteenhall, Northants 119,
    138, 149, 161, 163*ff*.
  origin of term 29, 164
Waltheof, Earl of Northumbria 15, 48, 56, 60,
    90–1, 163
Warrenne, Frederick 75–6
Warrenne, William, Earl of Surrey 75–6, 75–6,
    101, 121
Waters, Henry F. 167
Waverley, novels 123

Wessex 8, 10, 15, 31, 44, 48, 50, 54–6
Westminster 18, 50–1, 54, 85, 107
Wherwell, Hants. 47
Whittington, Salop 124
Whittlesey Mere 136, 141
William the Conqueror 1, 9, 34, 43–4, 49,
    51–3, 56–7, 72–3, 78–9, 84, 90–2, 96,
    117, 119–21, 126, 154, 158
  at Hastings 1, 6–8, 53–4
  commands Fenland siege 2, 35–6, 85–6, 92,
    101*ff*., 148
  cruelty 3–4, 54
  death of 25, 100, 106
  family 30–2, 59
  humour 111
  physical appearance 64–6, 65
  tactics 11–12, 27–8, 62, 76–7, 91–2,
    107*ff*.
  visits England 47
William of Malmesbury (*see* Malmesbury)
William of Poitiers (*see* Poitiers)
William Rufus 59, 106, 148
Willingham, Cambs. 137, 144–5
Winchester 25, 33, 45, 78, 92, 106, 111–12
Winter, Hereward retainer 74, 88, 132
Witan, the 41–3, 48, 51
Witchford, Cambs. 111, 145
Wright, Thomas 159–61
Wulfstan, Bishop of Worcester 54, 118–19
Wulnoth, King Harold's brother 106

Yonge, Charlotte 123
York 22, 52–4, 58–60, 95, 101, 107, 141, 163,
    163
Young, Michael 130–1